THE EARLY HISTORY OF
THE MONASTERY OF CLUNY

THE EARLY HISTORY

OF THE

MONASTERY OF CLUNY

BY

L. M. SMITH

SOMERVILLE COLLEGE, OXFORD

HUMPHREY MILFORD

OXFORD UNIVERSITY PRESS

LONDON   NEW YORK   TORONTO   MELBOURNE

CAPE TOWN   BOMBAY   CALCUTTA   MADRAS

SHANGHAI   PEKING   COPENHAGEN

1920

PREFACE

ALTHOUGH the importance of the monks of Cluny in the social, political and religious life of the tenth and eleventh centuries has been universally acknowledged, there has been no book in English dealing with the history of the monastery. Furthermore, in general histories, English, French, German and Italian, two misconceptions on the subject of Cluny had grown up: (1) that the Cluniacs were highly ascetic and uncompromising members of the Benedictine order; (2) that the Gregorian tenets originated at Cluny, and were promulgated by the Cluniacs who thus prepared the way for Gregory VII. From that standpoint the present writer began her work on Cluny, but on going to the original sources could find no evidence in support of either theory—a conclusion she put forward in an article published in the *English Historical Review.*

The theory that Gregory VII. was a monk at Cluny is no longer tenable; while Martens in his remarkable book on Gregory VII. maintains that the theocratic doctrine originated with Hildebrand himself, and was developed, not by the monks, but by a small group of ecclesiastics within the secular Church. The fallacy of the first theory was exposed by Sackur in his *Cluniacenser in ihrer kirchlichen und allgemeingeschlichtlichen Wirksamkeit.* Sackur, however, is interested in tracing the work of the monastic groups which emanated from or were influenced by Cluny, rather than in the history of the monastery itself. It therefore seemed to

v

the present writer that there was room for original work on the subject; for that work the storehouse of facts is the *Recueil des chartes de Cluny* published in Bruel's five volumes, which, as far as she knows, have not hitherto been worked over in detail.

As grantee, scholar and fellow, she wishes to acknowledge her indebtedness to the Carnegie Trust for the Universities of Scotland, and to express her thanks to Miss Duffy and the Rev. J. Richards for having read the proofs of this book.

L. M. S.

BIBLIOGRAPHY

ORIGINAL AUTHORITIES

Adalberonis Carmen.
Annales Benedicti. iii.
BALUZE, ii.
Benedicti Chron.
Benedicti Regula.
Boll. AA.SS. April II., May II., Sept. III.
BOUQUET, ix., x.
BRUEL. Recueil des chartes de Cluny, i.-iv.
Destr. Farf.
Flodoardi chron., iii.
Gall. Christ., ii.
Gesta abb. Gemblac.
Gesta episc. Tull.
HAVET. Lettres de Gerbert.
Joannis XIX. papae epist.
LABBÉ. Concilia, viii., ix.
MABILLON. Ann., v.
MABILLON. AA.SS., v.
MABILLON. Vetera Analecta, ii.
MANSI. Concilia, xix.
MARRIER. Bibl. Clun.
MIGNE. Pat. Lat. 103, 132, 133, 139, 141, 142, 159.
Miracula sci Mansueti.
Miracula sci Benedicti.
Miracula sci Gorgonii.
Mon. Germ. Script. Pertz, vii., viii., xiii.
Mon. Germ. Hist. Sickel, i., ii.
Udalricus Consuet. Clun.
Vita anonyma Odonis, Bibl. Nat. Paris, 5566.
Vita Halinardi.
Vita Joh. Gorz.

Modern Authorities

BUTLER.   Benedictine Monachism.

DRESDNER.   Kultur und Sittengeschichte der ital. Geistlichkeit.

GRUTZMACHER.   Die Bedeutung Benedict von Nursia und seiner Regel.

GRANDIDIER.   Histoire d'Alsace.

HUBERTI.   Studien zur Rechtsgeschichte der Gottesfrieden.

KLUCKHOLM.   Geschichte der Gottesfrieden.

LAVISSE.   Histoire de France, ii. 2.

Neues Archiv, vii., xv.

PIGNOT.   Histoire de Cluni.

PFISTER.   Études sur le règne de Robert le Pieux.

SACKUR.   Die Cluniacenser in ihrer kirchlichen und allgemeingeschlichtlichen Wirksamkeit.

CONTENTS

CHAPTER 1

MORE than a thousand years ago, on the site of duke William of Aquitaine's hunting-lodge, the little monastery of Cluny was founded, an event that seemed of such small importance that the founder hesitated to turn out his hunting dogs in order to make room for the monks. Yet in less than two hundred years the name of that small monastery had become famous throughout Europe, and Cluny head of an international system; where once the monks had built their wooden houses ' according to their skill and knowledge ' arose a new and famous school of architecture; where once the modest building had been retarded through lack of funds, rose the church of St. Peter, the admiration and wonder of the world; where once the dogs had barked, echoed the stately ritual of the most famous musical centre of Europe; and on the site of the former hunting-lodge rose a monastery so extensive in size, that St. Louis of France and his courtiers could stay there without one of the monks having to leave his cell. Cluny, once a tiny vill, hidden in the black valley, had by then become an international meeting-place better known than Paris itself.

But all these things had been added unto her. Cluny's chief work, a work which made her known as the spiritual head of Europe and her monks renowned as the savers of souls, lay in the reform she inaugurated, the spiritual enthusiasm she reawakened in monastic life, and the establishment of one uniform and universal rule in the monasteries of the West. This was no mean achievement, for society had been overturned by the invasions of the barbarians, and the monasteries, defenceless and rich, had been one of the chief objects of attack. There were monasteries to be rebuilt, restored, refounded, and, above all, to be brought under one rule.

It is very fitting that the *pied-à-terre* of the Cluniac abbots at Paris should have been built next the ruins of the *thermae* and palace of the Roman Emperors, for Cluny stood for the continuance of the old Roman tradition in the regular church, as against the Teutonic element. The Roman monastery had been a community possessing certain rights. The monasteries built or organised under Teutonic influence were rather the appanages or possessions of the founder and his relatives, the Roman idea being too abstract for the ignorant feudal baron to grasp. To the latter the monastery was another form of property which might be inherited, given away, split up, and divided according to the founder's wish, monasteries being held by seven or eight owners much in the same way as a fief. It followed from this that the right of electing an abbot was often claimed by the founder, and delegated by him to his descendants and relatives. St. Benedict, on the contrary, had laid down that freedom of election belonged to the monks. In consequence of the feudalising tendency the monk regarded his abbot somewhat in the light of a feudal chief. The vows he made on entering the monastery he made in the presence of the abbot, on whose death he felt himself free to leave the house.[1] Having dedicated his life voluntarily, the monk of the Teutonic school still felt that he remained an individual, with a right to his individual will and judgement. This was against the Roman principle strenuously upheld by the Cluniacs, i.e. the monk once a monk was a monk for life and one of a permanent community. His will had passed into his abbot's keeping.

In the Teutonised system, no one rule was accepted as the standard for the Empire. The founder could exercise his individual preference among the many rules, i.e. from the more

---

[1] It was quite usual for a monk to pass from one house to another. St. Benedict put an end to this by introducing the vow of stability.

ascetic Eastern to the more moderate Western.[1] Nor when a rule was once adopted were its tenets rigorously adhered to, again a consequence of Teutonic individualism. To the free Teutonic spirit, to the rough feudal lord, who at the end of a life of hard fighting founded or retired to a monastery, the monotony of regular discipline, however moderate, must have proved very irksome, and voluntarily to follow that discipline an idea almost beyond his comprehension. Hence abuses crept in, such as are mentioned in the *Vita Odonis*, e.g. change in the hour of matins that the night's rest should not be broken, richer and warmer clothing,[2] occasional changes from fish and vegetarian diet, holiday visits to friend and family, no fixed rules as regards fasting—the zealot being allowed to fast more, the indifferent less. All these points, which sometimes seem to be given an exaggerated importance in the *Vita*, yet fall into their places as the outward and visible signs of that larger significance, i.e. the maintenance of the Roman ideals of discipline and uniformity, as against the Teutonic ideal of individualism. This was the more important in that the monasteries were coming under the influence, not of the finer elements of the age, but of the reactionary tendencies of the feudal baron.

Before the Teutonic spirit could attain the old Roman ideal a long training was required. The Roman spirit stood for discipline, for the recognition of abstract rights, for the community. This was the training Cluny was to give, and the work Cluny was to do, i.e. to bring back to monasticism the ideals of discipline, uniformity, and obedience, a work successfully inaugurated by the greatest of her abbots. 'After Benedict and his disciple Maurus may come as the chief restorer of the monastic order in Gaul, and a distinguished reformer of the

---

[1] The best-known were those of Antony, Pachomius, Basil, Macarius, Aurelian, Cassian, Donatus, Caesarius of Arles, Columbanus, all of which were more severe than the Benedictine.

[2] St. Benedict allowed his monks eight hours' sleep on end for the greater part of the year, but they had to rise at 2 A.M. for matins. He also allowed for the climate and permitted warmer clothing than the Egyptian rules.

rule, Odo ; Odo, the first father of the order of Cluny who took up the task of renewing the dead and almost forgotten fervour of monastic life.'[1]

The rule which the Cluniacs followed was the Benedictine,[2] and one result of their work was to establish it throughout the West. It was eminently suited for their reform, in that it was not rigid and that it held up a standard of life attainable by the many. Unfortunately, little or nothing is known of the early history of this rule which had not been able to compete with older and better-known rules, and before the seventh century had received little or no recognition outside Italy.[3] In the South of Europe the rule of Caesarius of Arles had been generally adopted, in the North that of Columbanus of Luxeuil. Before the Benedictine could triumph, it required influential supporters. When Gregory the Great sent Augustine to England, he entrusted him with a letter addressed to the clergy of Gaul, advocating the adoption of the Benedictine rule. Little more is known about the rule till we find Charlemagne attempting to revive it in pursuance of the reform begun by Boniface and Pippin. He sent to Monte Cassino to have the rule copied and brought to Aachen. Not that the monastic movement *per se* owed much to Charlemagne, for his object in supporting it was educative rather than religious. He valued monasticism mainly for the opportunities it afforded for study, and the monasteries as a training ground for scholars whom later he might employ at his court, and in carrying on the administration of his empire.[4]

---

[1] Marrier, *Bibl. Clun.* p. 58, *Veniat post magnum Benedictum et eius discipulum Maurum, summus ordinis monastici in Galliis reparator, precipuus regulae reformator, Odo. Odo, inquam, primus Cluniacensis ordinis pater qui emortuum iam et pene ibique sepultum monastici propositi fervorem resuscitare suo conamine aggressus est* (Peter the Venerable's address to the priors and subpriors of Cluny, c. 1140).

[2] *Sci Benedicti Regula*, 116, *Constituenda est erga nobis dominici schola servitii In qua institutione nihil asperum, nihil grave nos constituturos speramus.*

[3] Grutzmacher, *Die Bedeutung Benedict von Nursia u seiner Regel.*

[4] Hauck, *Kirchengeschichte Deutschlands*, ii. p. 573. Charlemagne did not allow the rule to be followed in at least one point, viz. free election of the abbots by the monks: only four monasteries in Germany, Lorsch, Fulda, Hersfeld, St. Gumbert, were granted this privilege.

There was thus a wide field of work for the first purely monastic reformer who should arise, and he came in the second Benedict, Benedict of Aniane. He, however, began his career as an opponent of the Benedictine rule which he spurned, despising it as fit only for novices and weaklings.[1] ' He himself afflicted his body with the most rigorous fasts, and for so long left it unwashed that he resembled a beast rather than a man.' To his first religious fervour the Eastern rules alone seemed to reach a fitting height of asceticism, and he despised the Benedictine rule just because it held up a standard of life possible to the many. In time he learned to value it for this very reason, and to take it as his standard of reform.

Benedict had taken his vows at St. Sequanus', Dijon, where he remained for five years, till the brothers wished to make him abbot. Foreseeing the impossibility of turning the laxity of his fellow-monks to the strict observance of the rule, he fled to his boyhood's home There, near the little river Aniane, he built on his father's land a cell, nucleus of the monastery later to become so famous, where, surrounded by a few friends, he strove to enforce a régime in which religious contemplation and hard work were the ideals. That interest in reading and literary work which Charlemagne and Alcuin had fostered, was discouraged. Special importance was laid on manual labour, the monks themselves having to till any land they acquired. Extreme simplicity and even bareness characterised the architecture of church and monastery, the consecrated vessels being made of wood, and beauty avoided as a sin. The observance of the rule was so strict that only the strong could endure. Nevertheless the numbers grew, and three times Benedict found it necessary to extend the monastic buildings. The third time the severe simplicity of the earlier buildings was abandoned, and the monastery, which arose in pomp and splendour, was placed under the imperial protection.

Benedict instituted singers, taught readers, assembled gram-

---

[1] The first St. Benedict himself called the rule *minima inchoationis regula.*

marians skilled in the knowledge of the Scriptures, and collected a great number of books. Giving his heart to the investigation of the Benedictine rule, he went round the monasteries, questioning the learned on those points in which he was ignorant, and studying all the other rules he could find. By 813 his rendering of the rule was followed in the most important of the Burgundian monasteries. In Aquitaine Louis the Pious placed the monasteries under his direction, and these he visited and reformed with great activity.[1]

On Charlemagne's death the reform received new impetus from Louis the Pious, an ardent supporter of the movement. His first care was to call Benedict to the centre of the empire to Maurmünster, in Alsace. Later, that he might have him nearer his own person, he summoned him to Aachen, where two hours' journey from his palace the new and splendid monastery of St. Cornelius arose. This was to be the model monastery for the kingdom, though only numbering thirty monks.

With the imperial support Benedict's work prospered. Appointed by the emperor over the monasteries of the kingdom,[2] he (as the Cluniacs later) laid down the principle that uniformity of custom was to be strictly observed in the reformed houses,[3] differences which had hitherto been allowed to exist being ruthlessly suppressed.

In 816 a council of prelates was held at Aachen, when it was decreed that all monks should follow the Benedictine rule. A few months later (817) Louis summoned the abbots from all parts of the empire, and Benedict sat with them for several days,

---

[1] Hauck, ibid. Two of the points on which Benedict laid especial stress were zealously promulgated later by the Cluniacs : (1) the monk was to speak no superfluous word ; (2) he was to bear himself with extreme humility before his abbot ; at the name of God he was to throw himself prostrate on the ground, at the name of his abbot to bow the knee. Hoping to sever connection with the world, Benedict forbade his monks the use of their mother tongue.

[2] Migne, *Pat. Lat.* 103, *Vita Benedicti Anianensis*, cap. 50, *Prefecit eum imperator cunctis in regno suo cenobiis.*

[3] Ibid. 50, *Et una cunctis generaliter posita observatur Regula, cunctaque monasteria ita ad formam unitatis redacta sunt. . . . Uniformis mensura in potu, in cibo, in vigiliis, in modulationibus cunctis observanda est tradita.*

' discussing the first principles of the rule, elucidating obscure and doubtful points, abolishing previous errors, and confirming useful and effective customs '.[1] As a result the Aachen capitulary was drawn up, accepted by the abbots, and ratified by the emperor. The capitulary, which may be called a modified version of the Benedictine rule, was to be the standard of monastic life within the empire. *Inspectores* were appointed by the emperor to see that it was enforced. Free election of their abbots was assured to the monks. Taken as a whole, the characteristic of the Aachen resolution was the reaction against what Charlemagne had made of monasticism, and a return to the earlier ideal, i.e. asceticism before culture.[2]

The rule was not rigid. Benedict continued to seek out and question those skilled in its precepts, and in especial those who had been at Monte Cassino. Various considerations led him to admit or reject certain points, and where the rule was silent or obscure he supplemented it fitly and rationally.[3] He then wrote the *Codex Regularum*, a collection of all the rules prior to St. Benedict's. Working over it he next wrote the *Concordia Regularum*, a commentary on St. Benedict's rule, written to show the contentious ⁵ that the first Benedict had not tampered with the rules of his predecessors but had relied on them '.[4]

---

[1] Ibid. 50, *Regulam at integro discutiens cunctis obscura dilucidans, dubia patefecit, priscos errores abstulit, utiles consuetudines affectusque confirmavit . . . assentientibus cunctis . . . capitularem institutum.*

[2] Hauck, ii. 582 et seq. Each monk was to make himself acquainted with every word of the rule. In order to make it suitable for the climate of Gaul and Germany the monks were to wear thicker and warmer clothing and to have more food, which of course the first Benedict had permitted. Manual labour, which had been rejected in many monasteries, was reintroduced. There was no mention of theological studies, and the monks were forbidden to keep schools except for the *oblati*.

[3] Migne, ibid. 51, *Nonnulla praecipit quae aut propter concordiam unitatis aut certe propter observantiam honestatis, seu propter considerationem fragilitatis admittuntur. . . . Si qua nempe minus lucide pagina Regulae pandit, aut omnino silet, rationabiliter apteque instituit atque supplevit.*

[4] Ibid. 53, *Fecit denique librum ex regulis diversorum patrum collectum ita ut prior B. Benedicti Regula cunctis esset . . . quem ad collectam matutinam legere iussit. Ex quo rursus ut ostenderet contentiosis nulla frivola cassaque a Benedicto edita fore, sed suam ex aliorum fultam esse Regulam ; alium collectis*

With an enthusiastic reformer and a prince ready and anxious to support him, the work of reform went on apace. In his last years Benedict was unweariedly active in visiting and reforming the monasteries of the kingdom. On his death-bed he could rejoice at the extent of the work accomplished. The monks of St. Cornelius praised him as the man who had given back the Benedictine rule to Gaul. Nevertheless Benedict was perhaps too narrow in his outlook to carry through a universal reform. Laying over-much stress on single points, he did not see deep enough into essentials.[1] That he succeeded as far as he did was largely due to the imperial support without which the movement would have collapsed after his death (821). By 829 Louis had again to call the bishops' attention to the reform, and exhort them to further it.

His zeal, however, like that of the many, waxed faint. Later it was the bishops who had to remind him that the monks had been confirmed in the right of free election of their abbots. More and more the monasteries fell into lay hands, abuses crept in, and 'by the end of Louis' reign there was as little strict observance of the rule as there had been at the beginning'.[2] Then in Gaul came fresh incursions by the Northmen and Huns which prevented the development of peaceful monastic life. By the end of the ninth century only in isolated and rare communities did the observance of the Benedictine rule survive. It was in one of these, the little monastery of Baume, that the founder of Cluny's greatness received his training.

Regularum sententiis composuit librum . . . *cui nomen concordia Regularum* . . . *dedit ita duntaxat ut B. Benedicti praecederet sententia, eo vero rationabiliter convenientes iungerentur.* Hugo Menardus, who edited the *Concordia* (1638), gives a list of 26 rules from which it was composed.

[1] Hauck, ibid. iii. 591.
[2] Ibid.

CHAPTER II

In the life of St. Hugh of Autun [1] there is a story [2] which links the origin of Cluny to the mother of Western monasticism, Monte Cassino. In the sixth century certain distinguished men of Gaul, moved by God and the love of holy religion, sent messengers to St. Benedict begging him [3] to send monks from Monte Cassino to Gaul as instructors in the regular discipline. Benedict sent twelve monks, one of whom was his best beloved Maurus. They came to Anjou, where they founded the monastery of Glanfeuil, over which Maurus was made abbot. Under his direction the monastery prospered exceedingly. Its numbers increased, till an incursion by the Northmen forced the monks to flee farther south, where they settled at St. Savin's, Poitiers, and again by their zeal caused monastic life to flourish. St. Savin's became a model monastery which the kings of Gaul delighted to favour. Inspired by their example a certain Badillo was moved to emulation, and resolved to restore the ruined abbey of St. Martin, Autun. Having done so, he sent to St. Savin's and persuaded eighteen of the monks to settle in his new monastery, Hugh, who later became abbot, being amongst their number. Under Hugh's fostering care fruit a hundredfold was brought forth. From far and near men flocked to take their vows at St. Martin's. At this time monastic life was almost dead in Gaul, and the state of the few monasteries which had

---

[1] *AA.SS. Boll.*, Apr. II. cap.i . 3.

[2] Rodulf Glaber (eleventh century) gives the same story. That St. Maur ever came to Gaul has been disputed.

[3] *Vita Hugonis*: *Ut monachile institutum quod pene in illis partibus annullatum deperierat aliquatenus reformare satagerent.*

9

survived amidst the ruin and desolation caused by the incursions of the Northmen, a scandal. Of all the monasteries of Gaul that of Baume was the most lacking in regularity of life. The monks of St. Martin were asked to reform it, and sent thither Berno, who later became its abbot. With his name comes the connection of Baume with Cluny. Not only did Berno restore regularity of discipline at Baume, but also with his co-operation [1] duke William of Aquitaine founded the monastery of Cluny, over which Berno was appointed abbot. Thus the chain runs from Monte Cassino to Glanfeuil, from Glanfeuil to St. Savin's, Poitiers, from St. Savin's to St. Martin's, Autun, from St. Martin's to Baume, and hence to Cluny.

This information about Berno conflicts with that given in the anonymous life of Odo.[2] There we are told that Berno, scion of a distinguished and wealthy Burgundian house, despised the luxuries of this world, preferring to follow the precept of the Gospel and to lay up his treasure in heaven. Therefore, helped by his relative Laufinus,[3] he built the monastery of Gigny on his own land, and dowered it with no small riches. Monks settled there, and after a time Berno could rejoice that his prayers had been heard. The monastery stood forth an example of all that was best in monastic life. He endowed it with all his possessions, and himself took vows.

Later, when perfected in the rule, he, at the request of the monks and nobles of the district, became abbot. So prudently and well did he rule that his fame spread. He was asked to take over and reform Baume, a monastery said to have been founded by Columbanus himself, but which had lost both religious and temporal prosperity. Under Berno, its former reputation for holiness was restored.

These two accounts are contradictory, though they agree

---

[1] Bruel, *Recueil des chartes de Cluny*, i. 285, *Quod Wilhelmus quoddam monasterium Cluniacum per manus Bernonis construxit.* Cf. 253, 269.

[2] Discovered by Sackur, Bibl. Nat. Paris, 5566, fol. 21.

[3] *Gigny . . . a te tuoque consobrino nomine Laufino* (Migne, 129, p. 845, *Formosi papae privilegia*).

in the most important particular, that the reform of Baume was undertaken by Berno. The first account makes the reform emanate from St. Martin's, Autun, from which monastery the monk Berno was sent to reform Baume ; the second makes it emanate from Gigny, which was founded by Berno when still a layman. The evidence of later charters rather supports the second authority, for they show that Baume was dependent on Gigny. Also certain principles upheld at Gigny were later adopted at Baume and Cluny. Berno, when he proceeded to Rome (894) to have the charter of Gigny confirmed, placed the monastery under the protection of the papal see.[1] Its liberties were assured. The monks were free to choose their abbot,[2] and were not to pay tenths (conditions which obtained both at Baume and Cluny later).

Unfortunately very little is known of the history of Gigny, which Berno seems to have left after taking over the direction of Baume. From the latter monastery he evidently exercised his authority over Gigny. At Baume his connection with duke William of Aquitaine arose ; for William's retainers often visited the little monastery of Baume, and ever brought back to their lord reports of the abbot's excellent rule and administration. William, who had decided to found a monastery, felt he could not do better than consult Berno on the subject. He asked the latter about a site, but to his dismay the abbot fixed on Cluny, the favourite hunting-ground of the Duke, nay on the hunting-lodge itself.

'Impossible,' William replied, 'I cannot have my dogs removed.' Jocularly the abbot answered, 'Drive out the dogs,

---

[1] Ibid., *Ideo suggessistis nostro apostolatui ut apostolici nostri privilegii illud sanctione muniremus . . . confirmamus, munimus et in perpetuum sub iure et ditione atque potestate B. Petri et nostra confirmatum stabilimus. . . . Ut nulli homini quamlibet dignitatem fulcito licitum sit, aut etiam de ipsis donatoribus quamcunque vim aut aliquam oppressionem ibidem inferre . . . potius firmum et ab omnibus immutilatum custodiatur ad ius et protectionem beati Petri.*

[2] Ibid., *Congregatio . . . ex seipsis secundum Deum et regulam beati Benedicti quem idoneum praeviderint concordi voto habent semper eligendi et secundum morem in abbatem sibi praeficiendi.*

and put monks in their place, for thou canst well think what reward God will give thee for dogs, and what for monks.' [1]

Struck by these words William ordered the building to begin.

Apart from this legend, the origins of Cluny [2] remain in obscurity. In the three original sources, William's deed of gift, Berno's will, and the *Vita Anonyma*, no precise information is given about the founding of the abbey.

The *Vita* account, which is evidently based on Berno's will, runs as follows. When the success of Berno's reform at Baume was known, the religious and powerful men of the day, not only those living in the neighbourhood but even those from distant parts, being grieved that monastic life had almost perished in Gaul, resolved to place other monasteries under his direction. The famous duke William of Aquitaine gave him the two distant monasteries of Déols and Massay, where he instructed the monks in the regular discipline. Next William gave him property at Cluny where a monastery was to be built, a work which Berno at once began with as much zeal as goodwill. In a short time the walls of the church arose, a habitation for the monks was planned, and no small pains taken for the whole work. But alas, before even the walls of the monastery rose above ground, it was bereft of its master, nay rather of its parent, by the death of the duke, and left a posthumous child. As William died in 918, and the charter of foundation was drawn up in 910, the building could not have proceeded with any great

[1] *Vita Hugonis*, cap. ii. 13.

[2] Both the royal charters (anno 927) mention Berno as having built the monastery. (1) *Quod Wilhelmus quoddam monasterium Cluniacum per manus Bernonis construxit.* (2) *Quod a Wilhelmo per manus Bernonis constructum est.* The vill Cluny was given to the bishop of Mâcon in 802. He gave it and another vill to the count of Mâcon in exchange for 3 vills (Bruel, i. 4, 6). From the count it passed to Ava, sister of William of Aquitaine. She willed it to her brother (893) in exchange for an alod which she was to hold for life. The charter of gift (Bruel, 53) describes Cluny as a vill with churches, chapels, manors, vine-yards, meadows, pasture-land, plantations of trees, cultivated and unculti-vated land, waters and water-courses. All was given to William except twenty serfs. If William had a legitimate son or daughter Cluny was to descend to them.

rapidity. Even at the date of Berno's will (*c.* 926) the monastery was not completed.

William's charter [1] dealt only with the deed of gift, and with his intentions regarding the monastery. Freely he gave to the apostles Peter and Paul the vill Cluny, with *cortile*, manor in demesne, and chapel, dedicated to the Virgin and St. Peter. Everything belonging to Cluny went with the gift—vills, chapels, vineyards, fields, meadows, woods, waters, mills, serfs, cultivated and uncultivated lands. On the site chosen the monks themselves were to build the monastery according to their skill and knowledge.[2] There unceasing vows and prayers were to be offered up, so that with deep ardour and quick desire men might find the charm of intercourse with heaven. The Benedictine rule was to be followed. Berno was to be first abbot. On his death the monks were freely to elect their new abbot,[3] neither William nor any other person daring to interfere with the election. They were to pay Rome a tribute of ten solidi every five years, and to have the papal protection and guardianship.[4]

According as the possessions and opportunities of the monastery allowed, hospitality was to be given daily to the poor, needy, strangers, and pilgrims, and the monastery to serve as a perpetual refuge to those who, leaving the world stripped of its goods, and bringing nothing with them but their goodwill, might find in its superfluity their abundance. Notwithstanding this clause we know that Cluny was not richly endowed. It was ' poor in possessions ',[5] and endowed with but fifteen *coloniae.*[6] Lack of funds brought the building to a standstill,

---

[1] Bruel, i. 112.

[2] Ibid., *Pro posse et nosse suo, corde et animo pleno locum edificent.*

[3] Ibid., *Habeant idem monachi potestatem et licentiam quemcumque sui ordinis eligere, maluerint abbatem atque rectorem, ita ut nec nostra nec alicuius potestatis contradictione contra religiosam electionem impediantur.*

[4] Ibid., *Habeantque tuitionem ipsorum apostolorum atque Romani pontificis defensionem.*

[5] *Bibl. Clun.* p. 9 (Berno's will).

[6] Migne, 142; R. Glaber, *Hist.* iii. cap. 5, *Quod etiam cenobium in primo non amplius quam quindecim terrae colonias dicitur in dotem accepisse.*

a difficulty only overcome by the second abbot's enterprise, backed by the generosity of his friends in Aquitaine.[1]

The most important clause of the charter, in the light of Cluny's later history, is that which assured its freedom. The monks were subject neither to William, his relations, royal officials, nor any earthly yoke. No secular prince, count, bishop, nor even the pope himself, was to seize their property,[2] divide it, diminish it, nor give it to benefit another : nor were they to set an abbot over the monks against their will.[3] William called on the holy apostles Peter and Paul, and on the pope, to be guardians and protectors[4] of Cluny, and by canonical and apostolic authority to drive from the community of the church, and from eternal life, those who attacked or seized the property which with joyful mind and ready will he had given them. A tremendous curse was called down on any one who violated the charter.[5] Thus from its origin Cluny stood for monastic autonomy.

Berno's will gives little additional information. Berno administered six monasteries—Gigny, Baume, the abbey of Aethicens with the *cella* of St. Lautenus, Déols, Massay, and Cluny.

---

[1] Migne, 133; *Vita Odonis*, ii. cap. 2.

[2] Bruel, i. 112, *Ut ab hac die nec nostro nec parentum nostrorum, nec fastibus regie magnitudinis, nec cuiuslibet terrenę potestatis iugo subiciantur idem monachi ibi congregati ; neque aliquis principium secularium . . . non comes quisquam nec episcopus quilibet, non pontifex invadat. . . .*

[3] Ibid., *Non aliquem prelatum super eos contra eorum voluntatem constituat.*

[4] Ibid., *Tutores ac defensores.*

[5] Ibid., *Primum quidem iram Dei omnipotentis incurrat, auferatque Deus partem illius de terra viventium et deleat nomen eius de libro vitae, fiatque pars illius cum his qui dixerunt Dno Deo Recede a nobis, et cum Dathan et Abiron, quos terra ore aperto deglutivit et vivos infernis absorbuit, perhennem dampnationem incurrat : sortius quoque Judae proditoris Domini effectus, aeternis cruciatibus retrusus teneatur : et ne ei in presenti seculo humanis oculis impune transire videatur, in corpore quidem proprio future damnationis tormenta experiatur, sortitus duplicem direptionem cum Haeliodoro et Antiocho, quorum alter acris verberibus coercitus vix semivivus evasit : alter vero, nutu superno perculsus, putrescentibus membris et scatentibus vermibus miserrime interiit : ceterisque sacrilegis qui aerarium domus Dni temerare presumpserunt particeps existat, habeatque archiclavum totius monarchiae ecclesiarum iuncto sibi sco Paulo, obstitorem et ameni paradisi aditus contradictorem.* The final clause, that such sinners shall be compelled by the judicial power to pay a fine of 100 pounds gold, comes as an anticlimax.

Feeling death near, with the consent of the brothers, he appointed Wido, one of his monks, and his relative, abbot of the first three, and Odo, equally beloved, of the second.[1] Some of Gigny's property was given to Cluny, viz. the vill Alfracta, part of a meadow belonging to a certain Simon, and a fourth of the *caldariae*.[2] In return, the monks of Cluny were to pay Gigny twelve denarii annually in investiture. Berno begged the princes, *seniores*, and magnates who at the monastery had heard his will read by word of mouth to consent to monasteries, abbots, and monks remaining in that state sanctioned by royal decree, and indeed by apostolic privilege. If, as was not improbable, strife should arise from within or from without, he begged them to uphold justice and abide by the tenor of his will. There was no injustice in his gift to Cluny, which, left a posthumous child [3] by duke William's death and now by his, was still unfinished. Dedicated like Gigny to the apostles Peter and Paul, it was only fitting that the new son should receive a share of the patrimony. Besides, though Cluny was poorer in possessions it was greater in numbers,[4]—a surprising statement—; it may be, however, that the monks who were to build the monastery themselves were living at Cluny in temporary huts. Hoping for concord Berno exhorted them to observe uniformity in the manner of life (*modus conversationis*) at the six monasteries, if not better at least as well as they had done hithertofore, i.e. as regards ritual, observance of silence, food and drink, and above all the giving up of private possessions.[5] If any brother continued pertinaciously in error, the *priores* of the monasteries were mutually to decide how to correct him.

---

[1] *Bibl. Clun.* p. 9, *Uuidonem meum consanguinem atque Odonem edaeque dilectum una cum fratrum consensu mihi succedere delegavi.* The last mention of Berno's name as abbot is in a charter dated 926, and the first mention of Odo's in a charter, 927.

[2] *Caldaria*, large vessel in which water was carried to the fire (Ducange).

[3] Ibid., *Quasi postumus, morte . . . Guellelmi . . . atque nunc mea imperfectus deseritur.*

[4] Ibid., *Et certe pauperior est possessione et numerosa fraternitate.*

[5] Ibid., *Unanimitas . . . in psalmodia . . . et insuper in contemptu rerum propriarum, si non melius saltem sicut huc usque fecistis.*

After Berno's death concord did not long continue. Wido, though a signatory to the will, took by violence the property Berno had left to Cluny. This came to the ears of the pope (John X.), who wrote to Rudolf, king of the Franks, ordering the property to be restored (928). Wido argued that Berno's decree was illegal in that he had named no period of time nor persons in connection with the gift. The papal decision was that the monks of Cluny were to hold the land as long as any of those who had taken vows at Gigny lived at Cluny.[1] He commended the abbot and monks of Cluny to the king and his *fideles* who were able to further the abbey's interest. Wido, therefore, gave up what he had taken — Alfracta, an alod, and half a meadow, which were never to be alienated from Cluny unless, a somewhat malicious ending, the monastery and its inhabitants ever returned to canonical or secular life.

From our three authorities all that we know about the origin of the monastery comes to this. The charter of foundation was drawn up in 910. Forthwith the work of building began, but proceeded so slowly that at William's death only the church was finished. The work was then probably left over, so that by Berno's death little more had been accomplished. This delay in building was due to lack of funds. It was only under Odo that the building was zealously undertaken, and through the generosity of his friends in Aquitaine completed.[2] This, while putting forward the date of the monastery, renders more intelligible the fact that the royal charter was not obtained till 927, the papal 931.

---

[1] Bouquet, ix. 217, *Quod Berno hoc legaliter non fecit pro eo quod terminum temporis ac personarum in illo suo testamento non posuit. Quandiu ex illis monachis qui in Ginniaco professionem fecerunt aut oblati sunt apud Cluniacum aliquis vixerit.* The pope wrote directly to the king to explain the circumstances.

[2] Bruel, i. 425 (anno 935 ?). As their common father Berno had dedicated both monasteries to St. Peter, had begged the monks to continue in fraternity and love, and was buried at Cluny, Wido and his *domni fratres* freely gave up what he had willed. In return they were to receive annually *in vestitura* wax to the value of twelve denarii.

CHAPTER III

ODO, SECOND ABBOT OF CLUNY

THOUGH Berno [1] held the title of abbot of the yet unfinished
monastery of Cluny, its real history first began with Odo, the
second abbot. He it was who laid the foundation of Cluny's
future greatness and shaped the course of her later history.
Fortunately we are better informed about the circumstances of
his life than about the lives of his successors, for Odo had as his
biographer his enthusiastic and devoted disciple John,[2] whose
vivifying love, even across the cold centuries of history, performs
the miracle of making his master's figure live.

The details which John gives about Odo's childhood he
learnt from Odo himself. Once when abbot and disciple were
travelling together far from the monastery, John ' laid aside his
timidity, boldly raised his voice, and did not fear diligently to
ask Odo to deign to tell him about his childhood and his monastic
life. He, as was his custom, was silent for a little time, then his
face moved by emotion, he sighed deeply, and told the story
of his childhood,[3] his words broken by tears and groans.'

His father was a certain Abbo, different from the men of these
' modern times ' in that he was learned in the histories of old,
and knew by heart the *Novellae* of Justinian. He was also

---

[1] Bruel, i. 214, *President domno Berone abbate*. The date of this charter
is uncertain, 917–922. 253, *Sacrosanctae et venerabili ecclesiae St. P.P. . . .
in villa Cluniaco quam abb. Berno una cum monachis ad regendum habere
videtur* (anno 925). 269, *C un. quod monasterium iussu ac supplemento W.
decenter in P.P. honore sub providentia Bernonis construitur* (anno 926).

[2] Migne, 133, p. 43, *Vita Odonis a Joanne.*

[3] It is not known to what part of Gaul Odo's family belonged. In a vision
before his death St. Martin appeared to him and granted him leave to return
to his own land, Tours, where he was buried. According to the *Vita Anonyma*
he came from Semur. In another passage in the *Vita Joanne* he is called *Odo
Aquitanus.*

familiar with the Gospel, and was always ready to recite its precepts to those around him. Among his contemporaries he was held in such esteem that from far and near men came to ask for his decision in cases of dispute, assured of his impartiality. A deeply religious man, the vigil of a saint found him ever on his knees. One Christmas as he watched through the still hours of the holy night, he was moved to beseech God ever more and more urgently for the gift of a son, a boon hitherto denied him. His prayer was heard, and his wife Arenberga, though past the age of child-bearing, bore him a son.[1] As the boy grew older, often did the father dwell on the story of his birth.

Another story of his childhood Odo later learnt from his father's lips. One day Abbo entered the *septa cubiculi* and found the baby alone. Fearful of its safety he raised the child in his arms, and confiding him to St. Martin said, ' Oh, gem of saints, receive this child.' He told no one of this incident, but St. Martin did not forget.

A third story presaged the boy's future greatness. He was sent to a ' remote district ' to be educated by a priest, who was one day visited by the apostles St. Peter and St. Paul. They demanded the boy, whom they required for their service in Eastern parts. The priest, terrified at the thought of the parents' anger should the boy be missing, implored the apostles to give up their project. This they consented to do, but only, as they explained, for the moment. The priest hastened to send the boy home.

Then came a change in Odo's life. He had probably been a delicate child, but as he grew to youth he developed such strength and vigour [2] that his father repented of having destined him for an ecclesiastical, and resolved to train him for a military career. His literary studies were brought to a close, and he was sent as a page to the court of William of Aquitaine. There his life

[1] *Vita*; cf. Bruel, i. 584. This charter states that a brother (*germanus*) of Odo's gave a church to Cluny (942–53). There is also a story in the *Vita* about the infant son of Odo's brother.

[2] *Vita Joanne*, i. 8, *Strenuum et conspicabilem iuvenem.*

passed in hunting and military exercises ; but this, though it might please his father's pride, was not pleasing to St. Martin, who was not content to have so promising an acolyte escape. In sleep Odo was terrified by visions. Hunting brought him no pleasure, but immense fatigue. It seemed to him that his life was given over to evil. The change from the quiet life in some remote village with the studious priest to the coarse and rough pleasures of the hardy fighting baron must have been most distasteful to the boy's sensitive temperament, all the more if he knew the story of the apostles' visit, and in the quiet fields had thought and dreamed of the service for which they needed him. Very lonely and far away from that service he must have felt, in the court even of so pious a duke as William of Aquitaine, a court thronged by many a hard-living and hard-drinking feudal baron. As the years passed, the life grew more distasteful to him, and when he entered his sixteenth year his sufferings increased so much that Abbo in alarm advised him to follow his example, and to pass in prayer the vigil of each saint. This Odo did, but received no permanent relief. Then one Christmas, as he kept his vigil, he was seized by a passion of self-reproach and fear that his life was not pleasing to Christ. In anguish he poured out his soul to the Virgin. As if in answer a terrible pain in his head tortured him. It passed, but it returned, and for three years after this he was racked with pain, was taken home, and every medical aid of the time procured for him, but with no result. Finally, his father bethought himself that the son's suffering might be a sign from St. Martin, and, marvelling at the business-like spirit of the saint, told Odo the story of his early dedication. Then mournfully and reproachfully addressing St. Martin—

'Behold,' he said, ' what gratefully I offered exactly thou hast required. Truly as is fitting thou art quick to hear our vows, but expensive art thou in business.' [1]

---

[1] Ibid. i. 9, *Quod grate obtuli exacte requiris. Vere ut decet exaudibilis es in voto, sed carus in negotio.*

But here seemed a way of escape to Odo. At the age of nineteen he hastened to Tours, where laying his shorn hair before the tomb of the saint, he vowed himself to his service, and at last received relief from his pain.

Becoming one of the canons of St. Martin's, for six years he remained at Tours, second to none in his fervour for the cult of the saint ; always guarding him in his heart, telling of him with his mouth, and imitating him in his life. His fervent love for St. Martin found expression in the three celebrated hymns which at this time he composed and dedicated to the saint.[1]

At that time Tours, one of the most important towns in Gaul and famous throughout Christendom for the eminence of its saint, could offer every luxury of the day and every kind of dissipation to a young and distinguished clerk. As patron Odo had behind him no less a personage than count Fulc of Anjou, who was only too anxious to introduce him to the wealthy circle of aristocrats who visited Tours ; whither at one time or another, kings, princes, and the most eminent men of the day found their way. Nor for spiritual benefit alone was the pilgrimage undertaken. The religious duty fulfilled, there were open to the newcomer all the pleasures which one of the wealthiest towns of Europe could offer. Not the least luxurious life was that led by the young canons, most of whom were scions of some noble house ; Odo with count Fulc behind him might have lorded it with the best. He seems to have entered into the life with some zest for a time ; for John writes : ' What crowd of magnates surrounded him and what pomp of life was his I prefer not to dwell on lest I should do injury to that poverty which afterwards he followed.' [2] But that life soon palled on him, and he spurned it. Having learnt to despise the glory of the world he longed to live only in God.

His life of the next period was very different. During the day he fatigued himself by reading and during the night by prayer.

---

[1] Ibid. i. 10, *Tres hymnos in eius laude composuit.*
[2] Ibid. i. 11.

His reading was not confined to spiritual works. He began
to study the poems of Virgil, a study which came to an untimely
end. One night in a vision he saw a vase beautiful in form,
but full of serpents. Immediately he recognised in the serpents
the doctrines of the poets, in the vase the book of Virgil. From
this he understood that the right way to slake his intellectual
thirst was by Christ alone. Therefore, giving up the study of
the secular poets, he turned to the Gospels and prophets.[1]

Even here difficulties awaited him, for his zeal in poring
over the Scriptures seemed so unnatural to his fellow-canons
that they did their best to dissuade him from it.

' Why ', they barked, ' do you do such things ? Why do
you want to know about strange writers ? In such study you
will waste the flower of your youth. Spare yourself. Leave that
unintelligible stuff, and go instead to the psalms.' Odo possessing
his soul in patience paid no heed, and continued his studies.

Determined to give himself up wholly to spiritual contemplation, he retired to a little cell about two miles from the tomb
of St. Martin.[2] There for two years he lived a life of poverty,
following the Gospel precept and taking no thought for the
morrow. During this time his only food was daily a pound of
bread and a handful of beans, ' and what is contrary to the
Frankish nature, very little drink '. Having read in the rule of
St. Benedict that a monk ought to sleep in his clothes,[3] and not
quite understanding what was meant, he obeyed, and though
not a religious, yet bore the yoke of the monk. He never
closed the door of his cell. There was nothing within it to steal,
not even a bed, for he slept on the ground. ' Nevertheless his
body was not blackened by contact with the earth, nor his mind
weakened by the long continuance of his fasts.' It was
perhaps as well for Cluny's mission that its future abbot passed
through this phase of extreme asceticism when still a young man.

[1] Ibid. i. 13.
[2] St. Martin when bishop of Tours (fourth century) called monks to Mar-
moutiers outside Tours, where they lived a hermit-like life.
[3] *Vita Joanne* i. 15, *ut dormire debeant vestiti.*

Against so redoubtable an adversary Satan could not but pit his strength. Many and various were the snares he laid for Odo. One night, as he proceeded alone and unprotected to the tomb of St. Martin, the devil sent against him a pack of foxes. Guarding only his throat Odo went doggedly forward, till a deliverer appeared in the form of a wolf, who not only dispersed his assailants but thereafter became his constant companion.[1] Then in several of the manuscripts follows a delightful touch. ' If this story seem incredible to the reader, let him read Jerome's life of the blessed Paul, where he will find that two lions prepared the tomb of the saint. If still unconvinced, let him read further the life of Ammonius, whose cell was guarded by two dragons. Or again pope Gregory's life of Jerome where we learn that sometimes a lion, sometimes a bear used to guard his asses.' Scepticism is thus refuted.

At Tours Odo was attracted to the monastic life. Having read the rule of St. Benedict his sole desire from henceforth was to follow its precepts : ' Christ now throwing on the soil that seed which was to bear forth fruit a hundred fold.' It is not surprising that he did not at this time enter a monastery, for the condition of the monasteries in Tours was so scandalous as to revolt a religious mind. At the end of his life Odo's righteous indignation still boiled over at the remembrance of the life led by the monks of Tours. To his love of St. Martin it was as the ' abomination of desolation ' that scandal should ever have touched the saint's holy places. To his attentive disciple John he described those evil days when the monks began to follow their own desires, live corrupt lives, and give up monastic customs.[2] They would wear no longer the monastic habit, but paraded about in coloured garments, wore flowing cowls and tunics, and even covered these with a cloak. Worse still, to be in the height of fashion they wore shoes so coloured and shining that

[1] Ibid. i. 14.
[2] Ibid. iii. 1, *Persistente monastica congregatione apud ecclesiam beati Martini Turonis coeperunt modum suum consuetudinesque relinquere, ac propriis voluntatibus vitam suam propositumque corrumpere.*

they resembled glass, which they were so afraid of soiling that they would not venture to the nightly *Lauds*, but waited till by the light of day they might pick their steps ! These and similar things they did, defying the rule, but God was to put an end to these evils. One night, when all was quiet, a monk saw two men enter the dormitory, one with a drawn sword in his hand, the other directing him. Pointing out the monks in turn—' Strike ', the one called to the other, ' here and here.' In time all were numbered, and the sword came nearer and nearer to the watcher till it hovered over him. With a terrible cry he adjured them— ' By the living God slay me not.' Immediately the sword was withdrawn, and of all only he escaped.[1]

The evil condition of monastic life Odo attributed to the invasion of the Northmen, when many of the Benedictine order returned to the world and its pleasures, and forsaking their monastic communities enjoyed once more family life, and the society of their relatives and friends.[2] No longer working together for the prosperity of a particular monastery, they sought to enrich themselves. Tearing up their old garments, and not content with plain new ones, they arrayed themselves in fine colours. Even the few who remained constant to their profession preferred outside the monastic walls to dress like laymen. The terrible consequence of this one of these monks learnt to his cost. He was sent on business outside the monastery with a companion. Before starting he divested himself of his habit, an example which his companion virtuously refused to follow. On the journey the first monk was struck by mortal sickness. As the agony of death came upon him, he and his companion saw the vision of a throne on high, where

---

[1] Ibid. When Odo was instructing the young monks in the regular discipline he would often tell them of the miserable fate which had overtaken many monks, so as to restrain their youthful temperaments, and guide them like a shepherd by the staff of terror to the joys of heaven. On one such occasion John had asked how and when monastic life had degenerated and whether it had sunk as low in the rest of Europe as in Italy. In reply Odo told the two stories above. John first met Odo in Rome, and received his training at Pavia (p. 64)   [2] Ibid. iii. 2.

St. Benedict sat surrounded by an innumerable army of monks. Before the throne the dying monk saw himself lie prostrate, beseeching pardon. One of the monks near the throne interceded for him. St. Benedict replied that though he saw a man before him, yet, as he did not recognise the habit, he could do nothing ; it was not within his powers to discuss those of another order, or judge their lives.

At these words despair seized the dying monk, but in a passion of pity his companion took off his habit and wrapped it round the sinner, whereupon the saint commanded the latter to arise. Awakening from sleep the companion did as he had seen himself do in the vision, and strengthening his friend by prayer, and fortifying him with the holy Eucharist, sent him forth fearless on his last journey.

Such were the incidents which struck Odo most in the life of the monks of Tours, awakening in him the desire to dedicate himself to the work of monastic reform, as the closing words of his hymn in honour of St. Martin showed :

> *Monastico nunc ordini*
> *Jam pene lapso subveni.*

Meantime his fame had grown steadily. Notwithstanding his desire to remain hidden from the world in his little cell, he became one of the best-known figures at Tours, and to see him a coveted event of the pilgrimage. Those who had known him desired to recall themselves to his memory, and those who did not, sought the privilege of friendship. To all, like a flowing fountain, he offered delectable draughts ; to all, as an open library, he gave fitting example. He admonished and directed all who came to him, teaching one to condemn the world, and another not to covet its goods. He wept with prophetic soul over the evils to come, crying, ' Behold, Lord, how is the city which was full of riches made desolate.' The guilty, listening to him, were terrified. The guiltless, strong in innocence, rejoiced at the consolation of his words. Thus he saved many, who to show their gratitude wished to load him with gifts which he steadfastly refused. So it was he who, from being a pupil, began to lead his masters, and to be an example to his many followers.[1]

After a time, disappointed at having his solitude invaded, he betook himself to Paris in order to study.[2] There his teacher in all branches of the liberal arts was Remigius. Having finished his studies at Paris, he returned to Tours. This time the canons regarded his intellectual abilities with greater respect, and asked him to write an abridgement of the *Moralia* of pope Gregory the Great. Odo refused, feeling that it would be desecration to curtail so great a work. The canons accused him of laziness, ' and there was no small altercation between them daily '. Finally the pope himself descended in a vision and entrusted Odo with the task, when his scruples were removed.

It was at Tours that, through his connection with count Fulc, he made a friendship which was to change the course of his life. Fulc, fallen from grace had abstracted two golden vases from St. Martin's treasury, and refused to give them back. A mortal illness which attacked him witnessed to the weight of the saint's displeasure. No prayer nor gift could move him to bestow on Fulc the gift of health. In a dying condition the count was carried to the saint's tomb, when Odo went to him and fearlessly thundered, ' Give back, oh wretch, the vases which thou stolest, then only will St. Martin give thee back health.' Fulc obeyed, and straightway was healed. But to one of Odo's temperament it was not enough to have saved the count's body, he longed to save his soul by winning him to dedicate to God the life which had been miraculously restored to him. Grateful though he was, Fulc thought this asking too much. He proposed a substitute in his friend Adhegrinus, to whom on return-ing home he told the story of his miraculous healing. Fired by the tale, Adhegrinus hastened to seek the wonder-worker,

---

[1] Ibid. i. 17.
[2] Ibid. i. 19, *Ibique dialecticam sci Augustini Deodato filio missam perlegit et Martianum in liberalibus artibus frequenter lectitavit.*

and moved by Odo's words renounced his military career, gave his possessions to the poor, and shaving his head dedicated himself to the service of God. His example was followed by several of his companions, to whom ' suddenly the world stood revealed as a sink of iniquity, and men hastening towards the bottomless hell '. No escape seemed possible except in the monastic life, and straightway they sought throughout all *Francia* a monastery where they might live the regular life. Unsuccessful in their quest they returned sorrowful, to settle in the little huts which in their first religious fervour they had built.[1] But the soul of Adhegrinus was not content, and he resolved to go on pilgrimage to Rome. His way lay through Burgundy, where he stopped at the vill Baume, and received hospitality in the monastery of which Berno was abbot. There he found to his joy what he had sought in *Francia* in vain, a monastery where the regular life was lived, and where he could be received. Having obtained permission to remain and study the customs of the monks, and finding them all he could desire, he made known the glad tidings to Odo. The latter, taking with him his library of a hundred books (for he was a learned man), at once set out for Baume.[2]

Difficulties awaited him. Some of the monks, ' whose life and morals ', John severely remarks, ' can be judged by the following incident,' came out to meet him, and feigning not to understand his purpose in coming attempted to weaken it. ' Hast thou ', they cried, ' come hither for thy soul's health to join a monastery which we for our souls' health have resolved to flee ? Hast thou not heard of the severity of Berno ? Alas, alas, if thou but knew'st how he treats the monks. His corrections he drives home with the whip, and those whom he whips he binds with cords, he tames their spirits in prison, he afflicts them with fasts, and even after suffering all this, the miserable monks may not obtain mercy.'

---

[1] Ibid. i. 22, *Non fuit locus in Franciae finibus ubi audierunt adfuisse monasterium in quo aut per se non issent, aut suos perlustratores non misissent et non invenientes religionis locum inter eos in quo requiescere possent.*

[2] Ibid. i. 23, *Sumptis secum centum voluminibus librorum. . . . Quia erat vir scholasticus.*

Judging from the austerity of Odo's life at Tours, this account of Berno's severity might have attracted him, but this was not so, and trembling he resolved to flee. At that moment his friend Adhegrinus appeared, and vehemently taking up Berno's defence, denounced the speakers. Then, supported by his friend, Odo entered the monastery.

The friends did not remain long together. For Odo one phase of asceticism was past which for Adhegrinus was yet to come. After three years Adhegrinus begged permission to follow the life of a hermit, and retiring to a tiny habitation among the rocks spent in solitude and penance the remaining thirty years of his life. Odo on the contrary found his soul's salvation better to be attained within the monastic community. Having thus brought him to the haven where he would be, and where he was to pass the next fifteen years of his life, we may, like the author of the *Vita*, turn to consider some of the customs of Baume which later were followed at Cluny.

.   .   .   .

Unfortunately the author of the *Vita* gives little information about those customs, and much of what he tells is concerned with what now seem trivial details. One important fact he does mention, that Adhegrinus found the monks of Baume following the precepts of a certain father whom they called Euticus.[1] The account of the latter points unmistakeably to Benedict of Aniane.

Benedict of Aniane did not regard the Benedictine rule as rigid, but modified it as he thought fitting. In what was the chief duty of Benedictine life, the *opus Dei*, the monks of Baume followed his adaptation of the rule, i.e. the number of psalms and prayers to be said and sung were increased. At Baume daily 138 psalms were sung, though the number was later reduced

---

[1] Ibid. i. 23, *Fuit isdem vir temporibus Ludovici magni imperatoris carus regi, omnibus amabilis . . . in tanto amore apud regem habitus ut intra palatium illi construeret monasterium . . . ipse enim pater Euticus institutor fuit harum consuetudinum quae hactenus in nostris monasteriis habentur.*

by 14 because some weak souls objected that it was not fitting for the number of psalms to exceed that of prayers. During the octaves of Christmas and Easter only 75 psalms daily were sung. Every day also two masses were said and two litanies sung.[1] The same division was later followed at Cluny. The rule of prescribed hours of silence that obtained at Baume was also followed at Cluny. At certain hours which were called 'incompetent' no one dared speak within the cloisters, nor walk with another brother. In certain penitential seasons no one was allowed to speak except at the chapter.[2] In the last week of Advent and in Holy Week the deepest silence reigned day and night. On the vigil of a saint the abbot had the right of imposing silence. During prolonged periods of silence the monks either spoke with their fingers, or made signs with their eyes. By these means they could supply themselves with every necessary of daily life. According to John the life of a monk is edifying only if he has practised silence. 'Without that whatever his other virtues, even if he follow all the institutions of the fathers, his life is nothing worth.'[3]

A third point in which Benedict of Aniane's modification of the rule was followed was in still further increasing the powers of the abbot[4] and reducing those of the monk. The latter had to give up his own will, and in every trifle submit himself to his abbot. This was carried to such an extent that it has been said that whereas the first Benedict taught the monk to be humble, the second made him cringe. At Baume the monk when accused of a fault threw himself prostrate at the feet of the abbot without attempting any justification. This grace of excessive humility was one in which Odo excelled, to the deep admiration of his biographer, John. One night, in what was a case of necessity, Odo

---

[1] Ibid. i. 22.   [2] Ibid. i. 31.

[3] There were many other points which unfortunately John did not insert, being afraid of wearying the reader.

[4] Butler in his *Benedictine Monachism* points out that the first Benedict vested the sole power over the monastery in the abbot who had full patriarchal powers (p. 217 et seq.).

as *magister scholae* transgressed the rule by which he should not have been alone with one of the *oblati*. Delighted to have caught him tripping, several of the monks accused him publicly in the chapter. Odo, attempting no excuse, rose and threw himself prostrate before Berno, who marvelling at his humility, yet wishing to try him further, feigned deep indignation and condemned him to ' excommunication '. Not even then did Odo seek to urge the extenuating circumstance, but in a passion of still greater humility prostrated himself before each of his accusers in turn, praying them to seek his pardon. After this he was dearer than ever to Berno.

A charming story illustrates Odo's humility and at the same time one of the customs of Baume. During refection, one of the monks read aloud to his fellows till stopped at the end of the meal by a sign from the abbot.[1] Before this moment each monk had carefully to collect and eat his crumbs. Now among the monks there was one—i.e. Odo—who always listened to the reading with such rapt attention that frequently he forgot to eat, for before the spiritual food the earthly lost its savour. One day he was so engrossed that he forgot all about his crumbs. Full of remorse he did not know what to do, for after refection the monks went straight to chapel. He hastily collected the crumbs, joined in the prayers, and after chapel threw himself prostrate before Berno. Asked in what he had sinned he stretched forth his hand full of the crumbs, which in that very moment were changed to pearls ! Great was the admiration and amazement of the brothers. The practical Berno ordered the pearls to be made into church ornaments.

The rule about the crumbs was evidently considered very important. A monk on his deathbed was heard to call despairingly for help. He had seen himself before the judgement seat, where the devil, holding a little sack full of all the crumbs he had neglected to eat, stood ready to accuse him. Twice

---

[1] Ibid. i. 35. A change in the rule due to the second Benedict. Originally the abbot took his meals with the guests, but this was found impracticable.

with a terrible cry the wretched monk shrieked, ' Do ye not see, do ye not see that the devil with the sack is standing among you ? ' then fortifying himself with the sign of the cross he fell back dead. This dramatic end made a deep impression on the brothers. Ever after the crumbs were carefully collected by all.[1]

Odo also laid great stress on two other points which Berno before him evidently tried hard to enforce, (1) that no private property should be held by the monks,[2] and (2) that no flesh meat should be eaten. When he entered Baume the monks could not believe that he had renounced all his earthly possessions, and sent him forth with one of their number to fetch them. As a judgement the monk accompanying him fell ill and died.

To Odo the eating of meat was the cause of all fleshly lusts. Two stories from his lips showed what direful punishment would overtake the monk who was disobedient on this point. A monk on a visit to his sister, when offered fish, said he was sick of fish and demanded flesh and wine instead. When this was served he joyfully sat down to eat. His joy was short-lived, for unable either to eject or swallow his first mouthful, ' he lost ', as John quaintly puts it, ' both food and life '. [3] Another monk on a visit home was annoyed to find no food ready. His relatives refused to be browbeaten and explained that it was not dinner-time, whereupon the monk replied that he had not ridden all night on duty to be forced at the end to fast. To appease him he was offered fish, which incensed him the more. Seeing at his feet a brood of chickens, he snatched one up and cried, ' Let this be my fish to-day.' When his friends asked in surprise if he had a dispensation to eat flesh, he casuistically explained, ' Fowl is not flesh, and fowl and

---

[1] Ibid. i. 31.

[2] The first St. Benedict regarded this as of the utmost importance. The holding of private property was to him the worst of vices (*nequissimum vitium*). The monk was to have nothing of his own, and on taking vows was to give his possessions to the poor, or make them over to his monastery. In practice, however, this was found very difficult. Odo, like Pachomius, foresaw the ruin of monasticism from the holding of private property.

[3] Ibid. iii. 3.

fish have one origin and equal condition, as our hymn bears witness.' Then when the chicken was placed before him, he snatched up a bone. But he too was unable to swallow, and after being unmercifully cudgelled by the onlookers he died.[1]

During the fifteen or sixteen years that Odo remained at Baume his life probably passed in the quiet routine of contemplation and prayer; but not in idleness, for in a tantalisingly short sentence John explains that on his arrival at Baume, 'being a learned man, he was made schoolmaster'.[2] No further information is given about the *Schola*. The pupils were boys probably living at the monastery (*oblati*), and some of the monks. At that time Odo was thirty years old.[3]

Peaceful as the life was, friction was not lacking. Odo's virtues made him a prominent figure among the brethren, and this, joined to the fact that he was especially beloved by Berno, aroused the animosity of the reactionary party, those monks who found Berno's discipline too severe, and who had tried to keep Odo from entering the monastery. 'The head of this pest' was Wido. He with his followers did not cease to oppose Odo, and to hurl false accusations and insults at his head. Each instigated the other to tempt him, even though half afraid that they might themselves be the sufferers, if Odo, more learned than they, should refuse to teach them. Wido, however, knew his man well, and assured his followers that Odo would bear these and worse injuries without any attempt at retaliation. His only weapon against his persecutors was patience, and never

---

[1] Ibid. St. Benedict forbade the eating of flesh meat to all except the sick. But it was always a disputed point whether fowl was to be classed with meat, or with fish as in Genesis. Cf. also the hymn—

> *Magnae Deus potentiae*
> *Qui ex aquis ortum genus*
> *Partim remittis gurgiti*
> *Partim levas in aera.*

[2] Ibid. i. 23, *Nam patri Odoni quia erat vir scholasticus, laboriosum scholae imposuerunt magisterium.* By the Capitulary of 817 Benedict laid down that there should be no schools for outside pupils in the monasteries of *Francia*, but only for boys belonging to the monastery.

[3] Ibid. i. 33.

attempting justification he flung himself, at each new trial, seeking pardon at their feet. ' This he did not from timidity, but from brotherly love, in the hope that by his patience he might correct those whom he saw incurring the divine vengeance. Checked they were, yet ever like running water they returned to their evil ways, persecuting him whom they ought to have imitated.' After Berno's death these monks returned to the world and came to a bad end !

Apart from this ill-will Odo must have passed his days in peace and quiet. Yet he could not be happy when he thought of his parents still enmeshed in the snares of the world. Having obtained permission from Berno he sought out his father, and persuaded him to enter a monastery. His mother took the veil, and later became an eminent abbess. His brother Bernard [1] also took vows after his infant son (still unbaptized) had been carried off by the Northmen. Miraculously saved and restored to Odo's arms, in them the child was baptized and died.[2]

The name of Odo's mother recalled to John a story which illustrated Odo's feeling about monasticism. Once when absent from the monastery he stayed at the house of a nobleman who was away from home, but whose daughter watched him all evening eager to learn about his life. At night she came to him secretly, and falling at his feet begged him to save her from her approaching marriage. Odo did not know what to do, knowing he would be answerable to God for the girl's soul, yet foreseeing the scandal if he, a monk, dared to take her away. Finally, ' overcome by the love of God and the girl's sobs ', he rode into

---

[1] Bruel, i. 584. Bernardus gave Cluny a church near Lyons : *Pro remedio anime mee et amite mee, et fratris mei Odonis abbatis.*

[2] *Vita Joanne,* ii. 16. A pilgrim stopping at the monastery where John wrote, probably Salerno, on his way to Jerusalem long after told the story. The Normans when devastating the land round Tours carried off the child and his nurse eight days' journey from Tours, and across a river too deep to cross except by boat. There seemed no hope of escape. Yet the nurse passed through the ranks of the enemy, crossed the river, and in three days reached Tours, having suffered neither hunger, thirst, nor fatigue. Odo baptized the child and prayed it might die.

the night, ordering the servants to follow with the girl. Next day he left her in an oratory near Baume,[1] ' where noble women were wont to come for prayer '. When he told Berno, the abbot rebuked him for having dared to act on his own initiative. Prostrate on the ground, and clasping Berno's feet, Odo besought pardon. Only after reiterated questioning would he defend himself, saying : ' Oh lord and father, ever from the moment that thou didst deign to receive me, a sinner, I have seen that thy sole care was the saving of souls. Other abbots may study to gain material things and please men. Thou, relying on mercy and virtue, seek'st through the salvation of souls to please God alone. I wished to follow thy example in saving this virgin to the glory of thy name. For although in the end her tears overcame me, yet I was not unmindful of thy reproach, but I had rather suffer the flagellation of my holy father than be held guilty for her soul. And would that I could free all the women bound in the chains of the flesh who live in this province, and thou flagellate me for each in thy pious manner.' [2] Thus he turned aside the anger of Berno, who exhorted him to strengthen the girl daily in holy instruction, lest tempted by the devil she returned to the world. This Odo did, and a few days later took her to a convent near, where not long after she died : saved, as was evident to all, for St. Paul himself came to receive her soul.

The next event of importance in Odo's life was his ordination to the priesthood. Knowing that in his humility he would consider himself unworthy, Berno asked bishop Turpio of Limoges to ordain him, without telling Odo of his intention. When the bishop arrived, Odo was commanded on his obedience as a monk to receive ordination. So unworthy did he feel himself,

---

[1] Mabillon, *Ann.* v. p. 68. There were two convents for women near Baume, one founded by St. Romanus, and situated near the Jura mountains, the other near the river Doubs in the mountains of Besançon. Odo refers to one of them in the *Collationes*, iii. 21, when telling of the punishment which overtook two of the nuns there who returned to the world. *Duae sanctimoniales de monasterio puellarum quod iuxta nostrum Balma situm est.*

[2] To Odo as to Augustine marriage itself was wrong. *Coll.* ii. 204, *Si ergo tanta est culpa in coniugali concubitu ut infans pro illa sola puniri debeat. . . .*

that awakening that night and feeling the priest's stole round his neck, he gave himself up to lamentation, and for long through his excessive humility could scarcely summon up courage to go beyond the gates of the monastery.   Pitying his misery, Berno sent him to Limoges on a visit to bishop Turpio, a visit which led to the writing of his second book.   One day when he and the bishop were discussing the evil condition of the church, Odo taking Jeremiah as his inspiration spoke with such sombre eloquence that the bishop begged him to write his words down. When Odo objected that he could not write without first obtaining his abbot's consent, Turpio himself went to Baume to obtain it.   The result was the *Collationes*.[1]

Thus in teaching, in study, and in prayer, Odo's life at Baume passed.   He entered the monastery when he was thirty. Fifteen or sixteen years later, Berno, feeling his strength fail, summoned the neighbouring bishops to Baume, and divested himself of ' that office of which he a sinner had been unworthy '. Then he ordered the monks to freely choose an abbot.   With one accord they named Odo, whom resisting they dragged before Berno.   So passionately did he declare himself unworthy, that it required the bishop's threat of ' excommunication ' to make him accept the office.   Soon after Berno died (*c.* 927).

.   .   .   .

Whatever the contradiction of authorities as to the origins of Cluny, this fact at least is clear, that the monastery, as yet unfinished, came under the headship of the most eminent and virtuous monk of Baume.   The *seniores* followed him,[2] i.e. probably those monks who had supported Berno in his efforts to uphold discipline.   Henceforth while Cluny was to increase, Baume was to decrease.   The contrast between the histories of the two monasteries shows how much Cluny owed to the personality of her second abbot.

[1] *Vita Joanne*, i. 37, *Tres libellos composuit ex Jeremie vaticinio quorum textus per diversas ecclesias est translatus.*
[2] Ibid., ii. 1, *Secuti sunt autem eum seniores loci illius.*

Much of Odo's success may be attributed to the fact that he entered on his work as no young unbalanced monk, but as a man tried and trained in the discipline of life. Probably to that fact may be attributed his following the principle of moderation which so largely contributed to the monastery's success ; a principle befitting the times, in which, owing to the almost entire disappearance of monastic life, and the consequent licence, any attempt at discipline, however moderate, was resented. Almost fifty when he became sole abbot of Cluny, and having passed through a phase of severe asceticism at Tours, he was able to judge the evils as well as the merits of excessive devotion, in this resembling the first Benedict.

Apart from the personal character of her abbot, there seemed to be few factors working for Cluny's future greatness. The abbey was poor, and in a land to which many relics had been brought for safety, possessed none to attract popular fervour. Nevertheless in four years, thanks to the exceptional ability and deep spirituality of her abbot, Cluny had become known as a reforming centre. A great future clearly lay before her. For that future her geographical position was in her favour. She lay in the shelter of gently swelling hills, in a part of Burgundy into which neither Normans, Huns, nor Saracens seem to have penetrated. She lay near one of the pilgrim routes to Rome and near the highways of the Saône and the Rhone. More favourable still was her position for developing her principle of monastic autonomy, situated as she was in a part of Burgundy where independence was possible. For there the authority of both Frankish king and Teutonic emperor was negligible, what semblance of power the one possessed being neutralised by the other. Cluny conveniently distant from both was practically independent of either. Nor had she anything to fear from the dukes of Burgundy, who at this time were occupied in holding back the incursions of the barbarians. Besides there was no reason why any of the three powers should have troubled about the small, insignificant, poverty-stricken monastery, and Cluny was left free to develop. Her greatest struggle for independence, that against the attempted domination of her diocesan, the bishop of Mâcon, came after Odo's death.

Odo's first care at Cluny was to go on with the building of the monastery. Even after the work was well in hand the monks saw themselves threatened with disaster through lack of funds. Neither from Baume nor from Gigny was help to be expected. Gloom settled at Cluny. Not in vain, however, had been Odo's fervour in the cult of St. Martin. On the festival of that saint, a day ever to be celebrated with special honours at Cluny, Odo after morning celebration saw a venerable old man regarding the unfinished building. His examination finished, the old man informed the enraptured abbot that he was St. Martin himself, come to tell the monks that if they persevered and their courage did not fail, he would see that necessary funds were sent to them ! A few days after, 3000 solidi were brought as a gift from ' Gothia ' to Cluny, a sum sufficient to avert disaster and allow the monks to continue their labours.[1] Another wonder marked the completion of their work. When the monks had finished the oratory, they asked the neighbouring bishop to consecrate it. On the appointed day, having either forgotten or not having realised the poverty of the brothers, the bishop was seen approaching with many followers. Having no provisions to feed so many the monks were in despair, when a huge animal emerged from the forest, and came near the church door, upon which—a realistic touch—the guardian incontinently fled ! Quietly and peaceably the animal rubbed itself against the door, and remained there till the bishop arrived, when it offered itself a willing sacrifice for the needs of the brothers. They with fervent thanks to God were enabled sumptuously to feast their guests.[2]

Apart from the poverty of the abbey Odo at first met with other difficulties. As an old man he warned John of the many

---

[1] Ibid. ii. 2.
[2] Ibid. ii. 3. In some of the manuscripts the animal is called a boar, in others simply *immane*, probably to heighten the effect.

trials to his patience which he, as abbot, must expect. ' This he made clear, by telling of all he himself had suffered from his monks when he first became abbot, but as all of them since then have become eminent for their holiness and sanctity of life, it would ill beseem me to dwell on their earlier faults.'[1] Nevertheless from the beginning Cluny flourished under Odo's fostering care, and in 927 he obtained for it a royal charter from Rudolf of Burgundy, king of the Franks.[2]

How essential in his eyes the principle of the monastery's autonomy was, is seen from the fact that almost the whole of the charter is occupied with that point. The preamble recapitulated how duke William of Aquitaine had founded Cluny (*per manus Bernonis construxit*), had under a great and terrible oath freed it from all secular domination and subjected it to Rome alone, ' for protection not domination '.[3] Therefore Rudolf the king, rejoicing over the work and favouring the constitution, proclaimed that, according to William's testament, Cluny was freed from the interference and absolved from the authority of kings, princes, relatives of William, and all men whomsoever. What property the monastery possessed, or in the future would possess, was to be held without let or hindrance. No one was to take away its serfs or freemen.[4] The monks were not to pay tolls in the markets. In cases where they held part of woods or of ploughed land, they only were to receive *terraticum*. They could have tenths from demesne land for hospitality.[5] Alfracta was to be theirs with an alod, serfs, and a manor. Other two alods which they had received were to be held in

---

[1] Ibid. ii. 7.

[2] Bruel, i. 285. The charter begins :—As it is certain that God will not cast away the powerful without whom there would be no power, so it is certain that He will inquire about their works. Therefore it behoves the king to do good especially to holy church and thus to work with God, and win eternal reward.

[3] Ibid., *Ab omni seculari dominatu liberum sub magna et terribili adiuratione fecit. Apostolicae sedi ad tuendum non ad dominandum subligavit.*

[4] Ibid., *Homines eorum liberos ac servos nemo . . . distringat.*

[5] Ibid., *Decimas suas indominicatas ad hospitale habeant.*

perpetuity.   After Odo's death they were freely to elect their new abbot, and the monastery to continue in that order and administration which William had laid down.

The reform which Berno had begun, Odo not only carried out at Cluny but extended to other houses.   By 930 he reformed Romainmoutier, Tulle, and Aurillac, and in 930 the old and far-famed monastery of Fleury.

CHAPTER IV

FLEURY was at one time the most distinguished monastery of Gaul, its renown arising from the fact that the bones of St. Benedict had been translated to it from Monte Cassino. Hence its name, for on the arrival of the relics, though it was autumn the ground around the monastery burst into flowers.

By the tenth century Fleury had fallen from its high estate. Just because its reputation for holiness had been so high the scandal was the greater when the lives of its monks became a byword for infamy. 'After the end of the persecutions of the Northmen alas! though the bodies of the monks were reunited at Fleury, their souls were in a divided state, and the monastery fell into evil ways.' At last St. Benedict himself intervened. Appearing one day to a certain brother he told him that, horrified at the conduct of the monks, he was leaving Fleury, but would return bringing from Aquitaine a man after his own heart[1] Here was an opportunity for amendment if the monks had betaken themselves to penitence and prayer. Instead they rushed round the countryside on horseback, in the hope of finding the saint, and forcing him to return. Failing in their quest they jeered and mocked at the visionary.

Retribution swiftly fell on them, for count Elisardus, the famous warrior, 'hearing of their infamous life asked and received the monastery from Rudolf, king of the Franks, which he begged Odo to reform'. With his customary zeal Odo, accompanied by several monks, a bishop, two counts, and two of the chief men of the district, at once set out for Fleury. On

---

[1] *Vita Joanne*, iii. 8.

his arrival he found the monks prepared for resistance, ready to die rather than let any man enter. Several of them armed with spears and swords guarded the approach to the monastery. Others hurled down stones from the roof. Notwithstanding this brave array there was division among them. 'Alas, alas,' they cried, 'why did we not believe the story of our brother? All things that he told us have come true, for is not this Odo of Aquitaine? And did we not suspect that it was he of whom St. Benedict spoke? Why did we not take the initiative, and send to him, or invite him of our own accord?' Only one of the monks, Wulfaldus, kept his head, and seized on the one point which could justify his companions, and put the newcomers in the wrong. He appealed to the royal charters,[1] by which the abbey had been exempted from outside control, and granted priority over all other monasteries. How then dared the upstart Odo touch its rights? Odo could only reply that he came peaceably, with no desire to injure any one's rights or person, and simply to correct irregularities.[2]

Against this the monks protested, and threatened to murder him. For three days intermediaries went to and fro, and matters were at a deadlock, till Odo took the decision into his own hands. Without telling his companions he mounted an ass, and rode alone towards the monastery. When his intention dawned on his terrified companions, the bishop and the others ran after him, calling, 'Whither goest thou, father? Dost thou not know that they are ready to slay thee? nay, that at the very moment they see thee, thou shalt die the death? Dost thou then seek to cause them joy, and us inconsolable grief?' But not thus was Odo to be stopped, for the just man like the lion is without fear. And what seemed a miracle happened. At his approach the heart of his enemies was changed. With one accord they threw

---

[1] Ibid. iii. 8, *Precepta regalia in quibus continebatur ut nulli ex alia congregatione ullo unquam tempore liceret eiusdem loci prioratum subire.*

[2] Ibid., *Pacifice veni ut neminem laedam nulli noceam sed ut incorrectos regulariter corrigam.*

away their weapons, and embraced his feet. Great was the joy that day.

Odo then took over the direction of the monastery and remained alone at Fleury, while his friends returned home. He found it no easy task to carry out the reform, for though an outburst of emotion had thrown the monks at his feet, in the ' daily round, the common task ', they were not so ready to remain there. He met with stubborn resistance to the two first principles of his reform, that no private possessions should be held within the monastery, and that no flesh meat should be eaten. Rather than share all things in common the monks preferred to squander their possessions on profligates, or to bestow them on friends outside the monastery.

Over the second point, the giving up of flesh meat, Odo had foreseen difficulties, and had come provided with large supplies of fish. But the monks laid their heads together, and overcoming their aversion to that article of diet, eagerly devoured Odo's store, so that he would be faced with the alternative, of letting them starve, or return to the eating of meat. Every day, with malicious eyes, they watched Odo's dwindling supplies, rejoicing beforehand in his dilemma when he should find himself outwitted. But they had not reckoned with his unquestioning obedience to the Gospel precept, ' Take no thought for the morrow ' ; and no shade of annoyance nor doubt crossed his serene face. ' Intrepid in faith, secure in hope, and fortified in charity,' he knew that God would provide. And indeed St. Benedict intervened. Appearing to Odo he promised to send a hundred solidi to Fleury, and later such quantity of provisions, that for long the needs of the monks would be supplied.

Considering the circumstances in which the reform had been carried out, it is not surprising that doubts as to its permanency were entertained, and that Odo was glad to have behind him the support of the temporal power. This he had from Hugh, duke of the Franks, a fact stated in the papal charter of 938, when Leo VII., confirming the privileges of Fleury, referred to the reform, which he heard had been carried through by Odo, and Hugh.[1] The pope threatened with the anathema, monks or other persons who by creating disturbances over the election of the abbot, or by attacking the property of the monastery, or by seeking to seduce the monks from their new way of life [2] showed themselves inimical to the monastery's true interests. Fleury was to be under no power except the king's. Neither he nor any other prince was to give it to bishop, canon, layman or other abbot *ad dominandum*. Five months before, writing to the bishops of Lyons, Bourges, Sens and Rheims, Leo expressed his sorrow over the iniquity of the times and the decline of religion, but his joy over the reform of Fleury, the work of Odo and his monks.

The reform of so eminent a monastery aroused great expectations. ' It is our hope,' the pope wrote, ' that if religious observance flourishes again in that monastery, the head and chief of monasteries, others as members may also revive.' [3] On the whole this hope was fulfilled, and Fleury not only recovered its old reputation but became an active centre of reform.

Before considering the reform which emanated from Fleury we may mention two of John's stories about Fleury, the first showing the jealousy that even trivial points aroused between the old order and the new. Odo with several brothers was staying at the monastery. On the Saturday evening, according to the Cluniac custom, one of them began to clean his boots. This innovation intensely annoyed a Fleurian monk, who, although it was the silence hour, could not contain his wrath, and burst forth, ' Tell me in what passage St. Benedict ever ordered his monks to clean their shoes '. On the other circumspectly making

---

[1] Migne, 132, p. 1075, . . . *conversationis comperimus quod filius noster Odo, venerabilis abbas in hoc monasterio et venerabilis vir Hugo dux Francorum nuper stabilierunt alacrius et securius.*

[2] Ibid., *Sive in detrahenda vel impedienda conversatione quam novelli fratres tenere.*

[3] Ibid., *Spes nobis inest quia si in illo coenobio quod est quasi caput ac principium observantia religiosa refloruerit, cetera circumquaque posita quasi membra convalescant.*

the sign for silence, he still more furiously continued : ' Oh, thou ! who wast accustomed to gad about the countryside on business, hast thou now come hither to preach the rule and to correct the life of thy betters ? By swearing and perjury thou who like a bird of prey wast accustomed to snatch away the substance of thy fellow-men, now impudently settest thyself up for a saint, as if we did not know thee of old. God did not make me a serpent that after thy manner I should hiss, nor an ox that I should bellow, but a man to speak with the tongue He gave me.' Afraid to hear more the Cluniac monk fled, pursued by the insults of the other. Next day the scandal was reported at the meeting of the chapter, when the hardened sinner refused to seek pardon, and had even the audacity to maintain that he had done well, and that the other had no right to hold himself the better. Odo sorrowful at such pride adjourned the dispute to next day, that the peace and joy of the Lord's day should not be disturbed. But when the chapter adjourned, the offending brother was found to be dumb, and three days later, without absolution, he died.[1]

The second story shows the reverence with which Fleury was regarded. Odo was there one year for St. Benedict's day. Morning Lauds was celebrated before dawn, when St. Benedict appeared to a weary brother who had fallen asleep. With that charming familiarity incident to visions, the sleeping brother asked the saint where he had come from and what he was doing there. He had been absent from Fleury in the night, the saint replied, to rescue a monk who having left Fleury from pride had crossed to Britain, where he had died, and been seized by demons. This amazed the sleeping monk, when to his further amazement the saint explained that since its foundation there was no monk of Fleury but had been received into eternal

---

[1] This custom of cleaning the footgear was stopped in the twelfth century by Peter the Venerable. It had been useful in the days when the monks travelled, but when Cluny grew in size, though many of the monks never left the cloister, the rule was still obligatory. The monks would therefore wet two fingers, and smear their boots, so as to make a show of cleaning them.

rest. He then asked if the brothers were well supplied with fish, and learning they were not, said they should fish not in the river but in the marsh. That day he would be present with them and would give such a sign that none could mistake his coming. When the hour of speech came, the brother told all. Fishers were sent to the marsh, but fearful of ridicule went to the river and of course caught nothing. Questioned by the *oeconomus* they were ignominiously driven by him to the marsh, where their catch was so enormous that they could scarcely drag it back. Then the festival dawned, and crowds were seen at the monastic gates, the halt, the blind, the paralysed, the sick, all waiting for the hour of refection, before which mass was said. When the *Gloria* was sung, suddenly with a loud noise the doors of the church burst open.[1] All struck with terror looked round, when the blind saw, the lame walked, the deaf heard, the sick received their health, and the lamps of the church lit up. All understood that St. Benedict was with them, and none could restrain their tears of joy.

Odo would not tell the name of the monk who saw the vision, therefore it remains doubtful whether it was he or another.

Fleury's influence spread first to St. Evre's, Toul. Gauzlin, bishop of Toul, being interested in the reform movement went to Fleury to study it. On returning he brought a copy of the almost forgotten Benedictine rule, and reformed St. Evre's,[2] where he appointed Archimbald, a monk of Fleury, abbot (934). The bishop retained supreme authority over the monastery. No abbot was to remove it from his jurisdiction, and the election of an abbot was valid only if ratified by him. His zeal did not stop with the reform of this, the chief monastery of his diocese. With Archimbald's help he restored Bouxières (a convent) and reformed St. Mansuy's.[3] To the latter Archimbald sent monks

---

[1] Ibid. iii. 2. So large was the church that of all the vast multitude not one had to remain outside.

[2] *Gesta episc. Tull.* c. 31.

[3] *Miracula S. Mansueti, SS.* iv. p. 508.

from St. Evre's from which St. Mansuy's was subsidised, but it soon lapsed again from grace, and sank into so evil a state that it had to be reformed a second time by Gerhard of Brogne. A more scandalous state of misrule prevailed at Montiérender from which the abbot was expelled. The majority of the monks fled, and others under the leadership of a monk of St. Evre's were settled there.[1] Fleury itself was given full rights over three monasteries as far distant as Pressy in Autun, Sacerge, and La Réole in Gascony.[2] The possession of the last proved rather a misfortune than a blessing. Its monks were always turbulent, and the abbots of Fleury, though too far away to control them, were yet held responsible for the scandal of their lives. Finally, in an attempt to restore order Abbo, the greatest of the abbots of Fleury, lost his life.

Another important monastery reformed by Fleury, three years after Odo's death, was St. Rémi of Rheims.[3] Its monks had been forced to flee during the incursions of the Huns (926). For years after that. Rheims was the centre of the political intrigues of the Frankish king and his opponents and no thought was given to monastic revival. Finally, Hugh, the archbishop, was moved to restore St. Rémi's, and asked Archimbald of Fleury to help. By his efforts and the favour of Gerberga, mother of the Frankish king, the former possessions of the monastery were won back, and its old reputation restored. Within its walls Lothair was crowned, when he granted St. Rémi's full immunity from dues (953). In 972 John XIII. took it under the papal protection, and confirmed its freedom from royal, secular, and episcopal control.

By the end of the tenth century Fleury had attained a position, second if not equal to Cluny, with which almost all connection had been allowed to drop. In her reform propaganda the influence of the monastery extended chiefly to

[1] Sackur, *Die Cluniazenser in ihrer kirchlichen und allgemeingeschlichtlichen Wirksamkeit*, i. p. 176.
[2] *Mirac. S. Benedicti*, iii. c. 15, c. 4; cf. *Vita Abbonis*, cap. 20.
[3] Mabillon, *Acta SS.* v. 346.

the north and east of Gaul, and to Lorraine ; even more distant England [1] seems to have owed much of her monastic revival to Fleury. With the tenth century the most influential days of Fleury were over, and its abbots soon sank to being mere creatures of the Crown.

[1] Cf. *Vita Abbonis, Vita Oswaldi.*

CHAPTER V

THE fact that so celebrated a monastery as Fleury had been reformed by the abbot of Cluny, made a stir in ecclesiastical circles, and greatly increased Odo's renown. After that event, ' many from neighbouring regions came to follow the footsteps of the holy man, and under his direction to learn the way of obedience. In so much was the fame of his holiness noised abroad, that not only laymen and canons, but even certain bishops joined his community. Thus the ground which had been left uncultivated and choked with thorns began to bring forth new fruit ; and Odo began to shine like a star, known to kings, familiar to bishops, and beloved of magnates. And whosoever in those days built a monastery, delivered it to the authority (*ius*) of the father, that he might order and direct it '.[1]

In 931, John XI. granted a charter which contains a clause epoch-making in the history of Cluny. ' Because it is only too clear that almost all monasteries have erred from the regular life, we grant, that if any monk from any monastery should wish to pass over to your manner of living with the sole object of amending his life, that is, if his former abbot has neglected to provide regular means of subsistence for preventing the holding of private property, thou mayst receive him until such time as the conduct of his monastery be corrected.' [2] In the past

---

[1] *Vita Joanne.*

[2] Migne, 132, p. 1055, *Et quia iam pene cuncta monasteria a suo proposito praevaricantur, concedimus, ut si quis monachus ex quolibet monasterio ad vestram conversationem, scio duntaxat meliorandae vitae studio transmigrare voluerit sui videlicet eius abbas regularem sumptum ad depellendam proprietatem habendi ministrare neglexerit, suscipere vobis liceat, quousque monasterii sui conversatio emendetur.*

47

this privilege had been granted, but very rarely. The decree of the Council of Agde [1] had forbidden any abbot to receive strange monks within his monastery, unless with their abbot's goodwill and consent. Now, however, with the express sanction of the papal authority, the way was cleared for Cluny's propaganda. Possession of Romainmoutier was confirmed, and the papal licence granted Odo to receive any other monastery under his authority for reform. [2]

Other clauses in the charter witnessed to the papal goodwill; e.g. Cluny's quinquennial tribute of ten solidi was to be paid in order to make clearly intelligible to all, that it pertained to the holy see to guard and cherish the monastery. [3] Its freedom from outside domination [4] was again assured, and freedom of choice at the election of an abbot, though it was added, ' that should, what God prevent, an unworthy choice be made, then any one whosoever might annul it '. The pope confirmed Cluny's possessions, and the privilege of coining money (*monetam propriam*) granted by Rudolf, king of the Franks. No one was to take away its serfs or attack its property, Cluny being one of those holy places to which reverence was due. Tenths which had formerly belonged to its chapels and through the modern authority of any bishop had been taken away, [5] were restored (*vobis ex integro restituimus*). New chapels built in the neighbourhood were to diminish nothing from the tenths of Cluny's churches, [6] and the dues which bishop Berno had granted from

[1] *Labbe Concilia*, viii. p. 329, clause xxvii., *Monachum nisi abbatis sui aut permissu aut voluntate ad alterum monasterium commigrantem nullus abbas suscipere aut retinere presumat sed ubicumque fuerint abbati suo auctoritate canonum revocentur.*

[2] Migne, 132, p. 1057, *Si coenobium aliquod ex voluntate illorum ad quorum dispositionem pertinere videtur, in sua ditione ad meliorandum suscipere consenteritis, nostram licentiam ex hoc habeatis.*

[3] Ibid., *Ad tuendum atque fovendum.*

[4] Ibid., *Liberum ab omni dominatu cuiuscunque regis aut episcopi, sive comitis, aut cuiuslibet ex propinquis ipsius Willelmi.*

[5] Ibid., *Per modernam quasi auctoritatem sive licentiam a quolibet episcopo subtractae sunt.*

[6] Ibid., *Capellas si aliquae iam factae sunt vel faciendae inibi sunt, ita manere concedimus ut vestris ecclesiis nihil ex decimis minuatur.*

these churches were assured in perpetuity. Tenths from cultivated lands and vineyards could be reserved for hospitality. Then followed the anathema on those who broke, and the blessing on those who kept, the clauses of the charter. Next year the pope, at the request of Odo and Hugh, king of the Lombards,[1] reconfirmed Cluny's privileges. 'For the highest reward will be given to those venerable places which strive to increase holiness.' Cluny's possession of Carus Locus, a monastery belonging to the jurisdiction of Rome, was confirmed. Any one who went against the charter would be anathematised by Peter the apostle, and abandoned to the devil and his atrocious minions to be burnt in the eternal fire with Judas who betrayed the Lord, and sunk with the wicked in the abyss of infernal chaos.

Six years later John's successor, Leo VII., reaffirmed the privileges (938). He did so because of (1) his love for the apostles Peter and Paul ; (2) the good repute of the religious life at Cluny ; [2] (3) his love for his sons, kings Hugh and Lothair, who, as he had heard, cherished the monastery exceedingly.[3] He confirmed the privileges granted by John and declared Cluny free from all outside domination, as William the Pious had decreed. He reinstated Cluny in the possession of vills given by king Rudolf but claimed by the church of Lyons and of Mâcon. Leo based his decision on the fact that no person then living was old enough to have seen the aforesaid churches invested with any of the vills, and that the legal time for proving such cases had been spent in wrangling and dispute. All further discussion was to cease.[4] Any one who seized Cluny's possessions or the property given by the king would be excommuni-

---

[1] Ibid. p. 1058, *Quia supplicavit tua religio et interventio Hugonis glorissimi regis, dilecti filii nostri.*

[2] Ibid. p. 1074, *Pro religione quae ibidem tenetur.*

[3] Ibid., *Qui locum multum fovent.*

[4] Ibid., *Non est tamen aliquis tam longaevae aetatis, qui unquam in predictis ecclesiis vestituram de illis villis ullam habere vidisset ; et quia prestitutum legale tempus ad recuperandas huiusmodi querelas pertransiit, omnis repetitio conquiescat.*

E

cated. All who did good to the abbey would, if they wished to amend their lives, be absolved from their sins; all who did harm anathematised.[1]

Proofs of royal favour were also given. Three times in 931 Rudolf of Burgundy, king of the Franks, gave land to Cluny and confirmed gifts made by others. In the first charter he stated that as there was no power except from God, the powerful should humble themselves under His hand and be zealous to please Him with gifts. He therefore made known to all kings, counts, magistrates, and ministers of the kingdom that, at the request of his wife and *fideles*, he gave Cluny a vill and the third of a fishery (*piscina*), the middle part, with its serfs and whatever else belonged to it. No king, count, or person of inferior rank was to interfere with the gift:[2] at the same time he confirmed the gift of Blanuscus,[3] with a chapel and its lands, and reaffirmed the decree of bishop Berno of Mâcon over tenths (cf. i. 373), which were to be held by Cluny as of old, and not taken away by any modern authority. The second charter stated that by bending the royal ear to the just petitions of the faithful, the royal cult was furthered, and subjects made more zealous in their fidelity. Therefore, at the request of his wife and dearest brother, the king gave seven manors in three different vills to Cluny, confirmed his former gift of the third of a fishery, with the three servants attached to it, their children and the manors which they held (*quos ipsi*

---

[1] Ibid. p. 1068. The year before (937) the pope twice confirmed Cluny's possession of property. For it was right to give the apostolic defence to those places which asked it, and especially to Cluny, subject as it was to the papal *ius*. At Odo's request he confirmed possession of the *curtis* Escutiola with churches, houses, lands, fields, meadows, pasture, woods, thickets, apple trees, cisterns, fountains, rivers, fruitful and unfruitful trees, cultivated and uncultivated land, serfs, male and female, i.e. everything belonging to the *curtis* as left by count Geoffrey. A curse was pronounced on any one who attacked this property. In the same year at Odo's request he confirmed Cluny's possession of a vill and everything belonging to it, given by king Rudolf: the wording identical to the above.

[2] Bruel, i. 396.

[3] Ibid. Chapels, serfs, vineyards, meadows, waters, woods, mills, cultivated and uncultivated land.

tenent), also the abbey's right to property given by two other donors.[1] In the third charter, again at his wife and brother's request, he gave the vill Salustriacus (in which he had previously given three manors), with vineyards, fields, meadows, woods, and the fishery, etc., mentioned above.[2]

The next year the little society of Cluniac brothers, watched over by their gentle father and abbot Odo, remembering that ecclesiastical authority warns men in this miserable life and earthly pilgrimage to strive for eternal joys, and to flee from the waves of the world to the shore of eternal tranquillity, and afraid that they should be found unfruitful trees, built a chapel at Salustriacus, which they asked Berno, bishop of Mâcon, to consecrate, and in endowment (*pro dote*) to grant them tenths. He, not seeking his own with the consent of his canons, granted them all the tenths from the land given by the king in Salustriacus and the country around, tenths which formerly belonged to St. Peter's Massiacus, half of the tenths from Bulon, and other tenths from Salustriacus and Bulon which at that time went to St. Julian's Rocca, to which the new chapel was subject. No superfluous dues were to be asked from the monks, and at the synodal season the priest was to pay 2 denarii in *eulogiae* and 12 denarii in *paratae*. The bishop begged his successors to keep this agreement (932-33).[3] In 939 king Louis, at the request of Hugh the Black, son of the duke of Burgundy, also confirmed Cluny's possession of Salustriacus, two other places (*loci*), and a third of the fishery before mentioned. At the same time he confirmed the abbey's privileges. Cluny was to remain as duke William decreed, *liber et absolutus*, subject to the Roman see *ad tuendum non ad dominandum*: the

---

[1] Ibid. i. 397. Three in Salustriacus.

[2] Ibid. i. 398. Same preamble as 397.

[3] Ibid. i. 408, *Nos parvula Cluniensium fratrum societas cui Odo mitis pater et abbas pie patrocinatur utilitatem monasterii nostri pro posse providentes vel utcumque statum divini cultus nitentes augere. Capella omni tempore Sancto Juliano subjecta habeatur : obsequio non requirente superfluo ab abbate vel catervis pretaxati cenobii.*

monks to choose their own abbot : tenths to be as bishop Berno granted.[1]

From Hugh, king of the Lombards, and his son Lothair Cluny received the *curtes* Savigneux and Ambérieu, with chapels, land, vineyards, fields, meadows, pasture, woods, waters, mountains, valleys, hills, plains, houses, and serfs, the king retaining under his own power a fisher and five other servants (*servientes*). The gift was made because it was certain that for temporal gifts to venerable places dedicated to God an eternal reward would be gained. Any one disputing the gift would be condemned by God for sacrilege, and compelled to pay 100 pounds of the best gold, half to the treasury, half to the abbot (934).[2]

Several gifts were made to Cluny by bishops. As early as 929 Berno, bishop of Mâcon, perceiving that the love of the laity grew cold, and remembering it was necessary to provide for his spiritual sons wherever they were, proclaimed to all bishops, archdeacons, and chiefs of the church that he wished to solace Cluny, bound to him in special friendship.[3] There had been controversy about four of Cluny's churches in the time of his predecessor. As it was only right that the monks should enjoy tranquillity, the bishop and his congregation granted them all that his predecessors and the archdeacons had received from the four churches, with their chapels, excepting synodal *eulogiae et paratae*.[4] As long as the monks celebrated divine service there, they were to hold the churches and their tenths, or give them away if they wished. The bishop decreed this *pro signo societatis* that, alive and dead, he and the monks might share in one another's good deeds. He wished all in the present and the future to remember that by ancient custom his

---

[1] Ibid. i. 499. The preamble is the same as i. 285.

[2] Ibid. i. 417. Confirmed 937 by Leo VII. at the request of the king and his son. The anathema was called down on any one who went against the gift (Migne, 132, p. 1082).

[3] Ibid. i. 373, *In quantum possumus solaciari.*

[4] *Eulogia* : small gift. *Paratae* : expenses of receiving bishops and archdeacons when visiting rural churches (Ducange).

see had the right to do what it would with tenths.[1] If any of
his successors were tempted to go against his decree, let them
remember the text, ' Cursed be he who removeth his neighbour's
boundary '. The same bishop granted Cluny tenths when con-
secrating the chapel at Salustriacus (p. 51). In 938 another
bishop of Mâcon, Maimbod, gave Cluny a charter almost identical
with the above (373) to which he had been a signatory. An
eruption of pagans it seemed, and the violence of evil men had
almost destroyed the churches which bishop Berno had placed
under Cluny.[2] It therefore seemed only right to reduce their
synodal returns : hence one which had paid 8 was to pay only
4 denarii, and in *eulogiae* 5 denarii. One parish over which
the monks had been much distressed was restored to them in
its entirety, and from four churches, as granted by bishop
Berno, synodal *eulogiae et paratae* remitted. Three years later
Maimbod, with the wife of another man, gave a vineyard,
manor, and *curtilus* to Cluny.[3]

The bishop of Autun confirmed Cluny's possession of a
little chapel belonging to a church in his diocese. His predecessor had given it to a priest for life, and endowed it with
a little land. On his death certain evil men seized it, claiming
it as the bishop's heirs.[4] The priest therefore decided to give it
to Cluny, that fitting service should be rendered to God and the
legal dues restored to his church. The monks could do what
they wished with it, as long as they paid the parent church
12 denarii silver annually. The bishop renounced his episcopal
dues from it in favour of the monks.

From laymen in these early years there were a few gifts of
churches, e.g. a certain Leotbald and his wife gave four churches,

---

[1] Ibid., *Noverint lecturi . . . quod nostra sedes ex antiqua consuetudine pro
lege teneat, ut id de nostris dee mis facere liceat.*

[2] Ibid. i. 484, *Cum ipsas ecclesias irruptio paganorum, quin etiam violentia
quorumdam pravorum maxima ex parte annullasset visum nobis est . . . sinodali
reditu levigare.*

[3] Ibid. i. 534.

[4] Ibid. i. 474, *Iniuste et cum fas eandem quasi successores invaserant.*

a vill, its serfs, and other two vills with churches and serfs,[1] to be held by the donors for life, and on their death to revert to Cluny (927). Two years later they gave the whole entirely and unconditionally to Cluny.[2] A gift of a church[3] and of a chapel, St. Victor's, are also recorded.[4] The chapel was to pay no tenths nor dues to the secular power, for it was only right that the people's offerings should go to the monks. If any one went against the charter or asked, for the chapel, a little gift from the brothers, or seized its lands, at the day of judgement God, His holy apostles, and St. Victor, would withstand and confound him. Three deeds of sale are mentioned. A man, hoping to be snatched from the pains of hell, for 36 solidi paid by the monks gave the fourth of a church to Cluny.[5] Another man, remembering that in this fragile body all should prepare for the future, since no man knoweth the hour of his death, gave three churches with all belonging to them, i.e. tenths, cultivated and uncultivated land, meadows, plains, waters, woods, vineyards. He received 50 solidi from the monks.[6] In exchange for the vill Ambérieu and its church, a man and his wife willed a vill, its churches and serfs, to Cluny. They were to hold both properties for life, paying the monks 6 solidi annually. On their death all reverted to Cluny.[7] A man and his brother gave Cluny a *curtilus*, field, half another field, and the customs of a wood, for having burnt down a church.[8]

Of the charters, that of John XI. (931) is of course the most important as giving free scope to Cluny's reforming activity, to the consideration of which we now turn.[9]

[1] Ibid. i. 283.   [2] Ibid. i. 387.

[3] Ibid. i. 471. Any one who disputed the charter was to pay a fine of three pounds gold, *de auro libras iii.*

[4] Ibid. i. 378, *Aliquod munusculum pro ipsa capella expostulaverit.*

[5] Ibid. i. 239. *Accipio aliquod pretium 36 solidos.*

[6] Ibid. i. 486, *Pro ipsa scriptione accepimus 50 solidos.* Aymardus is mentioned as abbot (anno 938).

[7] Ibid. i. 509.   [8] Ibid. i. 310.

[9] Among the charters are a few which record marriage settlements. One man, for his love and goodwill toward her, gave his beloved wife a chapel in

Mâcon with all belonging to it and a vineyard, with all which she was to do as she willed. If the husband or his heirs later disputed the gift they were to pay a fine of three ounces gold (i. 254). Another husband, remembering that a man shall leave father and mother and cleave to his wife and that those whom God joined are not to be put asunder, gave to his beloved and amiable spouse, whom by the will of God and of his parents he had married, a vineyard and a manor with the trees and all else belonging to it—in *esponcalicio* as the Roman law laid down (*commemorat*). She could hold, sell, or exchange the property. If he took back his gift he was to pay a fine (i. 686). Another man gave in dower to his sweetest and most amiable wife a third of all he possessed or would possess, to have, hold, sell, or exchange. If he or any one else disputed the gift they were to pay a pound gold to the fisc (i. 687). Several other charters record deeds of gift or sale by women, e.g. Eva, a noble woman, sold the monks a vineyard given her in dower by her husband for two measures of wine and of wheat (i. 115). Another woman, for the love and goodwill she bore her son, gave him and his wife a manor with all belonging to it, vineyards, fields, meadows, woods, waters, mills, and adjacent to the manor three fields and four vineyards. While she lived she was to hold half of one vineyard and its serfs (i. 211). The same or another Eva, remembering that the divine mercy in pity for human frailty allows each of the faithful to buy an eternal kingdom by giving from what God gave them, and mindful of the precept to lay up treasure in heaven, gave St. Peter *in vestitura* property which came to her in hereditary right, i.e. her part of two vills (as apart from what belonged to her brothers and sisters); also a manor. She was to hold all for life, and on her death the whole reverted to Cluny (i. 141). An Eva again, who at the end of her life was fearful at the enormity of her sins, wishing to buy an eternal reward with earthly things and make friends with the mammon of unrighteousness, gave a manor and serfs to Cluny; also the third of a meadow and of a field (*contamina*, i. 153). A few other charters record gifts by women.

CHAPTER VI

ODO'S REFORMING ACTIVITY

THE time and the man go together. Great as Odo was, he could not have accomplished the work that he did had the times not been ripe. In the beginning of the tenth century a spirit of revolt at the coarse materialism of the day passed over society. As the best way to counteract that materialism, earnest men turned to the encouragement of monastic life. New monasteries were founded, and those that had fallen into disrepute were reformed.

But if the harvest was ready, the labourers were few, and a most important element in the reform was the personal. Without Odo, who towers like a giant head and shoulders above his contemporaries, Cluny's later eminence could hardly have been possible. This personal element had its disadvantages as well as its advantages. Extraordinary worker and indefatigable traveller as Odo was, he could not be everywhere, and often after he had reformed a monastery its connection with Cluny was allowed to drop. But as the reform in turn went forth from the new centre, the end after all was attained : Odo sowed the seed and cared not who reaped the harvest. Like the Psalmist he might have exclaimed, ' Show Thy servants their work, and their children Thy glory.' Because of his great zeal, and his indefatigable energy in answering any call however distant, it was impossible to build up a society looking to Cluny as head. That was to come later, when his successors had more time for organisation.

Characteristic of the reform was the fact that Benedict of Aniane's modification of the rule having been adopted, the Cluniacs showed no desire to heighten its standard of asceticism.

As the papal charter of 931 shows, Odo looked towards the reform of monasticism as a whole, and the ideal he set before him was the establishment of uniformity, similarity, and obedience in all monasteries, rather than the encouragement of isolated instances of individual perfection. Very wisely, considering the state of the times, he worked to uphold one standard, and that a standard attainable by the many.

As abbot of Cluny, the history of Odo's life is the history of the reform. The first monastery to come under his direction was Romainmoutier, which Adelheid, duchess of Burgundy, placed under him and his monks in order that they might transform it into a priory.[1] She exhorted the monks of Romainmoutier to follow the discipline and customs of Cluny.[2] Both monasteries were to be held and ruled by one abbot, and neither community to elect an abbot without the consent of the other,[3] nor were the monks of Romainmoutier to substitute another for him appointed. For it would be highly unjust if they who had been called to new life by the monks of Cluny should divide the fellowship of that monastery.[4] Nevertheless the regulation of St. Benedict held, i.e. if the minority of either congregation was moved by saner counsel and wished to choose a better person, the others (according to the rule) were to consent.[5] It was in the power of the abbot to transfer monks from the one monastery to the other as the common advantage, or indeed the state of supplies, demanded.[6] Like Cluny, Romainmoutier was to be

[1] Bruel, i. 379, *In priorem studeant reformare statum.*

[2] Ibid., *Modum conversationis . . . de Cluniaco transfertur ita conservent, ut eundem modum in victu e. vestitu, in abstinentia, in psalmodia, in silentio, in hospitalitate, in mutua dilectione et subiectione atque bona obedientia, nullatenus imminuant.*

[3] *Semper tamen velut una congregatio . . . sub uno abbate . . . non illis aut istis liceat sine communi consensu abbatem sibi preficere.*

[4] *Quoniam valde iniustum esset, si illi qui forte velut filii Romanis monasterio succreverint, socialitatem Clun. qui velut patres locum resuscitant, aliquando disciderint.*

[5] *Si vel illius vel istius congregationis minima pars saniori consilio meliorem personam eligere voluerit.*

[6] *Pro utilitate transmutandis, sive etiam de subsidiis quae forte uni loco plusquam alteri habundaverit.*

under the guardianship of Rome. Its liberties were assured and its freedom from outside control, the aid of the apostles and Rome called on, and the curse pronounced in clauses identical to those of Cluny's charter of foundation. Hugh the Black, like his mother, favoured Cluny, and intervened for Odo at the court of Conrad of Upper Burgundy. In 939 he petitioned Louis of Gaul to confirm the Cluniac charters.[1]

In Auvergne, Odo's opportunity came through the goodwill of the old friend who had ordained him, bishop Turpio of Limoges. Through the influence of the bishop and his brother Aimo,[2] Odo became abbot of Aurillac (928), a monastery which had sunk low under its last two abbots, men of infamous lives, but safeguarded by the papal protection and by the privilege of immunity from outside interference which John XI. had granted the monastery. This immunity the bishop and his brother overrode, and Odo as new abbot carried through the reform. He set over the abbey a co-abbot, Arnulf, under whom Aurillac turned from its evil ways and became a distinguished centre of reform. This success at Aurillac encouraged Aimo[3] to place Tulle under Odo's direction. In doing this he overrode the claims of another monastery, St. Savin's in Poitiers, under whose jurisdiction Tulle had been placed. This did not prevent Rudolf of Burgundy from declaring Tulle free from all previous jurisdiction, and Odo its abbot. Having inaugurated the reform, Odo appointed as co-abbot Adacius,[4] under whom the monastery flourished exceedingly.

It was also owing to bishop Turpio and his brother that two monasteries in Limoges,[5] St. Martial's and St. Augustine's, were reformed. Both were put under the direction of Martin, abbot of St. Cyprian's, Poitiers, a new monastery consecrated (936)

---

[1] Ibid. i. 499.

[2] Mabillon, *Vetera Analecta*, ii. 349, *Odo . . . rogatus a Turpione et Aimone Tutelense abbate.*　　　　　　　　　　　　[3] Sackur, i. pp. 78, 79.

[4] *Vita Joanne*, ii. 12, *Archembaldus . . . Adalasius viri nempe optimatissimi et multorum monachorum patres sunt effecti.*

[5] Sackur, i. 81 et seq.

by archbishop Teotolo of Tours. As Teotolo was the close friend of Odo, Martin may have been in sympathy with the Cluniac movement. He himself reformed two monasteries as distant as St.-Jean-d'Argély in Aquitaine and Jumièges in Normandy. Odo's next work was in Italy. Later in Gaul he reformed St. Peter le Vif.[1] Sens (937), a monastery whose lands and buildings had been laid waste by the Huns. A monk of Fleury was appointed abbot, but squandered the revenues and let the monastic lands lie waste. The monks who had no means of subsistence rapidly dwindled in numbers until only fifteen remained. Of these finally twelve were poisoned in one night, and the monastery left desolate. For a time the archbishop of Sens used the deserted buildings as a lodge for his hunting dogs. Years passed before they were restored, and St. Peter's repeopled by monks from Fleury and Cluny. The last Frankish monastery to come under Odo was St Julian's, Tours. St. Julian's had been devastated by the Northmen. For almost a hundred years monastic life there had ceased. Then archbishop Teotolo rebuilt the abbey (937), which he and his sister richly endowed. Hugh the Great also gave it land. When the restoration was complete, Odo was asked to inaugurate the reform. Soon St. Julian's became a well-known centre to which distinguished clerks and laymen flocked.[2]

In the meantime the abbots of Aurillac and Tulle extended Odo's work. In 936 Raymond Pontius of Toulouse, nephew of the founder of Cluny, built the monastery of Chanteuge,[3] which he wished to place under Odo. The latter, at that time occupied in Italy, appointed Arnulf of Aurillac abbot. Freedom from outside jurisdiction, and after Arnulf's death freedom in electing an abbot, was assured to the monks. The count and his wife also founded St. Pontius, Narbonne, and put it under Arnulf and his monks, one of whom was made abbot. Arnulf's success there won the approval of the bishop of the diocese who begged him to reform St. Chaffre du Monastier, from which religious

<hr>

[1] Ibid. i. 92.   [2] Ibid.   [3] Baluze, ii. 15.

life had quite disappeared. A monk of Aurillac was appointed abbot, who not only restored the abbey's reputation, but from it reformed Sainte Enimie's.[1] Another disciple of Arnulf's was made abbot of St. Allyre's in Clermont, which Raymond Pontius and the nobles of Auvergne had begged Arnulf to reform.

Nor was Tulle behind as a reforming centre. Its abbot, Adacius, reformed the ruined Sarlat, restored and given to him by Bernard of Périgueux and his wife Gersindis. Declared free from outside authority the monastery was placed under the protection of the king. At the election of an abbot the advice of Odo or his successors was to be obtained.[2] So worthily did Adacius rule at Sarlat that next year Bernard restored and gave him St. Sorus', Genouillac.[3] He also reformed Lézat in Toulouse (944).

In the last years of his life Odo was mainly occupied with the reform in Italy, where the state of religious life was worse even than in Gaul. The land had not recovered from the invasions of the Saracens and Huns. The whole church from the papacy downwards was secularised. Country appointments were in the hands of the nobles, who presented them to their favourites ; the sale of bishoprics and spiritual offices was quite common ; children were raised to the highest offices in the church. In the upper ranks of the clergy senseless luxury ruled, in the lower the priests shared the rude joys of the people. Even the cathedral clergy were not ashamed openly to parade their wives and concubines.

In the regular church conditions were just as bad ; monastic lands lay waste and the monasteries deserted. The monks, unable to withstand the depredations of the barbarians, had fled from their communities. Only in isolated groups had a few banded together and attempted to live by the rule. Meanwhile the lands of the abbeys were an easy prey to any freebooting noble who cared to annex them.[4] With the advance of

[1] Sackur, i. 87.   [2] Mabillon, *Ann. Ben.* iii. 405.   [3] Ibid. iii. 419.
[4] Dresdner, *Kultur u. Sittengeschichte der ital. Geistlichkeit in X. XI.* (1890).

the tenth century there seemed some hope of amelioration, one or two zealous abbots striving to win back their old possessions. They were too few in numbers to succeed, and it was evident that no headway could be made without some strong external support. This was to come from the temporal power, from Alberic of Rome himself, who but a few years before had been an unscrupulous oppressor of the monks. ' He was too terrible,' wrote a chronicler of the century, ' and cruelly pressed his yoke on the Romans and the holy see. He took over all the monasteries and their property, and with them rewarded his retainers.' [1] But after he had driven his stepfather from Rome, and had begun to find his position more secure, Alberic's policy changed. From being a most dangerous oppressor of the monks he became their ardent supporter. He had learnt that by enriching his supporters too freely with monastic possessions, he might make them a menace to his own power. At least so it appears to later historians, though the chronicler of the day is more charitable. ' Accordingly,' he wrote, ' our merciful Alberic struck with the fear of the Lord . . . began in all holy places with ardent mind to serve the servants of God, and to give rich support to the monasteries.' Political motives rather than this sudden conversion better explain Alberic's change of policy, which fortunately had begun some time before Odo's first visit to Rome (936). Whether or not Odo believed in the genuineness of Alberic's piety, he, seeing his opportunity, was quick to seize it. In the remaining six years of life, with the support of the secular power, he began the reform in central Italy. Under his direction several of the Roman monasteries were rebuilt. Perhaps at Alberic's suggestion, perhaps at the pope's, he first restored St. Paul's outside the walls,[2] which became his headquarters in Rome, and over which he placed his disciple Baldwin.

---

[1] *Benedicti Chron.* iii. cap. 32.

[2] Ibid. cap. 33. Cf. *Vita Joanne,* i. 27, *Dum Odo Romam pergeret ut monasterium intra ecclesiam beatissimi Pauli apostoli ut olim fuerat, reaedificaret cogente domno papa et universis ordinibus sacrae aedis.* Cf. ibid. ii. 22, *Ibi denique praeposuit discipulum suum abbatem Balduinum.*

Next Alberic transformed the palace on the Aventine in which
he had been born into the monastery of St. Mary's,[1] where
Hildebrand was said to have been educated. The monasteries
of St. Lawrence and St. Agnes, both outside the walls, were
then restored and reformed. Greater difficulty was experienced
with St. Andrew's on the Clivus Scaurus [2] where a few monks
remained. As they resisted the reform they were expelled, and
other monks settled. Alberic restored the possessions of the
monastery which had been appropriated by lay lords. Great
hopes were entertained of this abbey which pope Leo strengthened
with fortifications and towers. Under its abbot Alberic placed
St. Sylvester's and St. Stephen's.

Little more is known about the other monasteries restored
by Alberic in Rome. Probably wherever there was reform it
followed the Cluniac lines, for Alberic appointed Odo director
of the collective monasteries in Rome and its neighbourhood.[3]
He then looked to Monte Cassino, mother of Western monasticism, the condition of which could not have been more piteous.
During the barbarian invasions, the monks, unable to protect
themselves, had accepted the invitation of the prince of Capua
to settle near his capital. The few who remained at Monte
Cassino let the monastic lands lie waste, and led a life that was
far from edifying. To restore Monte Cassino to prosperity would
have required more time and labour than Odo was able to spare ;
he could only improve its condition,[4] and appoint his disciple
Baldwin abbot. The complete reform of the abbey came later.
In the same neighbourhood Subiaco was in a similarly evil plight,
its lands and buildings having been devastated by the Saracens.[5]
In 936 the buildings were restored by Alberic, who renewed its

---

[1] *Destr. Farf.* cap. 7.   [2] Cf. *Vita Joanne,* ii. 9.

[3] *Destr. Farf.* cap. 7 ; *Mon. Germ.* xi. p. 536, *Ut de Gallia faceret venire
Oddonem sanctum abbatem qui tunc temporis Cluniacum gubernabat monasterium
et eum archimandritam constituit super cuncta monasteria Romae adiacentia.*

[4] Ibid., *Cassinense monasterium sub illius magisterio ad normam regularis
ordinis reductum est.*

[5] Sackur, i. 103.

charters, which had been burnt. The pope confirmed them.
Another historic monastery, Farfa, which had fallen on evil
times, felt Odo's influence. The monks had been driven away
by the Saracens, and the lands left desolate. After some time
several of the monks returned, but only to appropriate the
abbey's remaining property. They murdered their abbot,
squandered the monastic revenues, and lived on the principle,
' Let us eat and drink, for to-morrow we die.' Alberic ended
this scandal. According to one account he put Farfa under the
authority of St. Andrew's on the Clivus Scaurus, according to
another Odo himself came down on the monastery, and caused
the terrified monks to flee.[1] For a time a better state of things
prevailed, but not for long.

A more successful reform was that of St. Elias', Nepi, given
by Alberic.[2] Here Odo appointed Theodorardus, one of his
disciples, abbot. Theodorardus had a hard fight to keep his
monks from eating meat. He had come well supplied with
fish, which his monks soon finished, and as there was no river
or lake near, he had to send round the country for more, ' till
the very horses which Odo had given him were worn out by
rushing hither and thither '. Finally, Odo's opportune arrival
miraculously caused a stream to flow from a mountain near,
and fish were kept therein.[3]

Odo's influence seems to have extended as far south as
Naples and Salerno, where he may personally have supervised
the reform.[4]

In Benevento, where Alberic's reforming zeal was also active,
the reform probably followed the lines already laid down by
Odo. In the North a new sphere of activity was opened to the

---

[1] *Destr. Farf.* cap. 7.
[2] *Vita Joanne*, iii. 7, *Concessit nobis Albericus.*   [3] Ibid.
[4] Ibid., *Praefatio*. John dedicates his life of Odo to the monks of Salerno
in a prologue which suggests that they knew Odo. He may have been prior
there. In the story of Odo's infant nephew he reminds the brothers that it
was told by a pilgrim who stopped at *our* monastery when going to Jerusalem
the previous year.

Cluniacs through the reform of St. Peter's, Ciel d' Oro, Pavia,[1] entrusted to Odo by Hugh of Lombardy.

Odo's work in Italy, aided mainly by the upper classes, and almost entirely dependent on Alberic's support, seems to have awakened in the lower classes little or no enthusiasm. That enthusiasm came after, through the reform of the Italian hermits. Yet Odo's work is striking, for he was already fifty-six years old when he began the reform in Rome. Four times in the remaining six years of his life he went that difficult journey.

A group of monasteries in Upper Lorraine, though neither directly nor indirectly reformed by the Cluniacs, seem to have felt their influence.

In Upper Lorraine the bishops had retained greater influence and power than in Gaul. The wealth of the church was in their hands, and in many cases the monastic endowments also. Their influence, however, made for political and social rather than spiritual success. The majority of them were too much occupied in worldly affairs to welcome a reawakening of spiritual life or a monastic revival, which might bring with it a recovery of monastic endowments. In that borderland, too, the disturbed years which followed the break-up of the empire were not favourable for religious revival. But at last the unsettled state of the times caused men's minds to turn with longing to some ' more abiding city '. A wave of religious fervour passed over the land, stirring up in particular the lower clergy who in the dioceses of Toul, Metz, and Verdun agitated whole-heartedly for reform, only to beat themselves in vain against the apathy of the higher clergy and bishops. In despair, therefore, many laymen and priests withdrew themselves from the world, some to seek abnegation of self in solitude, others to work out their soul's salvation in the monastic communities of more favoured lands. The most ardent,

---

[1] Cf. ibid. i. 4. It was at Pavia that John was instructed in the regular discipline. Odo first met him in Rome two years before his death, snatched him from earthly affections, and caught him in his net. He accompanied Odo to Pavia, where the latter was detained by king Hugh, and therefore entrusted John to the keeping and teaching of a certain Hildebrand.

whose dream it was to found a monastery in their homeland, tried hard to persuade Adalbero, bishop of Metz, to grant them a site on which to build. They asked in vain, and at last in despair resolved to set out for Italy. It was then represented to Adalbero that the scandal would be great if he let the best spirits of the diocese depart. He then reluctantly gave them Gorze.

Gorze, an old and famous monastery, founded by Chrodegang, had degenerated, and then been destroyed by the Huns (919). It was restored, and monks entered it (933). For the first three years they suffered extreme privation, for though the bishop held supreme authority over the monastery he did not trouble to provide for the maintenance of the monks. Having reached starvation point they decided to leave, when they were saved by St. Gorgonius, their patron saint, who appeared to the bishop and commanded him to relieve their necessities. ' Thank the saint, not me,' the bishop replied in exasperated honesty to their professions of gratitude, ' for not of my own will but of his have I acted.' [1] Henceforth, along with its spiritual renown, the material prosperity of Gorze increased. Monks streamed to it from Greece, England, Burgundy, Metz, Toul, and Verdun. It was even said that no monk knew the true monastic life unless he had passed some time ' at the beehive ' of Gorze.[2]

This movement arose in absolute independence of the Cluniac, and unlike it was a popular movement forced on those above from those below. Of the leaders who settled at Gorze not one was of good family. Most were of peasant birth, and only one a man of any education.[3] But all were inspired by a frenzy of asceticism in striking contrast to the Cluniac moderation. As time went on this extremist phase became modified, and though

---

[1] *Boll. AA.SS.* Sept. III. p. 343. *Mirac. S. Gorgonii,* cap. 7.

[2] *Vita Joh. Gorz.* cap. 16.

[3] Einold, archdeacon of Toul, was rich, and distinguished for his secular and spiritual learning. But he fled from the world, and gave up all his possessions in order to live a life of penance in a small cell near the cathedral. From there he went to Gorze.

F

the movement was always marked by greater asceticism than the Cluniac, in several points the latter's example was followed ; [1] e.g. exceeding fasting was discouraged, and the same fast days adopted as at Cluny ; in the recitation of the psalter, in the reading during meals, and in the division of vigils and prayers, the Cluniac custom was followed. The extreme submission of the monks to the abbot recalled the Cluniac tradition, as also the custom that the monks' boots should be cleaned on the Saturday evening. [2]

Though Gorze never reached Cluny's importance, it was the centre of a not inconsiderable reform. This was largely owing to Adalbero of Metz, who, from being a lukewarm supporter of the movement, awoke to the consciousness that it was better to swim with the tide than be submerged by it. In 941 he gave the monks the monastery of St. Arnulf's, Metz, which had fallen to secular canons. The latter were expelled and were replaced by monks, with Aribert of Gorze at their head. [3] More important, as extending Gorze's influence to another diocese, was the reform of the ill-famed Senones in the diocese of Toul (938), a reform carried through by bishop Adalbero, Gauzlin of Toul, and the monks of Gorze. [4] A second monastery reformed in Toul was Moyen-moutier, given to the monks by duke Frederick of Lorraine, who was won over to the movement by Aribert. Three monks of Gorze went there. [5] One became abbot, and from Moyen-moutier reformed Saint-Dié, which he placed under one of his monks. [6] The latter soon fell into evil ways and squandered the monastic revenues to such an extent that duke Frederick expelled him and his monks, and replaced them by secular canons.

In the diocese of Liége, owing to the enthusiasm of bishop

---

[1] Hauck, *Kirchengeschichte*, iii. 357, unlike Sackur, thinks that neither of these points was adopted from Cluny. He maintains, what seems highly improbable, that the fame of Cluny was unknown to Gorze; cf. Sackur, i. p. 160.

[2] Some of the monks attributed this rather to an old custom of Gorze fallen into disuse.

[3] *Vita Joh. Gorz.* cap. 67.　　　　[4] Sackur, i. p. 166.

[5] *Vita Joh. Gorz.* cap. 70.　　　　[6] Sackur, i. p. 168.

Richer, the reform met its greatest success.   He, with the help
of the monks of Gorze, restored St. Peter's, Liége,[1] and Stablo
Malmédy.[2]   The former destroyed by the Normans, the latter
devastated by the Danes, had passed to lay abbots.   Under
a former monk of Gorze, Stablo Malmédy arose more magnificent
than before, a magnificence for which it paid dear.   Its prosperity
aroused the cupidity of the lay lords of the district by whom
it was again despoiled.

More important was the foundation of Gembloux by the
warrior Wigert.   Having provided for the building of the
monastery he retired to Gorze, where he took the habit, and there
spent the rest of his life.   Only once did he leave Gorze to inspect
the new monastery, and appoint as its abbot his friend Erluin,
a canon.[3]   The latter met with some success in reforming St.
Vincent's, Soigniers,[4] but with failure at Lobbes, which for two
years he struggled to reform.   After that time, blinded by the
monks, and with his tongue pulled out, he returned to Gembloux.[5]

[1] Pertz, *Mon. Germ. Script.* iv. p. 63.
[2] Sackur, i. p. 169.
[3] *Mon. Germ.* xiii., *Vita Wicberti*, cap. x.
[4] Sackur, i. p. 171.
[5] *Gesta abb. Gemblac.* cap. 15.

CHAPTER VII

ODO'S LAST YEARS AND DEATH—HIS WRITINGS

IN contrast to the even tenor of his days at Baume, Odo's life during the fifteen years that he was abbot of Cluny was characterised by a varied activity. Not only was he a zealous reformer in France and Italy, but he is twice found working in the interests of peace between Hugh of Lombardy and Alberic his stepson.[1] Hugh had received the Lombard crown in 926, and through his marriage with Marozia was master of Rome. This led to discord with his stepson Alberic, who in 932 rose against his stepfather and drove him from Rome. Hugh retaliated by besieging the city, and laying waste the surrounding district. Intermittent warfare continued till both combatants were exhausted, when Odo was summoned to Rome by the pope to arrange terms of peace (c. 939).[2] He was well fitted for the part of intermediary, being on friendly terms with both sides. For long he had known Hugh, who had several times helped to protect Cluny's lands, in 932 had joined his name to Odo's in petitioning the pope to ratify Cluny's charters, and in 934 had

---

[1] *Flodoardi Chron.* iii. p. 389, anno 942, *Domnus Odo abbas pro pace agenda inter Hugonem regem Italiae et Albricum Romanum patricium apud eundem regem laborabat.* Cf. *Vita Joanne,* ii. 9, *Tempore praeterito dum Romuleam urbem ob inimicitiam Alberici iam fati principis praedictus Hugo rex obsideret, coepit ille intra extraque discurrere ut pacis concordiaeque monita urbem tueri a tanta obsidione.* John probably wrote in 943.

[2] Ibid. ii. 7, *Sub idem tempus Italiam missi sumus a Leone summo pontifice ut pacis legatione fungeremur inter Hugonem Longobardum regem et Albericum Romanae urbis principem.* John states that he first knew Odo two years before the latter's death, 941 or 942. Leo VII. died 939. Cf. *Vita Leonis Bibl. Clun.* p. 61, *Odonem vocavit Romam ut inter Hugonem regem Italiae qui Romam obsidere ceperat et Albericum Romae principem pacis componendae sequestrem ageret.* Cf. *Vita Odonis Nalgodo,* cap. 32.

presented the monastery with Savigneux and Ambérieu. In 936 Odo's relationship with Alberic began through the reform of the Roman monasteries, and helped to strengthen the chain binding Cluny to Rome, where the popes were but the tools of the prince. Peace was sealed by Hugh's giving his daughter Alda in marriage to Alberic. But concord did not long continue, and probably in 941 Odo was again in Rome working for peace.[1]

So in manifold activity and growing fame passed the last six years of his life. ' Let those who will ', writes John, ' praise men who expel demons, make the dead to live, and other men of ill-famed works. I, least among all, will praise my Odo, first for his virtue of patience, then for his contempt of material things, then for the souls he saved, for his restoration of monasteries, his clothing, and feeding of the monks, the peace he gave to the churches, the concord to kings and princes, his guardianship of all ways, his instancy in command, his persever- ance in vigils and prayers, his respect for the poor, his correction of youth, his honour for old men, his improvement of morals, his love of chastity, his encouragement of continency, his pity for the wretched, his undefiled observance of the rule, and finally for himself, the mirror of all virtues.' His doctrine and the fame of his virtues had made him celebrated throughout almost the whole of Italy. His journeys to Rome had brought his monastery into closer touch with the papal see,[2] and made him a well-known figure in the holy city, where the ardour with which he visited the sacred places became a tradition for later abbots of Cluny. In Rome he was jestingly called ' the Digger ', for so rooted in him was the practice of the rule, that wherever

[1] *Vita Leonis: Venit abbas sanctissimus suaque intercessione hoc obtinuit ut Albericus filiam Hugonis conjugem acciperet.*

[2] *Vita Joanne,* ii. 15. A story which to his monks was a proof of his pro- phetic gifts seems rather proof of his influence with the pope. Hearing the bishop of Nolana lament that he had twice gone to Rome for the papal benediction which his enemies had prevented his receiving, and that he was going a third time though he feared it was useless, Odo blessed him and said, ' Know of a surety that this time God will grant thy desire.' In fifteen days the bishop returned triumphant.

he was, standing, or walking, or sitting, he was ever to be seen with bent head, and eyes fixed on the ground [1] (*Reg.* cap. 7).

It was in Rome that the hand of Death touched him. ' The nearer he felt his vocation draw nigh, the more instantly did he afflict his body with fasting, vigils, and prayers, and the other works of holy virtue ; and as a true athlete wrenched his aged limbs with hard exercise.' As the monk's life was but the preparation for death, a long and beautiful account of his death is given in the *Vita*.[2]

When he felt death approach, the faithful imitator and vicar of the apostles, having completed his course of excellent virtue, longed for his flesh to be dissolved. He yearned to behold St. Martin, whom he had drunk in with his mother's milk, and who had separated him as another vase of election from his mother's breast. God was merciful. St. Martin, conspicuous in grace of form, appeared to him and said, ' Oh, holy soul, beloved of God, thy call draweth near, and the last dissolution of thy body approacheth. But I, St. Martin, grant thee strength to return to thine own land, where thy life will be exchanged for death, and Christ reward thee with the blessed society of the elect.' His strength returned, and thinking nothing of the hardships of the journey he started for Tours, arriving in time for St. Martin's Day. His coming caused double rejoicing in the city.

' My imagination ', John continued, ' is unable to conjure up his devotion at the festival, nor the prayers and groans he poured out to the saint. Nay, the stolidity of my mind and the rusticity of my style would but detract from the reality. After the first three days of the festival he groaned more and more anxiously for his promised reward. On the fourth day fever again attacked him, and cold blood flowing from his heart consumed his strength. His vow was heard : he grew weaker. Joyfully he saw God, he breathed, he sighed, his dying voice was heard. " Thou, oh Christ, spare Thy redeemed. Thou, oh Martin, receive me." '

[1] Ibid. ii. 9.   [2] Ibid. iii. 12.

From all parts monks flocked to his bedside. He instructed them and consigned them to God with the prayer of faith, strengthening them with his benediction, and with pious sobs bidding them farewell. On December 4 that blessed spirit, refreshed by holy unction, fortified by the life-giving chalice, and absolved from corruptible flesh, soared to the sky, where with St. Martin his master he presented to his Maker a manifold return for the talents entrusted to him, and received in Christ a gracious guerdon for his pious labours.

* * *

Odo may be called the first of Cluniac writers both in point of time and of importance. The list of his works includes (1) an abbreviation of the *Moralia* of St. Gregory the Great, written at Tours ; (2) the *Collationes*, the most important of his works, written at Baume ; (3) the life of Gerald of Aurillac, written at Aurillac ; (4) five sermons in prose, two in honour of St. Martin, one on St. Peter, another on St. Benedict, a fifth in honour of Mary Magdalene, and the *Occupatio* sermons in verse ; (5) a poem in twelve hexameters on the blessed Eucharist ; (6) twelve antiphones in praise of St. Martin, written on his deathbed at Tours. Besides these, four musical treatises were once attributed to him, the *Tonarius, Dialogus* or *Enchiridion, Regulae Rythminachia, Regulae Abacus*, and a little book on the building of organs, of which the authorship is uncertain. It would seem that his reputation as a musician was considerable in his own day, several of the later chroniclers giving him the patronymic, *Odo Musicus*, and stating that his chief study under Remigius at Paris was music and dialectics.[1]

The most important of his books was the *Collationes*,[2] which he wrote at bishop Turpio's request, and with Berno's permission.

---

[1] *Bibl. Clun.* p. 57 et seq. Sigebertus Gemblacensis (twelfth century). '*Gestorum Andegavensium*' (twelfth century), *magister scholae et precentor ecclesiae.* Vincentius Bellovacensis (thirteenth century), *Odo musicus . . . a Remigio in musica et dialectica . . . eruditus.* '*Chronicon Turonense*' : *Odo praecentor ecclesiae.* '*Chronici chronicorum*' : *A Remigio in musica et dialectica eruditus.* '*Liber de Scriptoribus eccles.*' : *Erat insignis musicus et archicantor ecclesiae Turonensis.*

[2] Migne, 133, p. 518.

After obtaining that permission, he could not bring himself to begin to write. At last Berno warned him that in a fortnight's time he must return to Limoges, so he set to work in earnest and wrote Book I. Winter set in early that year, and with such severity that his journey was postponed. Berno, having read his manuscript, pointed out that he had raised and left unanswered many problems, and advised him to take advantage of his enforced leisure to expand and amplify his book. So Book II. was written, and the two parts submitted to bishop Turpio, who with Berno united in asking for more. The completed work naturally suffers from this lack of distinct plan and definite scheme, and as a whole is marred by repetitions, brusque transitions, and unexpected returns to subjects already treated. In the preface to Book III. Odo likened his work to a vase already full. Water added to it would only overflow and form drops on the surface which would detract from the beauty of the form. All the same the third book, which is almost as long as the first two put together, contains the most vigorous writing.

The *Collationes*, one of the most famous books of its day, was inspired by a conversation between bishop Turpio and the young monk over the evil condition of the church. It is a Jeremiad and a diatribe, in which Odo lamented over and scourged the sins of the day. For the time was at hand, and Odo looked to the year 1000 as marching towards that end of which the Apocalypse speaks.

He went, not very deeply it is true, into the problem of evil in the world and its expiation by suffering. The world was once perfect, till God found it turning out evil, and brought punishment and suffering on men.[1] Satan brought moral evil by tearing God's word from the heart, putting pride, lechery, and wickedness in its place. Men brought on themselves a third kind of evil through persecution, injustice, and shame.

---

[1] Ibid. p. 637, iii. 52. Nor can man complain. *Cur itaque asperum creditur ut a Deo homo tolleret flagella pro malis, si tanta Deus ab hominibus pertulit mala pro bonis?*

God's creation ruined, the race which remained tainted was divided into the two great families of Cain and Abel. Odo fulminated against the evil race of Cain who gave themselves to the work of the devil. It is here that his style is most forcible. He may not be able to go deeply into the problem of the origin of evil, but he is graphic and telling in depicting its effects. Brief and trenchant in Book III. are his scathing aphorisms against the rich children of Cain. 'Open all the books of antiquity and you will find that the more powerful are always the worst.'[1] 'Not nature created the worldly rank of the nobility but ambition.'[2] It is the rich who grind the faces of the poor ; night and day they pass in feasting, play, drinking, dancing ; yet the food with which they gorge themselves, and the sumptuous garments in which they adorn themselves, are acquired by the sweat of the poor. 'If there is any beauty in such things, it is those who make them that should be praised, as Boethius says, and not those who use them.'[3] It is the poor who sow the seed, the poor who garner the grain. The many toil that the few may live at ease. Great will be the reward of the rich in hell.

Of all Cain's evil children he regarded the unworthy professors of religion as the worst, those hypocrites who cover their sins under the cloak of religion. He denounced the secular clergy of his day, as given over to carnal things, swollen by pride, hardened by avarice, eaten up by desire, inflamed by anger, torn by discord, ulcerated by envy, and vitiated by luxury. Nor did the monk escape, Odo, like Pachomius before him, foreseeing with deep grief the decay and ruin of the monastic order —a result which would follow from what he regarded as the greatest evil in the monastic life of his day, the holding of private

[1] Ibid. iii. 30, *Omnes libros antiquitatum considera, potentiores semper invenies peiores.*

[2] Ibid., *Nobilitatem quippe mundanam non natura, sed ambitio praestitit.*

[3] Ibid., *Si qua vero pulchritudo in eis est aut suavitas, artifices laudandi sunt ut Boetius dicit et non hi qui eis . . . utuntur . . . propriam sibi non sufficere produnt.*

property within the monasteries.   From this evil arose the occasion to greed, gluttony, and vice.   He brushed aside the monks'
plea that they were forced to infringe the rule through the
fault of their abbots, who neglected to provide for the necessities of the monastery.   In that case, Odo pointed out, they were
only justified in keeping sufficient for their needs, and not for
the luxuries with which they pampered themselves.   Their own
greed, and not only the abbots' negligence, was at fault.

He had his message also for the race of righteous Abel—
the perfect, and the less perfect.   He rejoiced over the former,
who are marred only by small unavoidable sins, who welcome
tribulations, recognising in them trials to purge them from their
faults.   He warned the less perfect, not to let their love for their
Creator be weakened by their love for His creatures, nor to be
too much engrossed by their own and their children's future.
Berno had objected that there was not enough said for the consolation of the elect in the first two books.   In the third Odo
dwelt on the futility and instability of earthly joys, the nothing-
ness of beauty, the example of the saints, and the horrors which
the evildoers in this world will suffer in the next.

Like the other writers of his age, Odo used the imagery of the
bestiary :   the eagle the symbol of pride ;   the mare of lechery ;
the dragon of violence ;   the rich man who preys on the goods
of others the fish, which, devouring its smaller neighbours, is
in its own turn swallowed up : so will Satan devour the rich.
The man who in the difficulties of life lives like the fathers in the
desert, he likened to the goat feeding among the mountains.   If
the goat falls, he alights on his two horns, and does himself no
harm.   The wise man, when he errs, is saved by the two horns
of the Old and New Testament.

An earlier work of Odo's, written when still at Tours, is the
abbreviation of the *Moralia* of Gregory the Great,[1] a book severe,
sombre, and dull, though Odo's quaint and florid introduction
describes it as a garden into which he entered to gather flowers,

[1] Migne, 133, p. 107.

whose unearthly beauty and wondrous perfume overpowered his senses.

More interesting is the life of Gerald of Aurillac,[1] which he was asked to write by Aimo, and other monks and priests. Gerald had recently died, and the many miracles which had taken place at his tomb were arousing popular interest. Men questioned whether this man who had lived in the world, who had partaken of flesh and wine, could be a saint. Odo too doubted, till he went to Tulle to collect the material for his book. There he interviewed four men who had known Gerald from childhood, a monk, a priest, and two laymen. Questioning each separately and all four together, he found that their witness agreed, and his doubts were laid at rest. Though Gerald lived in the world, he had wished to be a monk, and had only given up his intention when dissuaded by the bishop of his diocese ; though he had eaten flesh and drunk wine, he had done so in moderation and sobriety. His care to keep his body chaste and mind pure was in striking contrast to the customs of his contemporaries. The simplicity of his garments and of his manner of life was a rebuke and example to the priest who aped the great. His hospitality and charity were a lesson to those who, instead of receiving the poor in their homes, were content to distribute alms by the hands of strangers. Rich and powerful, he had despised ambition, pride, and outward pomp, keeping his mind lowly, simple, and humble. Living in the world, he yet in private life cultivated the virtues of the monk Unable to be a monk himself he had built Aurillac for the monk. The life is divided into three parts, Book I. giving the facts of Gerald's life, Books II. and III. the miracles which had taken place at his tomb. The life has also come down in another recension, a shorter form probably also written by Odo.[2]

Of the sermons, that on St. Benedict [3] is perhaps the most interesting, as showing Odo's veneration for the founder of his order, to him a second Moses. From the hard rock Moses and Benedict

---

[1] Ibid. p. 639.   [2] *Bibl. Clun.* p. 138.   [3] Migne, 133, p. 721.

had brought forth water, Moses for the earthly needs of his
people, Benedict for the spiritual needs of the monk. Far
greater was Benedict's glory than that of a king, if, as Solomon
said, the glory of a king is in the multitude of his people. What
king or emperor ever commanded so many legions in so many
parts of the world and of so many races as Benedict, who led
the militia of Christ, of both sexes and all ages, sworn voluntarily to God's service.

In the sermon delivered on the occasion of the third burning
of St. Martin's basilica [1]—a disaster which had caused the scoffer
to scoff and to murmur that the saint could not even protect
the church of which he was guardian—Odo returned to the
problem of the *Collationes*, the place of evil in the divine ordering
of the world, of which the destruction of the church was an
instance. He to whom all bowed could naturally have prevented
the disaster. It was but another proof of his love that he had
not done so. Caring nothing that his glory would be momentarily
obscured in the eyes of men, he had permitted the burning of
his church as a message, a warning, and a chastisement for sin :
and were not the lives of the canons of Tours such as to provoke
the saint's wrath ? Odo urged to repentance those who in
their foolishness and ignorance had reproached the saint, while
putting before them a work in which all might participate, the
rebuilding to God's glory and their own merit the basilica which
they mourned.

In the sermon on the Magdalen [2] Odo pointed out that as
by a woman death came into the world, so by a woman the glad
tidings of the resurrection was first announced. Thus by the
Magdalen the reproach of the female sex was removed.

At abbot Baldwin's request Odo ' elucidated and corrected
with a glossary ' the life of St. Martin written by Postumianus
and Gallus,[3] a task which caused his glory to shine forth. One
evening, he and a brother, Othegarius, were so engrossed in
their work that the signal for vespers found them still writing.

---

[1] Ibid. p. 729.   [2] Ibid. p. 713.   [3] *Vita Joanne*, ii. 22

Hastening to prayer, they forgot the book. It was winter time, and that night there was such a storm of rain that the cellars were flooded, and the place where the book had been left seethed like a torrent. Therefore great was the amazement next day when the news spread that, though the margin of the book was soaked through, yet the writing was untouched. But to the wondering monks the wise father joyfully cried, ' Why do ye marvel, oh brothers? Know ye not that the water feared to touch the life of the saint?' Then a monk ever quick in speech rejoined, ' But see, the book is old and moth-eaten, and has so often been soaked that it is dirty and faint! Can our father then persuade us that the rain feared to touch a book which in the past has been soaked through? Nay there is another reason.' The virtuous father, knowing that the speaker sought to suggest that the rain had feared to touch the book not because it was the life of the saint, but because it was his, hastily turned aside the remark to the glory of God and St. Martin.

CHAPTER VIII

ODO'S CHARACTER

In Odo is to be found a man who made real the teaching of Christ. 'He was', wrote John, 'like a four-cornered stone, divine, human, generous and filled with love.' Most beautiful was the relation between him and his monks. 'How can I, unworthy one, tell fittingly of him ? Verily, when we could not otherwise contain our souls, we kissed his garments in secret. But that was not surprising in us who were ever with him. For even strangers who entered our church to pray, immediately hurried to lift and kiss the hem of his mantle. And when with hasty step he would have escaped, they followed him as if they were persecutors.' [1]

Angel messengers watched over him, as Angelus the priest told and affirmed on oath to abbot Baldwin and his monks. One night at St. Paul's, when Odo, wearied after nightly Lauds and his private prayers, fell asleep, the priest saw a venerable white-haired old man cover him with a woollen garment. Taking him for Feraldus, deacon of the monastery, Angelus was indignant at his presumption in daring to act thus at one of the 'incompetent hours'. Next day, when his anger had cooled, he questioned Feraldus, who swore it was not he. Then to all it was clear that an angel messenger had watched over the father.[2]

Other stories showed that the divine grace was ever watching over him. Two priests who had gone with him to pray at Monte Gargano, on their return affirmed on oath that, though often during canonical hours he prostrated himself on the

[1] *Vita Joanne,* ii. 5.   [2] *Vita Anonyma.*

ground when it rained, yet never did a drop touch him. 'Protected by the divine dignity, even though the ground was soaked and wet, his garments remained dry.'[1] And once when Odo and his monks were crossing the Alps on which the eternal snows lay deep, he and his horse were shot over a precipice. Dropping the reins he raised his arms to heaven, and found between them the branch of a tree, to which he clung till help came. But never in that spot had a tree been known to grow![2] And once when he was crossing the Rhone, accompanied by the chief men of the district, one of the horses kicked a hole in the boat, which immediately began to sink. By the grace of God it reached the bank, and all landed, Odo last of all. The instant he set foot on land the boat disappeared beneath the waters.[3] What greater testimony of his merit could be given, 'since by this miracle he was held worthy to follow in the footsteps of St. Peter, St. Paul, and St. Benedict'. Often did John lament that he had been accounted worthy to be with his master only two years, and often did envy those who had been with him all their lives.[4]

Other stories throw a light upon Odo's character. Notwithstanding his deep sense of the sin of the world, and its misery, he set before his monks the example of spiritual joy. 'Such grace of the spirit filled him, that his joy not only rejoiced the joyful but cheered the sorrowful; making both participators of the eternal joy. His language was sweet and pleasurable, honey being as it were distilled from his lips, while the law of prudence was in his heart.'[5] 'His words were full of exultation, and often his remarks would make us laugh with too great hilarity. But he never let this degenerate into excess, and holding the reins of moderation in his hand he would check unseemly mirth by recalling the precept of the rule, "not to love much or excessive laughter"; and again, "let not the monk

[1] Ibid.   [2] *Vita Joanne*, ii. 18.   [3] Ibid. ii. 17.
[4] Ibid. iii. 5, *Sed felices illi qui eius presentiam cernere meruerunt quoad vixit. Infelix ego qui nec duabus expletis annis illi merui famulari.*
[5] Ibid. ii. 5.

be easily or quickly moved to laughter ",[1] for it is written, " the fool raiseth his voice in mirth ". In these and similar ways he restrained us, while his spiritual joy rejoiced our hearts.'

When travelling he joyfully uplifted his voice in the singing of psalms, encouraging his monks to do the same. If he met a group of boys he would ask them to sing, and then order a reward to be given them, for what was after all only their play. Laughingly he would say that for entertaining the monks the boys were worthy of pay.[2] ' These and similar speeches he made to rejoice us with his joy, and refresh us with the bowels of his mercy.' A charming instance of his sense of humour is seen in the story of the thief who in the night stole a horse from a monastery, and who was found in the morning motionless on a motionless horse. Dragged bound before Odo, the latter ordered him to be set free, and five solidi of silver to be given him, it being unjust, he gravely explained, that after having suffered all night, the offender should receive no pay.[3] This story evidently became the chestnut of the monastery.

Odo taught that the blind and the lame were the porters of the gates of paradise, and that it was suicidal to drive them from the gates. If a monk, impatient at the importunity of a beggar, answered him harshly or drove him away from the gates, Odo would call the beggar before him, and say, ' When he who has served thee thus, comes himself seeking entrance from thee at the gates of paradise, repay him in like manner.' [4]

Exaggerated asceticism he did not encourage. One young brother during his initiation strove by weeping and prayer to wipe out the cloud of his past offences. ' Giving up all else he sweated day and night in lamentation and remorse.' But

---

[1] Ibid., *Monachus non sit facilis aut promptus in risu.*   [2] Ibid.
[3] Ibid. ii. 10.   John often heard the story, for he later became prior of the monastery where the incident happened (probably St. Paul's, Rome) and found that the thief was the son of the miller. If ever the unfortunate miller refused to do something the brothers wanted, they bade John demand the five solidi back from him.   [4] Ibid. ii. 5.

Odo, skilled physician of souls, questioned the young zealot as to why he did not, like his companions, either teach or learn ; whereupon the novice revealed the agony of his heart, and his life of penance. Knowing that if a monk acts without the permission of his spiritual father his deeds are regarded not as meritorious but as showing presumption and vainglory, he begged Odo's approval of his manner of life. But Odo answered : 'Nay, wait to become a monk, till that spirit which has goaded thy mind with the sting of vainglory departs from thee.' In a year's time the brother was found worthy to be received.[1]

One of Odo's chief characteristics was his unquenchable charity. He at least carried out literally the Gospel precept, 'Take no thought for the morrow.' Even when supplies were not plentiful, no counsels of prudence could check his almsgiving. Before a journey he was careful to see that the purse-bearer had sufficient, not only for the needs of the monks, but also for the poor, and the latter fund often encroached on the former. Serenely he would give to all who asked, sure that at the worst God would interpose. Nor was his faith ever disabused.

A peculiarity of his almsgiving was, that if any one poorly dressed brought him a gift, he would ask him if he lacked for anything. If the answer was yes, he calculated the value of the gift, and commanded double the amount to be given to the donor—a procedure not always pleasing to the prior on whom the financing of the monastery fell.[2] Often, John confessed, when he saw Odo do this the sight distressed him. 'For though I had compassion on the poor, yet I was prior, and knowing the poverty of the monastery, and foreseeing the necessities of the brothers, I would point out that it was unjust to give all things thus indiscreetly away. I thought to act wisely, whereas I was only wrapped in the mist of darkness. But he, skilled physician of souls, put his finger on the pulse of my error and with this

---

[1] Ibid. ii. 14. Benedict did not encourage individual asceticism. The monk 'was to do nothing but what the common rule of the monastery and the example of his superiors exhorts', Reg. cap. 7.   [2] Ibid. ii. 4.

G

story cured the disease of my soul.' The story was, that one winter's night a youth set out for morning Lauds, and seeing a beggar lying half-naked in the porch of the church he covered him with his coat. When he returned to his cell half-frozen with cold he found a gift of gold, with which he was able not only to buy a new coat, but to give abundantly to the poor.

A charming incident of Odo's generosity occurred on a journey in Italy. The monks had set out well supplied with funds, thirty solidi silver, but before reaching Siena the greater part had been given away. At Siena there was famine, and John the purse-bearer, knowing that it would be impossible to check Odo's almsgiving, and that as a result the monks would be reduced to actual straits, secreted what solidi were left, and passed on first beyond the town. On entering Siena Odo was surrounded by beggars, beseeching that aid he had never been known to refuse. Immediately he called for the purse-bearer, to find him gone, but knowing he could not be far off, he told the beggars to follow. Nor was that enough. On leaving the town he noticed three men just as poverty-stricken as the beggars, but too proud to ask for help. With singular delicacy he asked them what was the price of some pots of laurel berries before their house. The men named a trifling sum, which Odo said was not enough, and that he would give them more. Meanwhile, John waiting beyond the town was amazed to see Odo approach, ' like a general starting out for war, though his troops were but beggars '. So pleased was Odo at having outwitted his disciple, that he almost forgot to give the customary benediction to John's salutation, and joyfully called out, ' These are the servants of God and our co-labourers, hasten therefore to give them their reward.' Having obeyed, John asked in real amazement what the laurel berries were for. The reply came in words such as John never hoped to hear again, while the monks laughed till they cried.[1]

---

[1] Ibid. ii. 7, *Adeo enim omnes exhilaravit ut prae nimio gaudio, ne quis ex nostris suas lacrymas posset continere, ut valeret alter alteri loqui.* A mediaeval joke somewhat difficult to see : either Odo chaffed his purse-bearer, or the monks laughed at seeing the well-beloved John rebuked.

When they recovered, John humbly begged that they might return the berries, but this Odo would not hear of, lest the sellers returned the price. Even when they had reached a lonely part of the road where there was no danger of being seen, he was with difficulty persuaded to let the monks throw the berries away.

It was not only in gifts of money that Odo's generosity showed itself. On his journeys if he overtook a weak or poor old man, he immediately got off his horse, made the other mount, and with a monk to hold him on, precede all the company. 'And though the other monks were on horseback, he himself would walk on foot, joyfully singing psalms and making the rest join in.' If one of the monks wished to dismount, Odo forbade him, knowing that his motive was rather respect for his abbot than love for the poor.[1] In this connexion John tells a story against himself. Once when he was travelling with Odo they overtook an old man carrying a filthy sack, full of bread, onions, leeks, and olives, whose combined odours caused John to flee. Odo as usual dismounted, gave his horse to the old man, and took the sack, a sight which moved John to shame. So he rejoined Odo, who received him with such words of rebuke and love that the disciple, forgetting the smell, was able to proceed at his master's side.[2] Another time Odo overtook a mad old woman and set her on his horse, when immediately she recovered her reason! The sequel shows why Odo was so beloved by the poor. He and his companions went on to Rome, leaving the woman at Siena. Some time later at St. Paul's, Odo signed to John to give money to a woman sitting with bent head at the church door. John asked why; but the abbot's old eyes had been quicker than the disciple's young ones, for the woman was she whom they had succoured by the way.

As Odo was sixty when John first knew him, these stories of his journeys show that he must have been of great physical strength. On the occasion of the journey to Siena, for example,

---

[1] Ibid. ii. 5.   [2] Ibid. ii. 6.

the season was winter, the roads bad, and the crossing of the Alps proved terrible. Heavy snow fell, the little company lost their way, and were so frozen with cold that they even lost the power of speech. Odo's suffering wrung John's heart, but all he could do was to force the abbot to wear his tunic. On their way home, when crossing the Juras at nightfall, they met a man who, with naked feet and body, stoutly advanced through the deep snow. Odo, letting the monks pass that they might not divine his intention, stripped off his mantle and clothed the stranger. In that vast solitude there was no inn near ; but the stranger said he would reach the camp that day, i.e. in an hour. Hence John knew that he was no man but a fiend in human form, since he was going to do in an hour what had taken them all day. A dream proved that he was right ; all the more did he marvel at his master's charity, which extended even to the wicked.[1]

If a soul were to be saved Odo could be pitiless. Once on his way to Rome he passed by the *vicus Vaduscinie,* ' where a man lived who, among the other crimes in which his mind revelled, had shamelessly taken to himself two wives '. Outside his door the way was blocked by a huge heap of mud, which the monks climbed over with the greatest difficulty. Odo passed safely and unhurt, his horse stepping as if he were on dry ground. Seeing this miracle, the evil man prostrated himself at Odo's feet, imploring him to enter his house. He consented, when the man rushed hither and thither setting the tables, doing service, and trying in every way to please the father. Seeing two women in the house Odo asked which was the wife. When he replied ' Both ', Odo said, ' I give you your choice : banish the younger woman or I leave your house.' Immediately the man thrust her forth, aroused from the death of the soul by the voice of the father.[2] What happened to the woman evidently did not matter.

Travelling as much as he did, Odo's life was frequently in

---

[1] Ibid. ii. 8, *Non fuisset homo purus.*   [2] *Vita Anonyma.*

danger.[1] Once forty robbers rushed at him, only to be checked by his intrepid bearing, for he advanced undauntedly with his monks, nor ceased to sing the accustomed psalms. This sight pierced one of the robbers to the heart, and he cried : ' Let us leave them alone for I never remember having seen such men before. We might overcome the company, but never their armour-bearer, that strenuous man. If we attack them it will be the worse for us.' When his companions replied that they would kill the armour-bearer, despoil the others, and flee, he rejoined, ' Then turn your arms against me, for as long as I am alive, no harm shall come to them.' Divided among themselves, they wrangled so much that the monks passed on in safety. But the first speaker followed Odo, asked what penance he should do, and thereafter ceased from his depravity.

Another robber having seen Odo on a journey, was struck by contrition before the gentleness of his face, and begged that he might become a monk. Odo told him to bring first ' some distinguished man from his district ' to answer for him. From the latter Odo learnt that the young man was a notorious robber. As it was dangerous to have such a wolf among his lambs, he said, ' Go first and reform your morals, and then seek our monastery.' In despair the robber cried, ' Father, if thou reject me to-day I shall go straight to perdition, and verily from thy hand God will require my soul.' So the pitiful Odo bade the young man precede him to Cluny, where after probation he was accounted worthy to be received. He was given the humblest of offices, that of servant to the cellarer, and as he was totally ignorant the monks tried to teach him. ' Most devout he was, patient under his yoke of obedience, and fervent in his study of the psalms.' His days passed laboriously till he came to die, when he begged to see the abbot alone. On Odo's asking whether he had transgressed the rule, he confessed with deep contrition that he had given ' their ' tunic to a naked man. Worse still, he

<hr>

[1] *Vita Joanne,* ii. 19, *Cum pro pace regum et principum et correctione monasteriorum impatienti amore arderet et ob hoc huc illucque discurreret.*

had stolen a piece of rope from the cellar, for on entering the monastery he had found it so difficult to restrain gluttonous desires, that he had taken the rope to tie round his body. When the rope was removed, so deeply had it eaten into the body, that the flesh came away with it. But the monk's pain was to him as a very little thing, for that night he saw a woman of glorious person and excellent power, who said she was the Mother of Mercy. True to his training in obedience he asked what she would have him do, and learnt to his joyful amazement that he was to join her in three days. Three days later he died, sure proof that his words were true. Ever after Odo called the Blessed Virgin *Mater Misericordiae*.[1]

Two stories tell of illness. Two monks, whose names John thought it better not to insert, suffered from a fatal disease, and often begged Odo to let them try medicine. At last he consented, though speaking in a parable he warned them that he had seen a monk who, suffering from the same disease, took medicine only to be tortured with pain. They, not understanding that he referred to them, took the medicine, suffered great agony, nor ever recovered.[2] Another monk at Rome, forced by necessity, bled himself at an ' incompetent ' hour, though terrified and remorseful because he had been unable to ask Odo's permission. And indeed the blood poured forth with such impetus that the vein burst and no remedy could save him ![3] The monks of that monastery said that whatever Odo foretold, good or bad, always came true.

A rather charmingly told incident shows how news was carried in those days. John had gone to Naples on the business of his monastery,[4] whence he hastened to return to Rome. At Porto he was received by certain noble men who had arrived from Rome that day. He immediately asked them about his beloved master. They, rejoicing as if over a friend, told him,

---

[1] Ibid. ii. 20. According to one MS. Odo ordered the monk to be whipped for his theft. When he returned to see him next day the monk told his vision.
[2] Ibid. ii. 14.   [3] Ibid. iii. 5.
[4] Ibid. ii. 21, *Cogente necessitate nostri monasterii missus sum Neapolim.*

inter alia, the following story.   On Assumption day Odo, who was staying at St. Mary's, Aventine, was asked by the abbot and monks to say mass.   He refused, but when they insisted he entered the church.   After praying for a little time, he hastily turned to leave, and when they tried to retain him, he cried, ' I beseech you let me go, for two of our brothers are at the point of death, and I must hasten to them lest they die in my absence. Behold, he who is sent for me is at the gate.'   Scarcely had he finished speaking when the messenger arrived !

CHAPTER IX

AYMARDUS, THIRD ABBOT OF CLUNY

ODO'S successor was Aymardus, of whom unfortunately little is known.[1] No biography was written of him, and what information we possess comes from scanty references in the *Vita Odonis, Vita Maioli,* and in later chronicles.

Aymardus must have been appointed Odo's coadjutor and successor as early as 938, a charter of that date [2] giving his name as abbot, though Odo's death did not occur till 942.[3] It is easily intelligible, that the frequency of Odo's absences from Cluny and his multifarious activity made the presence of a coadjutor at the Mother house necessary.

According to the *Vita Maioli,* Aymardus was not the first choice of the brothers, who twice begged Hildebrand, their prior, to become abbot, but he refused, ' preferring rather to obey than to command '. A legend of the eleventh century tells that Aymardus was chosen abbot on account of his humility. On the day of the election he was seen entering the monastery leading his horse, which was laden with fish. So struck were the brothers by this sight that they immediately elected him abbot. In the charters the adjective *humilis* nearly always precedes his name.

---

[1] Bruel, i. 217 (anno 920). A certain Aymardus, *miles clarissimus,* gave Cluny the *curtis* Silviniacus with its church and all pertaining to it, i.e. houses, vineyards, fields, meadows, and half a forest. Ibid. i. 443: an Aydoardus gave land in the province of Mâcon. Ibid. i. 460: A. gave land in the province of Autun, anno 936. Ib.d. i. 474 (anno 937): Aydoardus a priest gave a chapel to Cluny.

[2] Ibid. i. 486, *Ad Clun. ubi dominus Heymardus abbas preesse videtur.*

[3] Ibid. 534 (anno 941), *Clun. ubi preest Oddo abbas*; cf. ibid. i. 537 (anno 941), *sub qua congregatione Heymardus abbas.*

In the *Vita Maioli*[1] there is a passage about Aymardus which runs : 'Aymardus, son of happy memory and blessed simplicity and innocence, was zealous in increasing the property of the monastery and in acquiring material goods. Besides this he was devoted in the observance of the rule.' Rodulf Glaber described him as a simple man, who though not as famous as the other abbots of Cluny, yet like them carefully upheld the regular discipline.[2]

Perhaps Odo's rule though making for the spiritual renown of the abbey, had somewhat neglected the material interests. Here Aymardus' practical gifts came in, the more so as after Odo's death many gifts of land were presented to the monastery. To deal with these donations required organising talent which Aymardus evidently possessed.

In his latter years Aymardus became blind, ' an affliction which he bore without a murmur as he did all his other adversities '. It was probably on account of his blindness that after sixteen years of rule he retired from active participation in the administration of the monastery. His blindness was the occasion for an instance of ' marvellous humility ' of which Peter Damiani wrote to a friend. After Maiolus was appointed coadjutor and successor, Aymardus withdrew to the infirmary to spend his last years in peace. One day he wanted a cheese. When he asked the *cellarius* to fetch it, the latter roughly replied that so many abbots were a nuisance, and that he could not attend to all their commands. Cut off by his blindness Aymardus brooded over the insult as the blind are wont to do. Then he asked to be led to the chapter house, where approaching Maiolus he said : ' Brother Maiolus, I did not set thee over me that thou shouldest persecute me, or order me about as a master orders a slave, but that as a son thou mightest have compassion on

---

[1] *Bibl. Clun.* p. 269, *Vita Maioli Odilone, Hic in augmentatione praediorum et adquisitione temporalis commodi adeo studiosus fuit et in observatione satis devotus.*

[2] Ibid, Rod. Glab. iii. 5, *Vir simplex qui licet non adeo famosissimus, regularis tamen observantiae non impar custos.*

thy father.' After many more words he concluded, ' Art thou
indeed my monk ? ' Maiolus replied that he was, and never
more so than at that moment. ' If that be so,' Aymardus
rejoined, ' give up thy seat and take the one thou hadst before.'
Immediately Maiolus obeyed, and Aymardus seating himself
on the abbatial chair accused the cellarer, whom prostrate on
the ground he rebuked and enjoined to do penance. Then
descending from the abbot's throne he ordered Maiolus to
ascend, which the latter did without either haste or delay.[1]

The one event in Aymardus' life of which there is a sufficient
account is that of his retirement.[2] He was ill, weak, blind,
weary, and worn out with his struggles ; he knew that Maiolus
shone in good deeds and was raised to the heights on the wings
of virtue. So he called the brothers together and exhorted them
to choose a new abbot, as he in his blindness could no longer
watch over the interests of the monastery. The monks did not
know what to reply, till he, by divine inspiration, urged them to
elect Maiolus, as alone fit for the charge.

Nalgoldus [3] in his *Vita Maioli* expands this account and
makes Aymardus say : ' Ill, blind, and weary, I can no longer
be responsible for the interests of the monastery, nor fittingly
watch over its welfare. For it is well known that not only is
the spirit of bravery in soldiers derived from their king, and
their courage from his magnanimity and boldness, but that if
he, their leader, is remiss, they too lose their virtue. The
health of the whole body is in the head, and if it is sound, so are
the members. If the king loses courage, all his followers, even
the strongest and most manly, are overcome with womanly
fears. If the head is injured the whole body suffers. Now I
who lead you in the celestial militia before the whole church,
watch over your welfare as your head. I am old, infirm, blind,
and cannot longer retain this responsibility. Exercise, therefore,
your discretion and choose a father who will lead you in the way

---

[1] *Bibl. Clun.* p. 269.   [2] Migne, 137, p. 751, *Vita Maioli Syro*, ii. 2.
[3] *AA.SS. Boll.* May II. p. 658.

of God, and as a column of light in the night of offence direct your steps.   For if a ship without a rudder cannot reach port neither can your souls without a pilot.'

Suffering as he did from ill health and blindness, Aymardus could not have been even had he wished, the indefatigable traveller and reformer that Odo was.   We only know of two monasteries that came under Cluny's jurisdiction when he was abbot.   The first was Celsiniacus (Sauxillanges [1]), founded by count Acfredus (927), and given to Cluny by Stephen, bishop of Clermont (950), who with his father, and his father's wife, called Aymardus to Sauxillanges.   Aymardus was to send monks there.   No services nor dues were to be required of them, nor on the occasion of an episcopal visitation was there to be any attempt at usurping rights over the monastery.[2]   Louis IV., king of the Franks, at the bishop's request, confirmed Cluny's possession of Sauxillanges.

In 958 Conrad, king of Burgundy, at the request of Boso, count of Provence, gave Cluny the abbey of St. Amand's, near

---

[1] Bruel, i. 286.   The charter of gift is obscure and the Latin faulty. Acfredus, duke of Aquitaine pondering on human frailty and hoping that by the gift of a small portion of the land granted him by God, his sins might be remitted, gave to God the *curtis* Celsiniacus with its fields, vineyards, woods *appendariæ* (i.e. rustic buildings of small value.—Ducange), five mills, the woodland where he hunted, his own house, two churches, and everything which belonged to the *curtis* in various districts : i.e. three churches, seven vineyards, and a long list of manors, houses, and *appendariae*.   At Celsiniacus a house of religion was to be built, subjected neither to count, bishop, abbot, any of the count's relations, any mortal ruler, any saint nor angel spirit, but to God and the Trinity alone.   The servants (*ministri*) of God sent there were to have no *rector* over them, no judicial power was to use force against them, molest them, nor take unjust dues from them.   They were to put their trust in God only, and their serfs and *coloni* if accused or interrogated were to seek no other protector than Christ and the servants of God there : at one point these servants of God are called *clerici*, at another *monachi*.   The gift was made in honour of the twelve apostles, therefore twelve canons were unweariedly to pray day and night for the church, and for the remission of the sins of the count and of all the faithful.   The scheme was evidently found impracticable, but under Cluny Sauxillanges rose to great fame.

[2] Bruel i. 792, *Aut quodlibet servitium vel debitum ab ipsius loci potestate pro qualicumque ingenio exigere, seu occasione episcopatus aliquid illic iniuste ordinare nec sue rei potentatu cuiddam dominare.*   The bishop's father had been the count's almoner.

St. Paul-Trois-Châteaux, for he felt that if he were zealous in the restoration and care of ecclesiastical things he would not only rule on earth, but in heaven receive an eternal reward ; also that the nearer the day of death came, the more urgent he should be in doing good.   No count or magnate was to interfere with St. Amand's or its property, which was to be held for the use of the monks alone.[1] Next year Lothair, king of the Franks, at his mother's request also confirmed Cluny's possession in a charter which stated that St. Amand's was a ruined house without *rectores*, and situated in an uninhabited district.   The monks were to build there, according to their skill, a 'habitable place', and to hold the property : vills, meadows, vineyards, woods, waters, and serfs of either sex.[2]

After he had been seven years sole abbot of Cluny, Aymardus received a charter from a pope Agapitus[3] (sic), because Cluny was one of those holy places to which reverence was due (949). The monastery's liberties and privileges were confirmed, and its freedom from the domination of king, bishop, count, or relative of duke William the founder.   The monks were freely to elect their own abbot without consulting any prince.[4]   No bishop, count, nor other person was to enter the monastery, nor give orders, without the abbot's permission.   Tenths which formerly belonged to the monastery's chapels, and by the 'modern authority' of any bishop had been taken away, were restored in their entirety.   Bishop Berno's decree over tenths from their churches was to stand.   If any new chapels were built there, tenths of Cluny's churches were not to be diminished.   Part of those tenths and part of the returns from the vineyards and cultivated land belonging to the above churches could be retained for the

---

[1] Ibid. ii. 1052.   [2] Ibid. ii. 1057.

[3] *Bibl. Clun.* p. 273.   It behoved the apostolic authority to receive with benevolent compassion the vows of those who humbly approached it, and with swift devotion to answer their prayers.   In return the greatest reward would be given by the Maker of all : therefore the pope granted Aymardus' petition that Cluny should continue in that state which was decreed in duke William's will.

[4] *Nisi forte, quod absit, personam suis vitiis consentientem eligere maluerint.*

hospitale. No one was to seize or attack the monastery's *municipia* or property. Its possession of Sauxillanges, Carus Locus, the abbeys of St. John and St. Martin, Mâcon, the church of St. Saturn with its alod (the gift of archbishop Gerald), with other churches, vills, and alods, was also confirmed. To show that it behoved the Holy See to guard and cherish Cluny the monks were to pay Rome ten solidi every five years.[1]

Besides the papal, Aymardus received several royal charters. Three were granted by Louis, king of the Franks, at the request of Hugh, duke of the Franks, Hugh, duke of Burgundy, and count Letaldus, names that show Cluny to have had influential friends. In 946, the three nobles begged the king to ratify the gift of St. John's, Mâcon,[2] with its alods, lands, and serfs (confirmed three years after in the papal charter, see *supra*). Later in the same year they begged for the ratification of another gift, a vill with its vineyards, fields, meadows, woods, rivers, waters, fisheries, serfs, and *coloni* with their children ;[3] and finally for the confirmation of Cluny's possession of Carus Locus, the *cella* Regniacus, and abbey St. Martin's, Mâcon, with all belonging to them : churches, vills, vineyards, fields, meadows, woods, waters, serfs.[4] Duke Hugh and count Letaldus had influence also with Louis' successor, Lothair, who (955) at their request reconfirmed [5] Cluny's liberties and privileges, ' as conceded by former Frankish kings . The *castrum* of the monastery was to remain immune and subject to the monks alone, none daring to exercise judicial power within or without its circle, unless with their sanction. The monastery's property and possessions were to be held freely with no interference from outside authority, as former charters had decreed.

---

[1] Any one who did not observe the charter was to be bound with the chain of anathema, alienated from the kingdom of God, and tortured eternally by the devil.

[2] Bruel, i. 688.   [3] Ibid. i. 689.   [4] *Bibl. Clun.* 277.

[5] Bruel, ii. 980. ' If we strengthen holy places by our royal authority, without doubt we shall receive an eternal reward. . . . Assenting benignly to their request as is the custom of kings, we confirm whatever is known to have been granted Cluny by former kings of France, saving the apostolic right.'

In those early years, the kings of Burgundy continued to favour Cluny. In 943 Conrad, at the request of his relative count Hugh, ceded to Cluny a vill with its churches, and the little vills, lands, vineyards, meadows, woods, pasture lands, waters, and serfs belonging to it.[1] The same year, again at count Hugh's request, he ceded to Cluny another vill which Hugh had given him,[2] with everything belonging to it. Still, in 943, he supported the monks against his relative Charles of Vienne, who had disputed Cluny's right to the abbey of Carus Locus. The monks proceeded to Vienne and in the presence of the king pleaded against Charles, who finally acknowledged his error and signed Cluny's charter of possession. This was countersigned by the king, at whose command the decision of the case was written down.[3] Carus Locus proved a precarious possession. A certain Sobbo held it for some time. The monks again went to court, when Sobbo, convinced by the high authority on which their claim was based, ' broke the reins of his cupidity and withdrew his case ' (948). For the monks proved that Carus Locus had belonged to Robert, bishop of Valence, who built the monastery, and put it under the papal guardianship. By the pope it was given to Odo of Cluny, as its charters ratified by kings Hugh, Lothair, and pope John XI. testified. Sobbo made his retraction handsomely. Insatiable greed caused men to steal. He, Sobbo, was a sinner.[4]

A miserable sinner (remembering that now was the accepted time, etc.), whose father had left Cluny property which he through greed had withheld, at last recognised his sin, and with his wife's consent gave all with goodwill to St. Peter, i.e. a church with its vill and seven other vills, another church with the manor attached to it, serfs, land, mills, meadows, houses, moveables and immoveables. In reparation he also gave an alod of his own and hoped that God would forgive his sins, let him escape hell, and gain heaven.[5]

---

[1] Ibid. i. 627.   [2] Ibid. i. 628.   [3] Ibid. i. 622.   [4] Ibid. i. 730.
[5] 871 (954).   The preamble is the same as i. 726.

Of the other charters the majority deal with exchanges of land, evidence of Aymardus' good management and his care to round off Cluny's property. The charters dealing with these and with gifts of land follow the customary formulae. Several deal with disputes. In one case, heard before count Leotbald, his retainers, and the viscount, two men disputed Cluny's possession of a vineyard. To vindicate their rights the monks sent two *advocati*, who in front of the church of Mâcon successfully pleaded their suit, and proved that the vineyard belonged to St. Peter.

Before the glorious marquis Hugh, the monks sued Ademar, viscount of Lyons, for taking property assured to them by royal charter. When Ademar learnt that his *senior* was on their side, and that their charter of gift had been signed by the king, he renounced his claim and bound himself before Hugh not to offend again.

The chief monks of Cluny, i.e. Hildebrand, Leotbald, and many others appeared before count Leotbald, bishop Maimbod, viscount Walter, and their retainers, to accuse a certain Hugh,[1] who held two churches bequeathed to Cluny by the late duke William of Aquitaine, and other property which had passed from the countess Ava to her brother the duke, and from him to Cluny. Hugh, in the presence of all, stood up and protested that the property belonged to him by deed of gift from his mother, and showed the charter signed by his *senior*, Leotbald. Judgement was given that this plea was not valid, and that if he could not advance further evidence he was to restore what he had taken. He thereupon admitted St. Peter's right and withdrew his claim.

Count Leotbald and his wife gave an alod with an *ecclesia*, vineyards, meadows, woods, pasture, mills, houses, water, serfs, the whole to revert to Cluny when either he or his wife died, but for which till then they were to pay two solidi annually. Wherever the count died, the monks were to fetch his body and

---

[1] Ibid. i. 656.

bury it at Cluny.[1] Later they gave a manor with a church and everything belonging to it except one alod and a plantation of trees. The count was to hold it in usufruct for his lifetime,[2] paying the monks twelve denarii annually. He finally gave another church, eleven manors, and thirteen servants (servientes).[3]

Several gifts came from bishops. Maimbod, bishop of Mâcon, gave a curtilus, with old vineyards part sown with grain, five fields, a meadow, and half a wood[4] (947). In 945[5] and in 953[6] he exchanged land. In 956 when he was holding a synod, surrounded by a multitude of clerks, nobles, and laymen, Hildebrand and Maiolus, with other monks of Cluny, came before him, and humbly begged him to give them tenths of two churches which belonged to his cathedral, and to allow that the churches with their tenths, property, and everything belonging to them, might always and without opposition be secured for their use. The bishop, having consulted his archdeacons and clerks, assented, ' without any gift having passed between the parties '.[7] He also, at the request of Aymardus and count Leotbald, consecrated a chapel dedicated to the confessor Taurinus and built by the monks in a vill which they had received from kings Rudolf and Louis.[8] A nice discrimination was evidently necessary on such occasions, the bishop having first diligently inquired (1) whether the chapel recently founded would prejudice other churches, (2) would be of advantage to all Christians who cherished Christ in their hearts and the aforesaid confessor. The chapel was to be endowed by the monks with a colonia, three serfs, and a field (950).

An archbishop Gerald, oppressed by the enormity of his sins, bequeathed all his possessions to Cluny, remembering ' that now is the appointed time, now is the day of salvation ',

[1] Ibid. i. 625.
[2] Ibid. i. 655, Mansus indominicatus.
[3] Ibid. i. 768.
[4] Bruel, i. 707.   [5] Ibid. i. 667.   [6] Ibid. i. 842.
[7] Ibid. ii. 1000, Vice domni abbatis Eymardi et reliquorum monachorum Cluniaco degentium.
[8] Ibid. i. 780, Nec congruum erat ut tam gloriosus confessor et sincellite inibi commorantes diu sine benedictione episcopali persisteret.

i.e. a church with three vills and islands, a manor, lands, and houses in various districts. He intended to take the habit at Cluny, hoping thereby to escape the flames of hell, and to gain the celestial kingdom [1] (948). Manasses, archbishop of Arles, reflecting on the enormity of his sins, fearing the last secret judgement, remembering that now was the accepted time, and that as he could do no good after death it was wise to do good to those who without doubt would judge souls in the future, gave property to Cluny, ' where Aymardus rules with pious moderation ' : i.e. Juilly with three churches, vineyards, meadows, plains, pasture, woods, water, cultivated and uncultivated ground, buildings and serfs.[2] Burchard, archbishop of Lyons, consented to Aymardus' request that the services due to the cathedral from two of the Cluniac churches should be reduced. For the parish had lost in numbers owing to its men having become vassals and to the unsettledness of the times. The archbishop recognised the justice of this plea.[3] The bishop of Grenoble was not behind. In his diocese no synodal service was to be required from the monks except the customary wax.

A few churches were given by laymen. A woman, for her father's and son's souls gave a church with tenths, *presbiteratus*, *parochia*, and all belonging to it.[4] Three brothers, wishing to save their own and their parents' souls from hell, gave a chapel with all belonging to it, i.e. vineyards, meadows, fields.[5] A donor and his wife weighed down by their sins, but hoping that the pious and merciful God would save them and their relatives from the jaws of hell, and that they might merit to be set, not with the impious, but with the elect, and hear the words, ' Come, ye blessed ', gave a vill with its chapel, fields, woods, meadows, apple trees, and waters to Cluny.[6] Another

---

[1] Ibid. i. 724. Fields, vineyards, meadows, woods, waters, mills, houses, buildings, cultivated and uncultivated ground, furniture.

[2] Ibid. i. 726.

[3] Ibid. i. 734, *Cogitans diminutionem parochiarum quę per vassionem quorundam et temporis instabilitate facta est.*

[4] Ibid. i. 657.   [5] Ibid. i. 773.   [6] Ibid. i. 838.

H

donor had not hardened his heart but intently listening in church had heard that Christ, grieved at seeing the human race spotted by sin through the cunning of the ancient enemy of the race, had deigned to give salutary medicine for the many wounds of sin of which the most efficacious was to make friends of the Mammon of unrighteousness and thereby receive entrance to an eternal home. Remembering the enormity of his sins and fearful of his last hour he gave a manor, chapel, seven serfs and their families to Cluny.[1]

Parts of churches were also given, e.g. a third of a church ; [2] half a church and quarter of another, given by a woman, with a vill and serfs ; [3] a sixth of a church and its property ; [4] half a vill with half its church, lands, fields, waters, mills. In the last case the donor and his wife, not wishing to spend all they had for their own bodies, rejoiced that the divine clemency allowed the faithful to give from the transitory possessions which they had gained by just labour, and thereby obtain eternal reward. All the same it was only after their death that the monks could hold, order, and dispose it as they would. Any one who disputed the donation was to feel the anger of the Virgin's son, find himself shut out from paradise by St. Peter, and lest he should seem to escape punishment in this life, pay 100 pounds gold to the monks.[5] Parts of churches to be held for the donor's lifetime were also given, e.g. viscount Ratburn and his wife gave a church with its *presbiteratus* and *parrochia* and a third of what belonged to the church, i.e. *curtilus*, mountains, woods, thickets. They were to hold it in usufruct for life and pay St. Peter annually tenths *in vestitura*. On their death the whole reverted to Cluny.[6] A man and his wife, to make friends with the poor in Christ, who would receive them into their eternal habitations, gave Cluny half a chapel and a manor, which they were to hold for life and pay the monks twelve denarii annually.[7] Another man and his wife, reflecting on the enormity

[1] Ibid. i. 875.   [2] Ibid. i. 789.   [3] Ibid. i 651.   [4] Ibid. i. 706.
[5] Ibid. i. 876.   [6] Ibid. i. 546.   [7] Ibid. i. 746.

of their sins, but also on what was better, the sweet voice of Christ saying, ' Give alms ', gave Cluny land near Mâcon and a *curtis* in Auvergne with its chapel, which the monks were to hold *in vestitura*. On the death of the donors the *curtis*, chapel, fields, serfs, freedmen, mills, houses, moveables, immoveables, and any new buildings there reverted to the monks.[1] A count gave an alod with two churches and a vill. For the dispensation of God allows all who reflect sanely to give from their transitory goods in order to receive an eternal reward. He was to hold all while he lived and pay Cluny twelve solidi annually.[2] A priest sold half of two churches with their *presbiteratus* to the monks, and received from Aymardus 9 pounds silver that the sale should be firm and stable. He was to have usufruct for his lifetime and to give the monks *in vestitura* for the church a vineyard and a field. Any one who made trouble about the sale was to pay 4 pounds gold, half to the royal fisc, half to the monks.[3] One man and his wife gave a vill with its church and all belonging to it to his son. If the latter died without a legitimate heir they passed to Cluny.[4] One sinner and his wife made their donation because God said, ' Give alms and all worldly things will be yours ', and, ' As water extinguishes fire, so alms extinguisheth sin.' They hoped not to be thrust away with the impious into the jaws of hell but to merit to hear the joyful words, ' Come, ye blessed.' [5] The rest of the charters record gifts of vineyards, land, property, and vills. From the numerous exchanges of land it may be inferred that Aymardus was carefully rounding off the Cluniac property.

---

[1] Ibid. i. 825.   [2] Ibid. i. 797.
[3] Ibid. i. 751, *Ut certius credenda sit accio nostra, accipio de vobis in argente aut in valente libras viiii, et inante venditio ista firma et stabilis permaneat. Eo tenore dum ego Ado advixero usum et fructum: . . . et dono vobis de ipsam ecclesiam interim in vestitura . . . vineam unam.*
[4] Ibid. i. 653.   [5] Ibid. i. 838.

CHAPTER X

MAIOLUS, FOURTH ABBOT OF CLUNY

MAIOLUS, fourth abbot of Cluny, lived in very eventful times. He saw the extinction of a dynasty in Gaul, the rise of the Capetian house, the disappearance of the independent kingdom of Burgundy, and the march of the Teutonic eagles to Italy.

The date of his birth is unknown. The marriage settlement of his parents was drawn up in 909. His father, a *miles*, was of an old provincial family of Avignon, his mother of no less noble birth.[1] His father, Fulcher, must have had a goodly inheritance. His marriage settlement [2] on his wife Raimodis included three vills in Apt, two vills and a church in Aix, two vills and a church in Sisteron, two vills with two churches and two vills without churches in Riez, also ten serfs with their wives and children : altogether a hundred manors and fifty serfs (*mancipia*). The marriage settlement was drawn up publicly at Avignon ' according to the Roman law of the husband '. Raimodis was to do whatever she wished with this property, having most free and firm hold over it. If Fulcher, his relations or other persons interfered with it they were to pay a heavy fine.

Two sons were born of the marriage, Maiolus and Cynricus.[3] Probably Cynricus was the elder as Maiolus seems to have been early destined for the church, and as a child was given to ' literary studies '. [4] He was so precocious in mind and morals

---

[1] Migne, 137, *Vita Maioli Syro*, i. 1, *Ex Avenicorum oppido parentibus splendissimis.*

[2] Bruel, i. 105, *In dotalicium. Finat in summo mansa* 100, *in sponsalitium istud et mancipia* 50.

[3] Ibid. ii. 1071, *Fratri meo Eyrico ; anno* 959.

[4] *Vita Syro*, i. 1, *Ab ipsis infantiae rudimentis studiis litterarum traditus.*

that his future greatness was foretold by many. His name itself, Maiolus, i.e. *magnus oculus*, seemed sure proof that God had chosen him for Himself. ' Like a splendid star he was destined to raise human conditions.' [1] While yet a boy he lost his parents.[2] About the same time the family lands were devastated by the barbarians. The boy therefore went to Mâcon, where he was received by a relative, ' one of the chief men of the city '.[3] In time the bishop of Mâcon, having heard of his reputation for learning, asked him to join the college of canons. Maiolus refused, as he wished to study under Antony, a teacher of Lyons, famous not only for his wisdom but for the virtue of his life. He went therefore to Lyons, which as a scholastic centre still retained something of the renown which had been hers in Roman days, ' excelling all towns far and near in the opportunities she offered for the study of religion and the liberal arts. Nurse of philosophy and mother of all Gaul, she upheld not unworthily the keystone of ecclesiastical right. Her fame had spread across the seas, and to her flocked men eager to learn wisdom '.[4]

At Lyons Maiolus sought and enjoyed the companionship of good men, keeping himself aloof from the pleasures and vices indulged in by many of his companions, fearing lest, once infected by them, he should be unable to free himself later. So great was his reputation for holiness that he was already considered a monk.

From Lyons he returned to Mâcon, and was ordained priest. He laboured gladly in the vineyard of the Lord, ' kind to all, just to all, harming none, doing good to many, and striving to perfect himself in wisdom. Never was lying, detraction, or flattery heard from his mouth. Nor did he hesitate to be severe, if by admonition, exhortation, or rebuke, he could win a brother to the truth '. Fearful lest he should be condemned for hiding his talent, and eager not only to inform his own mind but to help others, he gathered round him a large body of clerks

---

[1] *Vita Odilone.* [2] *Vita Syro*, i. 4. [3] Ibid. i. 4. [4] Ibid. i. 5.

and taught them for nothing.   In time he was appointed arch-deacon.[1]

To gratify that love of solitude and meditation which was one of his chief characteristics, he built at some distance from the town, and on the opposite side of the river, a little oratory to which he could retire for silent prayer.[2]   The withdrawal from the world of so young and eminent a priest caused his fame to spread, and when the bishopric of Besançon fell vacant, the see was offered him ' by the unanimous voice of princes, ecclesiastics, and people '.[3]   His humility would not let him accept. Moreover he was afraid that, in a position where necessarily he would be involved in a certain amount of secular business, his soul might be led to seek the gains and glory of a world he despised.[4]   There seemed to him a higher calling, a more perfect vocation than life in the secular church, i.e. the monastic life. Disciplined therefore in ecclesiastical studies and despising the fleeting glory of the world, he sought the monastery of Cluny in the vale between the hills.   He had often visited the little monastery so celebrated for its spiritual life, and often the brothers, struck by his ' sweet speech, his angelic face, the wonderful intelligence of his mind, and his mellifluous eloquence ', had wished that he were one of them.   The wish was granted. Maiolus, ' with deepest humility from being a doctor of grammar began to study the wise stupidity of God, and to be the disciple of simple men '.[5]

At Cluny his pre-eminent virtues soon made him a conspicuous figure.   In the virtue of obedience especially he surpassed all his companions, and, as St. Benedict taught, bore himself most humbly not only towards his abbot but also towards the brothers.   ' No one is worthy to command until he has first learned to obey, so by the divine dispensation Maiolus was for long submissive to others, that later he might himself know how to rule without error.'   When Aymardus saw him more

[1] Ibid. i. 7.   [2] Ibid i. 10.   [3] Ibid. i. 12.
[4] Ibid   [5] Ibid. i. 13.

responsible and wiser than his fellows, he appointed him *apo-crisiarius*, whose duty was to guard the church treasury and receive the offerings of the faithful.[1] So well did Maiolus perform this work that he was made librarian, an office for which he was well fitted. ' Having himself read the philosophers of old and the lies of Virgil, he no longer desired either to read them himself or to let others do so.' He was very urgent in exhorting the brothers not to pollute their minds with the lecherous eloquence of Virgil, and in reminding them that the divine word was sufficient for them.[2] ' Indeed, he fulfilled his duties with such strictness and care that he was a terror to all converts.'

He was already a leader among the monks when an event occurred which caused his merit to shine forth : Sent with a fellow-monk to Rome, on the return journey his companion fell ill. For three anxious days and nights Maiolus watched by the sufferer. At last in utter weariness he fell asleep, when he saw a white-haired old man who said :—

' Why art thou cast down in idle grief ? Hast thou forgotten what my brother James orders for the sick ? ' Awakening from sleep, he remembered the apostolic injunction, and rubbed his brother with holy oil. From that very moment the sick man began to recover. When this miracle was told at Cluny, the brothers held him in ever greater veneration, to his great dismay, for he wished to be despised rather than honoured. But the more he fled the praise of his fellows the greater grew their devotion and esteem.[3] ' So having avoided vice, having risen from virtue to virtue, he reached through the *quadrivium* of obedience the supreme height of humility.'

It was to Maiolus as successor that Aymardus looked when he felt his own strength fail : ' Maiolus distinguished in merit and nobility, excellent in dogma, generous of soul, known to princes,

---

[1] Udalricus, iii. 12, *Consuet. Clun.*: *Apocrisiarus est qui custodit ecclesiae tresaurum, et in cuius manu est quidquid a popularibus ad altaria offertur.*

[2] *Vita Syro*, i. 14. [3] Ibid. i. 15.

revered by all.'[1] The monks were eager to hail him as pastor,[2] but in accordance with the usual convention he at first refused, though the monks, prostrate on the ground, implored him to consent. Even after the monks, clerks, and the chief men of the district, with the common people of the country and of the town, had assembled at Cluny to hail him as father, Maiolus held to his decision for three days. Then worn out with anxiety, and wearied with much thought, he passed a sleepless night. At dawn a vision was vouchsafed him. A monk of beautiful face appeared and told him to accept the responsibility of office, in which he would be guided by God. Holding out a little book, ' Here ', he said, ' you have a guide, act according to its precepts.' He who spoke seemed to be none other than St. Benedict himself ! Strengthened by this vision and throwing his care on the Lord, Maiolus hesitated no longer. Next day in the chapter, prostrate on the ground, he acknowledged that he had sinned by his refusal. Addressing the monks, he said :—

' Oh, father and brothers, do not judge from my contumacy that through obstinacy of soul I refused to obey your command. Indeed I longed to accept the greatness of the office, the governance of souls, but I was yet conscious of my weakness, and felt myself most unfit for the task. Hence my hesitation in obeying you, for I feared to be hurled to destruction under the weight of so great a responsibility. None knows another as himself, and if you but knew me as I know myself, you would not compel me to undertake this office. But as you urge and command me, I dare not say you nay. Now in Him who is able to smooth rough places, to raise up heavy burdens, and to overthrow the adversary, I place my hope, and submit myself to your unchanged command.'[3]

Aymardus then announced to the assembled nobles, bishops, pontiffs, and abbots that Maiolus was abbot. Great was the

---

[1] Ibid. ii. 1, ' *Solum hunc esse ad id offitium idoneum affirmans.*' ' *Hunc clarum meritis, tunc nobilitate legendum, dogmate precipuum, generoso pectore primum, principibus notum et nonnulla parte verendum.*'

[2] *Unus omnium consensus, nec dispar fuit effectus.*   [3] Ibid. i. 2.

rejoicing and giving of thanks. The election was inscribed, the antiphon sung. Maiolus, amid the joy of all, was led into the church, received the benediction, and seated on the abbatial chair.[1]

The charter of election is dated 954,[2] but Aymardus' name, with the title of abbot, still appeared frequently in charters up to 956, less frequently from 956 to 960, after which date his name disappears till 965, when it is mentioned for the last time.

. . . .

It would be interesting to know, but in the absence of contemporary records it is impossible to tell, what part Maiolus played in the social and political life of his time. He was known to princes, French kings, and Saxon emperors.

Otto I., who married Adelheid of Burgundy (951), may first have heard of him from his wife, who venerated the abbot deeply.[3] He was presented at the imperial court in Pavia at Otto's request, by a friend of the emperor, a wealthy nobleman of Pavia, who had left wife and children, renounced his riches and military career, and entered Cluny as a monk. The emperor kept Maiolus long at Pavia. ' He was the ear and depository of the imperial secrets : those who had any dealings with Otto seeking him out as intermediary.' [4] Definite proof of the imperial favour was seen when Otto appointed him abbot of St. Apollinare in Classe, near Ravenna.[5] The emperor also gave him a *corticella* in Italy, for it ' behoved him to cherish the church of God and thereby be sure of a temporal and eternal reward '.[6] He made the gift at his wife's request, who also asked Maiolus to help with the building of St. Saviour's, Pavia.[7]

---

[1] *Vita Odilone, Electus advocatur, invitatus restitit, rogatus contradicit, adiuratus tremiscit, interdictus quiescit.*

[2] Bruel, ii. 883, *Cluniacum cum omnibus abbatiis, locis et cellis ordinandum tradimus. Et abbatem unanimiter omnes proclamamus.* Two bishops, one of whom was Maimbod of Mâcon, two abbots, and 132 monks were present at the signing of the charter.

[3] *Vita Syro, ii. 21, Ac si ancillarum ultima, impendere cupiebat ei devotionis obsequia.*   [4] Ibid.   [5] Ibid. ii. 22.

[6] Bruel, ii. 1143 (962–973).

[7] *Vita Syro, ii. 22, Desudare coepit in fabrica.*

Maiolus is said to have foretold Otto's death. Once returning to Cluny he said, ' Last night as I slept I saw a mighty lion
in a cage, burst through his chains. Of a surety this year Otto
the Great will die.' Soon after a messenger arrived from
Germany with the news of the emperor's death.[1]

The imperial favour continued under Adelheid and her son.
Indeed, according to Sirius, they wished to nominate him to
the papacy. ' He was summoned to Italy by Otto II. and his
mother, who received him with the greatest veneration and
urged him with insistent prayer to ascend the summit of the
apostolic dignity.' [2] But he who sought lowliness rather than
exaltation could in no wise be moved to that sublime ambition.
He was unwilling to leave the little flock it had pleased Christ
to put under him, preferring to ' live a life of poverty with Him
who descended from the heights of Heaven to the lowliness of
earth '. Imperial son and mother were so insistent that he asked
time for consideration and betook himself to prayer. Rising
from his knees he saw a New Testament lying near, and opened
it, convinced that the first passage he lit on would reveal the will
of God. It ran, ' See that no man deceive you through vain
philosophy.' So, though whipped by the reiterated prayers of
the emperor and his mother, he persisted in his decision. Finally
to the imperial prayers were added those of the nobles and chief
ecclesiastics. But Maiolus was firm, and with skilful prudence
explained that (1) he had not the qualities required for such an
honour, nor felt himself able to bear a responsibility so great
that none should undertake it who felt himself unfit ; (2) he was
unwilling to forsake his flock at Cluny and the monastic life ; [3]
(3) he and the Romans being of different countries would agree
very little *in moribus*. Therefore they must choose another
pope, for he would never ascend the apostolic height nor leave
the flock committed to his care.

---

[1] Ibid. iii. 10.   [2] Ibid. iii. 8.
[3] Ibid., *Pusillum gregem nolebat dimittere quem Christo placuit sibi com-
mittere.*

As the nomination is not mentioned in Odilo's life of Maiolus, nor elsewhere,[1] the accuracy of Sirius' information has been questioned. But in view of the fact that the Cluniacs have been represented by modern writers as zealously upholding and promulgating the strictest theocratic ideals, the way in which Sirius regarded the imperial offer is really more important than the fact itself. Sirius did not criticise the validity of imperial interference in the papal election, nor was indignant at the papacy's being regarded as a sinecure determined by the imperial will. Such an attitude would have been out of keeping with the spirit of his age and order. Men had grown accustomed to the papacy's being regarded as a perquisite to be scrambled for by ambitious families. As a good Cluniac, his interests lay with the monastic order and its reform. But the incident served to glorify his master, and from that point of view he regarded it. He rejoiced that through humility his abbot could refuse such an honour and withstand the express command of the greatest prince of the world. Others, distinguished by neither knowledge nor virtue, thrust themselves forward to gain high places, degrading themselves by bribery and simony to attain papal rank. Maiolus fled from earthly glory, and far from the world came the nearer to God.

Though Maiolus had withstood the imperial will, not long after he acted as peace-maker between Otto and his mother. Otto II. had married a beautiful and gifted Greek, whose great influence over her husband may have aroused the jealousy of his mother. At any rate Adelheid was accused of being a menace

---

[1] Mabillon noted the omission, which he discounted partly on the somewhat surprising argument that Odilo was avowedly writing a panegyric, not a biography : the more need, it would seem, to mention the proffered honour. Sackur like Mabillon accepts the story, Schulze rejects it, taking Odilo's silence as in itself criticism and proof of the story's falsity. His argument is weakened by the fact that Odilo, though he knew of Maiolus' championship of the empress, did not mention it in his *Vita Maioli*, though he did so in his *Vita Adelheidi*. Mabillon puts the date of the nomination 974, after Boniface VI. had been thrown into prison and strangled by the men of Francone, who became Boniface VII.

to the empire and was banished from the imperial councils. When the sunshine of the imperial favour was turned from her, none, not even those who owed their advancement to her, would risk defending her ; for this cowardice they gave the easy excuse that the imperial majesty must not be contradicted. Finally, Adelheid was banished from the kingdom, and took refuge with her brother, Conrad of Burgundy.

But if all others forsook her, Maiolus stood by her, went to her, and comforted her. Then journeying to Pavia he sought out the emperor, and rebuked him for having forgotten that Christ, who deigned to subject Himself to His mother, commanded men to honour their parents. In spurning his mother Otto had acted presumptuously, and had forgotten that God who raised him to his transitory dignity could also bring him down to the dust. At this rebuke the emperor ' moderated the flames of his fury and his ferocious wrath against his mother '. [1] Seeking out Adelheid he threw himself at her feet, and yielded to her as a son should ; the charge against her was investigated and was found to be false. When it was known how Maiolus had commanded where others had not dared even to plead, his fame grew, and the emperor honoured him more and more. Probably about this time he again obtained the imperial ratification of Cluny's rights over Peterlingen.

In 983 he was with the emperor at Verona and advised him against his Italian campaign. Taking Otto's hand, ' Open thine ear ', he said, ' to the counsel of Frater Maiolus, and return whence thou camest. For know of a surety that if thou goest against Rome, thou wilt never see another Christmas, but in Rome find thy sepulchre.' [2]

The importance of Maiolus' name is also seen in an event which caused no small stir in monastic circles, and throws an

---

[1] *Vita Syro*, iii. 9. An account of this incident in the *Annales* (978) Magdeburg is more matter of fact. When exiled Adelheid went to Lombardy, then to Burgundy. One party at court worked for her. Finally, Otto asked Conrad of Burgundy and Maiolus to effect a reconciliation, and met her at Pavia. [2] Ibid. iii. 10.

interesting light on the Cluniac position, i.e. a disputed election at Fleury. A new abbot, Oilbold, had been appointed at the command of Lothair, king of the Franks.[1] As this was a flagrant infringement of their right of free election, several of the monks refused to recognise him. It is important to learn what part Maiolus as head of the Cluniac community took, and significant that the opposition that might have been expected to come from him, came instead from Gerbert.[2] Gerbert, at that time abbot of Bobbio, wished to unite the monastic order under the leadership of Maiolus, to isolate Oilbold, and force him to leave Fleury. Maiolus, though he condemned Oilbold, was prepared to bow to the *fait accompli*, a passive attitude to Gerbert reprehensible and incomprehensible. The points at issue and the standpoint of the two men can be judged from Gerbert's letters to Maiolus and quotations from Maiolus' reply.

Maiolus, as Gerbert knew, watched over his own flock with vigilant care, yet it would be a greater charity if he cured the disease of an alien flock [3] (i.e. the connection between Cluny and Fleury had evidently been allowed to drop). Gerbert was indignant at a reprobate's usurping what was almost the highest position in the monastic world. To let the scandal go uncorrected would encourage others to follow this example. If Maiolus kept silence who would speak ? The whole matter ought to be examined and sentence passed on Oilbold. If judged *probus* he should be recognised as abbot, if *improbus* cut off from fellowship with the monastic order and left to his own damnation. He was anxious to know Maiolus' opinion.

What stirred him most keenly, Gerbert wrote to Edward, abbot of St. Julian's, Tours, was such a scandal having arisen at Fleury, that eminent monastery where of all places the rule

---

[1] *Oilbold ad prelationem Floriacensium fratrum ipsorum electione et regia principis Lothairii ascendit donatione* (*Mirac.* II. xviii. p. 121).

[2] Gerbert was educated at Aurillac where Odo had been abbot. He was afterwards Sylvester II.

[3] Havet, *Lettres de Gerbert*, No. 69, *Etsi vigilanti cura super vestro grege assidue occupati estis, propensioris est tamen caritatis, si alieni gregis contagio interdum medemini.* Fleury was reformed by Odo.

ought to have been most strictly kept. He begged Edward to take action. If leaders of the monastic order kept silence who would take upon himself to correct the evil ? [1]

Maiolus' letter to Gerbert is lost, but Adalbero, archbishop of Rheims, who answered it at Gerbert's request, fortunately quotes from it.[2] Maiolus had justified his non-intervention in the dispute by pointing out that Oilbold lived under a different ruler and in a different land from himself. This to Adalbero was merely begging the question. The fathers of the church had never regarded proceedings against heretics in any country as beyond their ken. The Catholic Church was one and indivisible throughout the world. Maiolus himself had said that Oilbold's audacity and ambition were detestable to all the faithful, yet, though admitting his guilt, he still communicated with him ! Others of the monastic world had cut him off from their fellow-ship. He begged Maiolus to do the same, and to let Oilbold feel the weight of his displeasure. Then all the Cluniac monks would be turned against him, and even those of the papal entourage might be influenced.[3] Adalbero and his friends would gladly follow so revered a leader, and have nothing further to do with Oilbold (*pervasor ac tam probo improbo approbato*), June-July 986.

The prospect of leadership did not move Maiolus : ' Though he wisely and rightly condemned Oilbold, he maintained that the dispute concerned him and Cluny very little.'

His opinion in itself was sufficient to influence his co-abbots at Rheims. Writing to the recalcitrant monks at Fleury,[4] they expressed their deep sympathy with the injustice the monks had suffered, and condemned Oilbold. At first they had sinned by admitting him to their fellowship, but that was through ignorance. As soon as they learnt that Maiolus and Edward of Tours, ' those truest fathers and brightest stars in the church of God ', had

---

[1] Ibid. No. 80.   [2] Ibid. No. 87.
[3] Ibid., *Ac per vos, non solum quosque religiosos vestri ordinis sed etiam si fieri potest Romani pontificis se maledictis urgeri.*   [4] Ibid. No. 95.

condemned him, they accepted their judgement, '*An non lucidissima stella reverendus pater Maiolus : an non prefulgidum sidus pater Edradus.*'

Maiolus, as they learnt from his letter to Adalbero, had known Oilbold formerly, as notorious for the infamy of his life and beyond redemption in this world. He had promised to warn his neighbours against him, so that even if the scandal could not be blotted out, at least it would be known that Oilbold was cut off from the fellowship of the saints. The future must be left to itself.

Edward of Tours had also condemned him, a decision from which he declared not even the chiefs of the church could make him swerve. He called on the latter to judge the case without fear or favour of the secular power. The abbots were ready to abide by the decision of these two illustrious men.

'Take heed to these things,' the letter ended, ' oh comrades and fellow-soldiers. Withdraw yourselves, oh sheep of Christ, from him who is no shepherd, but a wolf ravening the sheep. He has not blushed to thrust himself forward, he who should have rather meekly effaced himself. Let him boast that by the favour of kings, princes, and dukes, he was set over the monks. Condemned by two such fathers as Maiolus and Edward he is cut off from our fellowship.' [1]

There the matter seemed to have dropped. Closely bound as Fleury had once been to Cluny, Maiolus refused actively to intervene. The Cluniacs had a due respect for dignitaries, and Oilbold had been appointed by the king. For two years he retained his office, from which death alone removed him (988), when Fleury was freed from ' the mouth of the lion ' [2]—to Gerbert's outspoken joy.

In 987 Maiolus made what was probably his last journey to Rome. On his way there he stayed at St. Michael's, Locedia, where he met the young William of Volpiano. From Locedia

---

[1] *Careat nostro consortio qui talium patrum dampnatur iudicio.*
[2] Ibid. No. 143.

he went to Pavia, and thence to Rome, where he consulted the
pope about the reform and rebuilding of Ciel d' Oro.[1] On his
return from Rome he stopped again at Pavia, and then proceeded to Locedia, where William of Volpiano begged to accompany him to Cluny. As abbot of St. Bénigne's, Dijon, William
became one of the most famous of the Cluniac alumni.

From this point the *Vita* hastens on to an account of Maiolus'
death.[2] His was rather a pathetic figure in his latter years. As
he mournfully pointed out, he had outlived his contemporaries
and those religious men who had fought the good fight and did
rest from their labours. His beloved books were his only consolation.

He was eighty-four when he died. Two years before his
death he felt his strength fail, and, assured that his call drew
near, he retired either to Souvigny or to one of the smaller
Cluniac houses. There he devoted his time to correcting the
brothers, stimulating them to ever better life, and in reading
and prayer gave himself wholly to God. In no way did he
spare the weakness of his old age. He died when on his way to
reform St. Denis, Paris, ' compelled by the too great importunity of the king of the Franks '.

He set out, not ignorant that his death was near, but glad
to end his days in doing a good work. He did not get far.
At the little monastery of Souvigny (Auvergne) he fell ill. He
rejoiced that the hour of his death had come,[3] but deep and
profound was the sorrow of the brothers, and one the voice of
weeping which arose. To the last his members remained free
and unimpaired. With beautiful face, sound hearing, sane
memory, and freedom from disease and blot, he advanced to
his immortal reward. He had nothing to grieve over, he told
the questioning brothers ; he regarded all things quietly and

---

[1] *Bibl. Clun.* p. 1775 ; cf. charter of John XV.

[2] *Vita Syro*, iii. 19. The beautiful simplicity of Sirius' account is missed
in the more ornate versions of the other lives.

[3] Ibid. iii. 19, *Nihil se habere molestiae sed omnia quieta et tranquilla
perspicere et videre bona Dei in terra viventium.*

tranquilly, had no pain, and saw all things good in the earth
for those who worked with God. Asked to whom he would
commit his flock, he answered that they would have Christ,
the Great Shepherd, as their protector.[1] Prostrate on the
ground the brothers besought his prayers, confident that one so
dear to God could obtain whatever he asked for. He gave them
absolution, then ceased from common speech, though ever and
anon he repeated little verses—' Lord, Lord, I have loved Thy
house,' etc. Then raising his eyes to heaven he signed himself
with the sign of the Cross, whispering to himself till his breath
failed.

The monks who had accompanied him wished to carry his
body to Cluny. Against this the monks of Souvigny protested.
Finally the inhabitants of the vill forcibly prevented his body
being removed. He was therefore buried in the church of St.
Peter, and Souvigny from being a small monastery became a
centre of pilgrimage. Many were the miracles worked at his
tomb.

[1] Nevertheless according to a charter he had appointed Odilo abbot. Bruel
iii. 1965, *Clun. cui domnus reverentissimus pater Odilo preest, iussione sci
patris Maioli* (993–4).

I

CHAPTER XI

UNDER Maiolus Cluny stood in the forefront of the reform. Her abbot was one of the best-known of the monastic leaders : ' the brightest star in the monastic firmament ', that ' archangel of monks '.

At his warning many renounced their possessions and gave themselves to the regular discipline. An innumerable multitude gathered under him from every part of the world. Of different race and tongue they were yet so united that in them were fulfilled the words of the apostle, ' There was one heart and mind among them '. Their pastor, watching over them with zealous care, rejoiced in the increase of his flock and in their zeal for their work. He corrected the discipline of the regular life which had fallen away by the negligence of old. He watched his flock with skilful care, and even in this life merited to see the fruits of his labours. Many monasteries which had left the straight path were corrected by him and by his monks, many of whom he appointed abbots. He rejoiced greatly that those whom he had trained were accounted worthy to rule in their turn.[1]

Cluny was ' especially dear ' to pope John XIII. Writing to the bishops of Arles, Lyons, Vienne, Clermont, Valence, Besançon, Mâcon, Chalons, Lérins, Viviers, Avignon, Geneva, Lausanne, Le Puy, to them as the light of the world and the salt of the earth, he commended Cluny with the houses under it.

---

[1] *Vita Syro,* ii. 6.

As faithful lovers of St. Peter he begged them to defend the monastery. If any one, however powerful, attacked Cluniac property the bishops were to excommunicate him until restitution was made. The bishop of Clermont, for instance, was to excommunicate one of his *fideles* who had taken land from Sauxillanges if he refused to restore it. The pope specially commended Cluny to the bishop of Mâcon, its near neighbour, asked him to give ' swifter aid ' to the brothers in their necessity, and to protect them. They had always loved him and desired his love.[1]

Neither Odo nor Aymardus had attempted to bind the reformed monasteries to Cluny. When Maiolus became abbot only five of them were subject to Cluny : i.e. Romainmoutier, Carus Locus (*Charlieu*), Sauxillanges, and two monasteries in Mâcon. The policy of building up an organised system of dependent houses, looking to Cluny as head, was only definitely undertaken by Maiolus' successors, Odilo and Hugh, though under Maiolus the tentative beginning of the system may be seen. Several monasteries were placed under him. In 958 Conrad, king of Burgundy, gave Cluny St. Amand's, St. Paul-Trois-Châteaux,[2] and two years later at his mother's request Lothair of Gaul confirmed the gift.[3]

Four years later Maiolus received Peterlingen, situated in the Juras, and the first Cluniac monastery on German soil.[4] Founded by Bertha, queen of Burgundy, she did not live to see it completed, but bequeathed to it all her property in that district. She was buried there. Her daughter, the empress Adelheid, completed her mother's work. Both she and her brother, king Conrad, gave land to Peterlingen, Conrad granting the monks an alod with the right of minting [5] (963), and later Crottas, with mill and all belonging to it.[6] The Ottos gave several charters to Peterlingen.[7] Protected by the great, the monastery

---

[1] Migne, 135, p. 990.   [2] Bruel, ii. 1052.   [3] Ibid. ii. 1067.
[4] Bouquet, ix. 667.   [5] Bruel, ii. 1127.   [6] Ibid. ii. 1152
[7] *Diplomata Ottonis II., Mon. Germ. Hist.* ii. No. 51. Maiolus with all

flourished, and its abbots in time gained much property in Alsace, Colmar, and Huttenheim.

St. Saviour's, Pavia, founded by the empress Adelheid, adorned with ornaments and richly endowed, was given by her to Maiolus. John XIII. in a charter addressed to Adelheid took St. Saviour's under the papal protection (972), and declared it free from all other authority, ecclesiastical or secular. Freedom of election was assured to the monks, who could receive ordination and the chrisma from any bishop the abbot chose. Bishops were never to demand tenths. Baptism could be celebrated in the monastery's chapels.[1] Ten years later (982) Otto II. confirmed St. Saviour's privileges, rights, immunities, and possessions, at Adelheid's request.[2] The monks could choose an abbot from another monastery if they wished. Monks leaving their own monasteries and wishing to enter St. Saviour's were to be received only if the brothers of St. Saviour's consented. St. Saviour's had already two monasteries under it. As Cluny is not mentioned in either of these charters, it must have been given to Maiolus after the date of the second.

The Cluniacs held another house in Pavia, the gift of a priest (967). He bought the chapel of the Virgin and St. Michael with much land from an imperial judge and his wife, and gave it the same day to Maiolus on condition that it was ' constituted a monastery for men '. Maiolus was to send monks there, and the new monastery, which was richly endowed, was to be always subject to Cluny.[3] The old Lombard capital was an important

the congregation of brothers came before the emperor at Aachen, 973, and asked him to confirm his father's charter to Peterlingen. He did so and confirmed its possessions in Alsace, etc., which with the monastery were to be held in security under the imperial defence : *sub nostra tuitonis immunitate . . . libere et securiter.* In 983 at Verona, at the request of his mother and his wife, Otto again confirmed Cluny's rights over Peterlingen.

[1] *Mon. Germ. Hist.* i. 307.
[2] *Mon. Germ. Hist.*, Sickel, i. 281.
[3] ii. 1229. The charter of sale and the charter of donation to Cluny are dated the same day : *Constitutum monasterium virorum.*

centre for Cluniac influence, for Pavia, likened to Tyre and Sidon, was still a cosmopolitan town to which thronged men of every nationality and tongue.[1]

In his first visit to Rome as abbot (probably 967) Maiolus went to St. Paul's, 'the house of the celebrated Doctor', reformed by Odo.[2] He found only a few poverty-stricken monks there whose necessities he supplied and whose customs he corrected. It was from St. Paul's that later the ashes of St. Peter and Paul were sent to Cluny for safety.[3] At Pavia he restored Ciel d' Oro, which was almost entirely in ruins.[4] Also in Italy a priest gave land, fields, vineyards, waters, pasture, on condition that the *seniores* of Cluny built a place (*locus*) there, where monks in return were to instruct his nephew in letters and make him a monk. The priest was to be dominator and rector of all the land he had given till his death, when the whole reverted to Cluny (966).[5] He made the gift remembering that it was written, ' Make friends with the Mammon of unrighteousness', ' Lay up for yourselves treasure in Heaven ': not wishing to hear the words, ' Depart into eternal fire ', but rather, ' Come ye blessed of my Father '.

Another priest, remembering the injunction to give alms, grateful to God for having preserved him from poverty, hoping to escape the devil's dark pit, and to reign in that Heaven where there is no terror, nor illness, nor hunger, nor sin, gave part of his hereditary possessions to the priory of St. Andrew's, Rosans,

---

[1] *Bibl. Clun.* p. 1775, *Vita Maioli Anony.*: *Pavia quae multiplicibus populorum referta turbis nobilium et diversarum mercium speciebus insignis, quasi quaedam Tyrus et Sydon videtur remanisse, quibus complacet ad sui mercimonii comparationem et venditionem venire.*

[2] *Vita Syro,* ii. 17.   Cf. Peter Damiani, *Opusculum,* xxxiii. 8.

[3] *Bibl. Clun.* p. 560, *Tandem seditionis urbe turbata motibus . . . malis urgentibus monachi discedentes vas illud apostolicorum cinerum sacra secum pignora detulerunt sicque Cluniacum propere pervenerunt.*

[4] *Vita Maioli Nalgoldo,* iii. 22, *Monasterium . . . collapsum paene fuerat in ruinam, restauravit ad unguem.* Cf. *Anony.* cap. 18.

[5] Ibid. 1200, *Ac nepotem meum litteris imbuant et monachum faciant : . . . Ego donator vester, quamdiu dominator et rector his rebus sim, secundum Deum et ad voluntatem meam omnia habeam.*

which he subjected to Cluny. He begged Maiolus to send virtuous monks from his own congregation to the priory (988).[1] In Italy also St. Apollinare in Classe Ravenna had earlier been put under Maiolus (p. 105).

Outside Italy, an important monastery to come under Cluny was Paray, founded by Lambert, son of the viscount Robert (973), on a site chosen by Maiolus. Paray was richly endowed, and monks sent to it from Cluny. Four years later (977) the church was consecrated with great pomp, three bishops officiating.[2] In 976, on condition that he and his monks built a monastery and sent monks there, a man and his wife gave Maiolus Mons Rompons, with its two churches, land, woods, meadows, pasture, rivers, fountains, waters, streams, and twelve serfs.[3] In 978 a similar gift came from the archbishop of Lyons, who, feeling his death draw near, gave Cluny ten vills in Nimiasus where the monks were to build a small *cella*. In return he begged to be mentioned in their prayers, ' for he had loved them before all their fellows '.[4] In the same year Maiolus begged the pope to give Cluny the island of Lérins which, by the decree of Gregory the Great, belonged to the papal jurisdiction. In 410 a monastery for men and a convent for women had been founded at Lérins by Honoratus. Attacked by the Saracens the monks and nuns had been driven away. They returned and lived in security for some time, many withdrawing themselves to live as hermits in solitary parts of the island. The Cluniacs were to pay from Lérins five solidi annually to Rome.[5] At the request of the saintly bishop, Bruno of Langres, Maiolus reformed

---

[1] Ibid. iii. 1784, *Deum et redemptorem meum glorificans, qui mihi corpus et animam gratuita pietate concessit et me nonnullis subsidiis humanae paupertatis constipavit.*

[2] *Chronicle of Paray-le-Monial*; cf. Bruel, iii. 2484. Paray, with its wonderful old church built, though on a smaller scale, on the model of Cluny's, is now the centre of pilgrimage for the cult of the Sacred Heart.

[3] Ibid. ii. 1434.

[4] Ibid. ii. 1450, *Concedo quasdam res meae adquisitionis, quas propria mea adquisivi substantia.*

[5] Bouquet, ix. p. 245. In the fifth century Lérins became famous as a school of theology, and many of its sons became the bishops of southern Gaul.

St. Bénigne's, Dijon.[1] The bishop, distressed at the decadence of the once famous monastery, and having heard much of the holy lives of the monks of Cluny, visited Maiolus to ask his help. Maiolus sent to St. Bénigne's twelve of the most perfect of his monks, ' wise in holy discipline, learned in human and divine wisdom, noble according to human rank ', with William of Volpiano over them. Owing to William's great merits and skilful administration the renown of the abbey was restored, and it stood an example to all and a new centre of learning.

Another famous monastery reformed by Maiolus was St. Maur des Fosses.[2] Favoured by kings of old it had passed to the Robertian house, under which its condition was worse than any other monastery in the kingdom. Its lands were lost by careless abbots, and its monks lacked even the necessaries of life. The abbot at this time, a man of very noble family, placed the interests of the world before those of soul and spirit. When he went out hunting, a sport he delighted in, he would strip off his habit, and clothe himself in costly skins, nay more, he covered what ought to have been his humble head with the finest *calamantium*. His monks followed his example as far as their means allowed, nor did this seem specially reprehensible, seeing the other monks in the kingdom did the same.[3] At last a hermit heard of the state of affairs and protested to Burchard, count of Paris, a noble whose many services and great valour had advanced him far in the royal favour. He asked the king to let him take over the monastery. The latter hesitated to give up what had belonged to his house for so long : also he was afraid that on Burchard's death his heirs might claim St. Maur's to the infinite prejudice of the monks—a sin for which he would be held responsible. When Burchard explained that he wished to hold the monastery only till it was reformed, the king consented. Now in those days the fame of Maiolus had spread throughout

[1] *Bibl. Clun.* p. 208, *Ex chronico S. Benigni Divionensis.*
[2] Ibid., *Ex Vita Burchardi Comitis Paris.*
[3] Ibid., *Hic mos a cunctis monachis istius regni agebatur.*

all Gaul. To him Burchard proceeded. Arrived at Cluny, Maiolus, true to his reputation for humility, prostrated himself before the count and asked why he had come so long a journey. When he heard the reason he pointed out that the count would have done better to go to one of the many monasteries in Gaul. It was difficult for him to leave Cluny for such distant and unknown regions. Only after Burchard had thrown himself again and again on the ground did Maiolus consent to go. Then taking with him the most virtuous of the brothers he started for St. Maur's. Arrived at the river near the monastery Burchard called on the monks to cross. He then told them that those who were ready to obey Maiolus in all things might return to St. Maur's. The rest must disperse where they pleased, ' taking nothing with them '. The most of them chose rather to follow the way of their hearts than to submit to Maiolus' strict discipline. The former abbot went to St. Maur's, Glanfeuil, where, as he was of noble birth, he was made abbot, and remained there till his death.

Maiolus brought St. Maur's back to the strict observance of the rule, ' permitting no point to be passed over '. He had Hugh Capet's and Burchard's help for the material welfare of the monks. He then returned to Cluny, entrusting the administration of the house to one of his monks. Time passed, and as Maiolus did not return, king Hugh and his son Robert, at Burchard's suggestion, appointed this monk abbot. This caused the monks at Cluny to sorrow greatly, for they had meant to hold St. Maur's as a dependent house (*ad cellam redigere*).

At the request of Odo of Champagne and his wife Ermengard, Maiolus reformed Maior Monasterium, to which he sent thirteen Cluniac monks.[1] So great was the sanctity of their lives that the king heard of them, and having obtained the papal consent,

---

[1] *Bibl. Clun.* p. 296, *Author. Gestorum abbatum Maioris-Monasterii anno 1494: Maiolus qui inter cetera suae sanctitatis indicia, monasterium quod est iuxta urbem Turonicam ab Hunis eversum ad pristinum revocavit statum.*

suggested to count Odo that one of the thirteen should be appointed abbot, and the monastery declared independent of Cluny. Royal and papal privileges were granted and the monastery declared the special child of Rome, and subject neither to church, archbishop, bishop, nor abbot.

To the Cluniacs this was a disappointment and a loss. Maiolus proceeded to Maior Monasterium to protest. He was received by the monks with honour and dutifully served as a reverend father. Next day he addressed the thirteen Cluniac monks.

' Alien sons,' he said, ' why have you lied to me and Cluny your Mother, who trained you in the delights of virtue ? Why have you alienated yourselves ? '

On the advice of their abbot, the monks kept silent with prudent simplicity. Maiolus then vehemently reproached the abbot for having led the brothers into error and ambitiously usurped the *ius* of Cluny. The abbot, but lately consecrated and a man of wonderful simplicity, replied :

' Be not indignant, oh lord abbot, with these thy servants. If any can be said to be in fault it is not ourselves, but the pope and king to whose command we bowed. We could not do otherwise. Indeed, as can be read in authentic books, from the days of St. Martin, abbots (not priors) have always ruled over the monastery. What is done cannot be undone. Your holiness, oh beloved father, must consider whether the statutes of the highest and universal pope ought or ought not to stand.' [1]

Maiolus saw the point and acquiesced. Though bewailing that the house beloved of St. Martin should be lost to Cluny, he declared it free and immune from his yoke and authority.[2] The monks were to have the right of choosing their own abbot. St. Martin's was thus restored to its original dignity.

· · · · · · ·

---

[1] Ibid., *Utrum summi et universalis papae statuta stare debeant.*

[2] Ibid., *A iugo et subjectione Cluniaci . . . emancipetur.* The above is an interesting example of the feeling (which modern writers have overlooked) which grew up against Cluniac policy. As a contemporary record it is, however, suspect, as the story comes from a fifteenth-century manuscript.

The goodwill of early days between Cluny and the neighbouring bishops continued when Maiolus was abbot, and took concrete form in donations of ecclesiae and land.

In 962 Odo, bishop of Mâcon, gave Cluny six churches, their tenths and property, reserving only the *eulogiae* and synodal service. Neither he nor his servants were ever to require hospitality from the monks, nor any dues. If any one asked why he alienated so many churches from the cathedral at one time, the answer was that their *beneficia* belonged to Cluny.[1] In 982 John, bishop of Mâcon, exchanged lands with the monks,[2] and six years after Milo, bishop of Mâcon, gave them an *altare*. In 967 Burchard, archbishop of Lyons, gave Cluny a church and tenths,[3] and later land on which a small monastery was to be built. He asked Maiolus to grant him Cluniac property, not that he wished to deprive St. Peter of it, but that he might guard it from evil men. On his death it would be restored to Cluny with any improvements made. He promised in return to stand Cluny's *adiutor, defensor, custos et advocatus*.[4] His successor Milo, with the consent of his canons, gave Maiolus two churches, their tenths, and all belonging to them, but reserving to himself synodal service, *paratae* and *eulogiae* (981).[5] The bishop of Chalon confirmed to Cluny, ' casting no envious eye on the gift ', land and a house which one of his archdeacons had built at his own expense, and according to his own skill. He did this the more gladly because he had heard tell of the glory with which God had exalted Maiolus, that great man arisen as a star over Gaul, to the admiration of the century and for the example of all.[6]

From Walter, bishop of Autun, Maiolus received two deeds of gift. In 983 the monks begged him to increase their daily dole from churches in his diocese and their *obedientiae*, where they daily said mass. The bishop made inquiries, and finding the request just granted them tenths from the churches in question to provide for their daily food (*ad sustentandos suorum*

---

[1] Ibid. ii. 1139.   [2] Ibid. ii. 1620, anno 982.   [3] Ibid. ii. 1227.
[4] Ibid. ii. 1508.   [5] Ibid. ii. 1553.   [6] Ibid. ii. 1537.

cotidianos victus). He did this the more willingly knowing that God had greatly favoured Cluny in the past, and that the brothers flourished in nobility as of old, worthily upholding the standard of their order, which he hoped would not be lowered in his time.[1] In 993, because the congregation of Cluny had always been joined to him in special love and had kept alive the true religion of God, he granted the monks six churches and their tenths, to be held as long as they celebrated divine office there. They were to pay no dues except synodal *eulogiae*. Neither the bishop nor his successors were to ask hospitality or housing from them. He made the gift *pro signo societatis* that alive or dead he and they might participate in each other's good deeds.[2] From a bishop Hector, Maiolus received half a church with half its *presbiteratus* (969).[3] Seven years later the bishop's brother gave Cluny the church in its entirety.[4]

Not long after he became abbot Maiolus gave part of his own and his brother's hereditary possessions *in precaria* to Arnulf, bishop of Apt, in whose diocese they lay : i.e. nine vills and a *locus* won in conquest by his grandfather and father : also an alod which his grandfather had bought. The bishop was to pay Cluny five solidi annually, and on his death the property with any improvements he had made reverted to the monastery.[5]

It is difficult to remain aloof from the evils of the day, and Maiolus ' with the consent of his monks ' is to be found giving several Cluniac churches *in precaria* to laymen. To one man and his wife he gave a church with tenths, oblations, dues for burial, gifts in kind, and other dues. The recipients gave in return a *curtilus* with house, vineyard, three fields, and a meadow. On their death and that of their two sons the church reverted to Cluny.[6] Another church was given *in precaria* to a man and his wife who paid *in vestitura* one *colonica* with fields, vineyards, meadows, woods, and waters.[7] Another man who had willed property to Cluny was given half an ecclesia with half the

[1] Ibid. ii. 1628.   [2] Ibid. ii. 1947.   [3] Ibid. ii. 1271.   [4] Ibid. ii. 1429.
[5] Ibid. ii. 1071.   [6] Ibid. ii. 912.   [7] Ibid. ii. 920.

presbiteratus. He was to pay *in vestitura* half the returns from three vineyards belonging to the *presbiteratus.* At his death the church reverted to Cluny.[1] To another man and his son Maiolus granted for life a church with everything belonging to it : fields, woods, waters, and tenths. They were to pay *in vestitura* eight denarii for lighting.[2] A noble clerk, very dear to the monks, asked and was given in usufruct a vill belonging to Cluny, with its church, for which he was to pay annually five solidi denarii. After his death the vill and church, with any improvements he had made, reverted to Cluny.[3] Another priest asked and was given for life a church with tenths, oblations, burial dues, food dues, and all else belonging to it. In return he gave a *curtilus* with vineyard and house, and four fields in a vill, in which he reserved one vineyard in usufruct. He also agreed to work in the vineyard and labour in the fields for the brothers like any *homo externus.*[4] Two instances of sale are mentioned : (1) three brothers sold to Maiolus[5] and his monks a chapel, for which they received 30 solidi ; (2) a priest, 'compelled by need', sold a church in Vienne with its property to the illustrious and famous Maiolus and the other lords of Cluny. He received the stipulated price of 100 solidi for it.[6] In another case Maiolus gave a church and its lands to a woman and her four sons, who gave three churches with their lands, tenths, and *presbiteratus* in exchange.[7]

Occasionally Cluniac land was given *in precaria.* A clerk asked and obtained property of St. Peter's : i.e. manors, vineyards, fields, meadows, woods, waters, serfs in various districts (all the gift of one donor to Cluny), and ten other manors. He was to pay 24 denarii annually *in vestitura*, and after his death the whole returned to Cluny.[8] A man, his wife and son, were given two vills and serfs. Maiolus held *in vestitura* one serf, his wife, children, and the manor where they lived. When one of

---

[1] Ibid. ii. 1271.   [2] Ibid. ii. 1501.   [3] Ibid. ii. 1073.
[4] Ibid. ii. 1529.   [5] Ibid. iii. 1859.
[6] Ibid. ii. 900, *crevit mihi voluntas et quodammodo compulit necessitas.*
[7] Ibid. iii. 1933.   [8] Ibid. ii. 1460.

the three recipients died, half the property was to revert to
Cluny ; on the death of all three the whole.[1]   Another man and
his wife were given three manors and half a church in one of
the manors.   The other half with its *presbiteratus* the monks
held *in vestitura*.[2]   In one case of exchange of land the dimensions
were carefully given.   The field Maiolus gave was 16 poles long,
and on one front 4 poles on the other 3.   The field he received
was 36 poles, 4 feet long, 4 at one end, 3½ at the other.   It was
bounded on three sides by St. Peter's land, and on the fourth
by the donors'.[3]   To another man, his wife and illegitimate son,
Maiolus gave a vill.   If a legitimate son was born it was to pass
to him, but if the illegitimate son had a legitimate son the
latter inherited.   On the latter's and the parent's death, the vill
reverted to Cluny.   The monks, however, retained the church
of the vill, its *presbiteratus*, tenths, land, and a female serf with
her children.

Of the 1372 charters which cover the period that Maiolus
was abbot the majority record deeds of gift from the laity.   Of
these the majority deal with donations of land, especially of
vineyards.   Gifts of churches are as yet comparatively few :
thirty-four churches and chapels and half of six churches were
given, and two bought.

Several charters recorded the gift of a church, and then
stated that the donor was to hold it for his lifetime, e.g. the
chapel of St. Columba was given to Cluny with everything belonging to it, vineyards, meadows, plains, woods, waters, apple trees,
tenths, and serfs.   During his lifetine the donor was to hold it
in usufruct, and to pay Cluny annually four denarii, or wax to
that amount.   On his death it reverted to Cluny.[4]   In another
case a donor gave half an ecclesia which he was to hold for life,

---

[1] Ibid. ii. 1064.
[2] Ibid. ii. 1088 (anno 960).   The charter is signed by *Maiolus peccator
et humilis abba et Heymardus abba*.
[3] Ibid. ii. 1463.   The last clause is curious.   *Et terminatur a mane terra
sancti Petri a medio die via publica, a sero ad ipsum Arleum a cercio similiter.*
[4] Ibid. ii. 1098.

and pay the monks annually six denarii *in vestitura*. In return he and his wife were to have part in the society of Cluny.[1] A father and son gave three churches, with tenths, parochial dues, and *presbiteratus*, the third to be held *in vestitura* during their lifetime. Another gave a church with fields, waters, mills, meal, all of which he held for life. He paid at once *in vestitura* the tenths of the church.[2] Another man and his wife gave a church, its tenths and land, which they were to hold in usufruct for life. They received twelve solidi (which they promised to repay in four years).[3]

A donor who felt the end of his life approach, remembering the promise that all the world would be theirs who gave alms, gave a church to Cluny, with tenths, fields, meadows, woods, vineyards, and waters. He was to hold the whole till his death, paying annually *in vestitura* a measure of grain and one of wine.[4]

The donations of land sometimes gave rise to disputed claims, which were usually settled at the monastery. Sometimes the abbot would plead his case or lodge his complaint before the local magnate, e.g. Maiolus, Hildebrand, and two monks before count Alberic at Mâcon proclaimed a man who held property belonging to St. Peter, i.e. vills, land, and half a church.[5] The *actores* of Cluny before count Leobald and his retainers proclaimed a man and his wife for seizing a manor and its church, which the latter claimed as theirs by hereditary right. But moved by the fear of God and love of St. Peter, or perhaps by the advice of the count and his men, they gave up the property.[6] Before the famous count Hugh and his mother, Vivian, the prior, and three monks of Cluny proclaimed a woman and her sons for unjustly holding property left to the monks. The offenders admitted their offence and promised that neither they nor their heirs would cause further trouble (*nausiam*).[7] Before count Lambert, a man, whom the monks had often proclaimed and complained of for having despoiled one of their chapels, swore

---

[1] Ibid. ii. 1189. [2] Ibid. ii. 1433. [3] Ibid. ii. 1325. [4] Ibid. ii. 1049.
[5] Ibid. ii. 1087. [6] Ibid. ii. 1037. [7] Ibid. iii. 1789.

that neither he nor his relatives would attack the possessions of
the chapel, great or small.[1]

One offender came before archbishop Teubald 'as he sat in
council surrounded by many monks, clerks, laymen, the *missus
indominicatus* of the king, and many other men of the best
testimony'. Before this august assembly he promised that he
and his wife would no longer exact the dues and customs which
they had unjustly taken from land given to abbot Berno in the
past, and since then held by Cluny.[2]

Nor were the monks afraid to defend their rights against the
great. Vivian, the prior, with other monks of Cluny made
known before count Hugh that he and his father had unjustly
taken dues from a vill which belonged to them. The count,
having consulted his retainers, found that the holy brothers were
right. He ordered a notice to be written to Cluny that neither
he nor his, in the present or the future, would exact dues or
services from the free men (*francis hominibus*) and the serfs
living in the vill, nor build houses there.[3]

The bishop of Riez had been at strife with the monks over
tenths of the church of Valensolle, which they claimed in virtue
of their labour there, and over land which he demanded in
the name of the church's endowment. The bishop came to the
church and on the holy relics contained in the image of St. Peter
gave up his claim to all, not only to dues which were admittedly
unjust, but to others to which he seemed to have some claim.[4]

Several charters show the hold which the monks had over
the consciences of their fellow-men. In one case Maiolus, who
had thought of excommunicating a man for the innumerable
evil deeds he had committed against Cluny, made him instead
responsible for guarding and defending certain *obedientiae*, thus
giving him an opportunity of making reparation for his sins.
He was not to levy any dues or customs from the said *obedientiae*.
If he happened to be passing through them, accompanied by not
more than sixteen soldiers, and the monks voluntarily invited

[1] Ibid. ii. 1249.   [2] Ibid. ii. 1437.   [3] Ibid. iii. 1794.   [4] Ibid. iii. 1866.

him and his men to refection, he might accept, on condition that
he left immediately afterwards. This charter was signed by
Albericus, who praised the decision. For the love of God a
woman gave up the quarrel and ill-will she had cherished against
the monks about an alod, thereby offending the apostles Saints
Peter and Paul. To be reconciled with them she withdrew her
claim to the alod, although it had been part of her dowry, and
promised that no son, daughter, nor relative of hers would
dispute her deed.[1] In another case, for many days and months
the monks sued a man for keeping property left to Cluny by will.
Before Vivian, the prior, and many others the accused at length
made restitution, hoping thereby to obtain St. Peter's pardon.
Indeed, the conflict between the monks with the eternal powers
behind them, and the laymen with their terror of those
powers, was not an equal one, e.g. a man who for long had disputed Cluny's right to a church gave up his suit because his
wife had died and he wished her to have Christian burial. One
generous donor gave all his possessions to Cluny on condition
that the monks provided him with clothing as long as he lived,
' for a gift to God is repaid a hundredfold '. Another donor
gave Cluny all he possessed—quite a considerable amount of
property—and went out into the world with nothing. If he or
any of his heirs repudiated his gift they were to pay a fine. One
case was settled by arbitration. Pasture-land left the monks by
will was claimed by another heir. Judgement was given that the
disputants should share the land in question. In another case
an offender, with great temerity, presumed to set up a claim to
a right of way leading from Cluny to the Grosne, and to the mill
of a vill. The monks satisfied his claims by giving him a horse
worth 40 solidi. In one charter a priest explained that he had
bought houses (costing 210 solidi) inside the cloister of St. Mary's
Le Puy. They had been burnt down, and it had cost him great
labour and expense to have them rebuilt. He evidently felt

---

[1] Ibid. ii. 1496, *Si aliquam rationem in ipso alodo habeo per dotalium quod
mihi senior meus fecit.*

that they would be safer under St. Peter's protection and gave them to Cluny on condition that he and a nephew held them for life. A father gave part of his lands to Cluny—a *curtilus* and a vineyard—on condition (*ea ratione*) that his son should be received by the monks and with them serve God for all time. Another donor, who gave two *coloniae*, laid the following curse on any one who disputed the gift : ' Let the anger of God and all the saints come upon him, and all the curses of the New Testament. Let him be cursed in the town and cursed in the field ; cursed in his going out and cursed in his coming in ; cursed in the fruit of his body and cursed in the fruit of his ground. Let God cut him off with incurable disease, let his enemies persecute him till he perish from the face of the earth, and all his substance be reduced to nothing. Let his part be with Dathan and Abiram, with Judas who betrayed the Lord, and with those who have said to the Lord God, Depart from us.' [1]

Several charters might be quoted in disproof of the statement that no one but a monk could enter the chapter (*capitulum*), e.g. a soldier who had quarrelled with the monks about an alod came to see the home of the apostles. Before his departure he attended the council held in the chapter,[2] was reconciled with the brothers, and withdrew his claim to the alod.

Most of the charters frankly state the reason of the gift and the *quid pro quo* expected. Thus William, the famous count who trembled when he thought of the day of judgement, made a donation of land to St. Peter's, Cluny, because to St. Peter was given the power to bind and loose. He expected the apostle to free him from his many sins, that he might merit to hear the joyful words, ' Come ye blessed of My father.'

The preamble of many of the charters runs : ecclesiastical authority and Roman law have ordered that any one making a donation of property should do so by will, in order to make the transfer legal.

---

[1] Ibid. ii. 1430.
[2] *Secundum morem monasterii in constituto capitulo.*

K

CHAPTER XII

MAIOLUS' CHARACTER—MIRACLES

IN Maiolus was fulfilled the ideal of the monastic character. His was a meditative, spiritual, almost mystical temperament. Less virile than Odo, he possessed those qualities of gentleness, humility, and self-effacement which rank so high in the monastic virtues. His love of peace, solitude, and prayer, his refusal of high office in the secular church, his dislike of public praise, gained him a reputation for sanctity above that of his fellows. The good he did he did in secret to avoid the occasion of vainglory, yet because he shunned the praise of men it followed him the more.

Odilo described his appearance. He was dignified in his bearing, cheerful in manner, angelical of face, serene in expression, possessed a beautiful voice, and was eloquent of speech. His every movement was graceful, and to Odilo he seemed ' of all men most beautiful '.[1]

In Maiolus we meet again that ' sweet religion of tears ', to Renan a characteristic of the early Christian church. At the end of a journey, in whatever house he happened to be, he retired to a secret corner, where, alone and unobserved, he might join his soul to God. ' And there none could tell with how many groans, with how many tears he was afflicted, the ground before him being watered with tears as if flooded by a wave.' [2] Whenever he travelled to Rome, he stopped at every wayside shrine, and, bursting into rivers of tears, prayed the saints to succour him, and to free him from the vile sepulchre of the body. But once in the Eternal City he exulted in all the

---

[1] *Bibl. Clun.* p. 284, *Vita Odilone.*   [2] *Vita Syro*, ii. 9.

joy of his heart, as if he saw the glorious princes and apostles before him.

Like Odo he encouraged innocent joy, and loved to see others happy.   A charming picture is given of his arrival at Le Puy,[1] which may have been his native town.   'Men and women rejoiced to see him : the whole town danced at his sight : all sought his benediction : all hoped to hear his holy speech : a procession was formed : the chief men assembled together : the common people hastened towards him : the holy priests of the church advanced in a dense throng.   They applauded and cheered him with dancing and clapping of hands.   Accompanied by the crowd, he proceeded to church, and, prostrate on the ground, adored his Christ, calling on Him with beating of the breast and watering the ground with his tears—tears which winged their flight to the sky.'

But though he rejoiced to see others happy, above all things he loved solitude.   Unlike Odo, who on a journey proceeded on his way singing cheerily and encouraging his monks to do the same, Maiolus rode alone with an open book in his hand.   'His reading was not restricted to ecclesiastical works alone, though when he read philosophy and books of secular wisdom, he always kept in mind the teaching of the divine word.   Passages about love and the conduct of worldly affairs, to him superfluous, he passed over as if poisonous.' [2]   Rarely did his book leave him, and he read both by day and by night.   He delighted also to listen to the conversation of the wise, and to follow discussions on any point of Scripture   In his knowledge of the Scriptures he was accounted second to none, yet never spoke in a discussion unless his opinion was asked, when he replied prudently and well.[3]   He could quote all the evangelical and apostolic precepts, and his reputation for learning was great, though, unlike the learned, he never boasted.

Characteristic of Maiolus was his love of moderation, an interesting point when it is remembered that the Cluniac School

---

[1] Ibid. ii. 11.   [2] Ibid. ii. 4.   [3] Ibid. ii. 8.

has been misrepresented as inaugurating and upholding an extreme standard of asceticism. As a discreet father he was abstinent in all things (but allowed no one to praise him for that). Tempering the apostolic injunction, he used a little wine, though sparingly. He also availed himself of the concessions of the rule, not from any desire to cherish volupty, but in order to supply his bodily needs. When present at the tables of the great he partook of whatever was set before him, not too much and not too little, ' for the mean is praiseworthy, and in all things, even in good things, whatever exceeds the mean is a vice '.[1] In dress he followed the same principle of moderation, his garments being neither too fine nor too shabby, in this unlike the generality of men who valued dress either too much or too little.[2] He never appeared filthy and ragged, in order to arouse admiration by an outward semblance of sanctity.

His charity was marked by the same rule of moderation. Though always ready to relieve the necessities of the poor, he never let his almsgiving degenerate into excess.

His speech was marked by brevity, ' whatever he said was weighty with the weight of wisdom, seasoned as with salt, grave in its virtue, and precious for its prudent sweetness '. He would reason with sinners with pious love, but when it was necessary, and when he could thereby lead an erring soul to truth, he was severe in rebuke, when his words were ' sharp and cutting as whips '. Having administered a rebuke, it was wonderful how holily and piously he could console the sinner.[3]

Asked to appoint one of his monks prior of St. Paul's, Rome, he chose one who, after many excuses, at last refused to go. Maiolus bore his disobedience quietly and started without him. The monk was so vehemently reproached by his companions for ' his obstinate hardness ' that ' panting with anxiety and haste ' he followed Maiolus. He reached a river, and seeing his master on the opposite bank, flung himself on the ground to

[1] Ibid. ii. 8.   [2] Ibid.   [3] Ibid. ii. 5.

beseech with his body the pardon he was unable to ask with his tongue. Maiolus sent a boat for him. Asked if he would do penance he answered ' Yes ', whereupon Maiolus said, ' Kiss that man ', a leper whose face was covered with sores. The monk immediately obeyed, and the leprosy vanished.[1]

His knowledge of human nature was great. On one sinner he would work by blandishment, on another by admonition, on a third by terror. Following the apostolic injunction he was urgent in all things both in season and out of season. ' Beloved by God and man he studied to please men that he should not be displeasing to God, and to please God that he might be useful to men.' His standard of life was the Gospel precepts. He studied himself as in a mirror, and whenever he discovered a fault in himself immediately corrected it, ever striving to adorn his mind. His chief counsel to his monks was to keep peace with all men. Like the apostle he could say, ' I have been all things to all men '.

Deeply compassionate when it was a question of helping others, he cared nothing for his own comfort. On one journey he took off his cloak and wrapped it round a poor man whom he was distressed to see without either shoes or coat. Nor did he hesitate to draw a moral from the incident, for when the bishop of the town gave him a new cloak, better in cut and material, he turned to his monks and said, ' Let us not hesitate to give to Him who so abundantly and speedily can return what we give.' [2]

In Sirius' judgement [3] he possessed all the virtues. ' Where divers faithful men are praised for different virtues,' he wrote, ' the blessed Maiolus is to be praised as possessing not one but all. Besides, he excelled in the greatest, the virtue of despising

---

[1] *Bibl. Clun.* p. 294, ex Petro Damiano, *De toto corpore linguam facit.*
[2] *Vita Syro,* ii. 18.
[3] Ibid. ii. 10, *Verum nos eas in eo laudare debemus, quas tota novit Italia, non ignorat Germania, in quibus tota exsultat Gallia : restaurationem coenobiorum, pacem ecclesiis redditam, regum et principum concordiam, intemeratam regulae observantiam, lucrum animarum.*

the glory of having virtue.' 'Among all men of his time he shone pre-eminent, honourable in action, sober in counsel, humble in prosperity, patient in adversity. He was affable to the gentle, terrible to the proud, generous when it was fitting, sparing when it was right.' [1]

'How pleasing Maiolus was to God was seen by the signs and miracles God worked through him. He healed many who were sick, many who were blind, many bitten by serpents, by wolves, or by dogs, many possessed by devils, and rescued many from death by drowning or by fire. The number of souls he saved was known to God alone.' [2] Only one gift was denied him, as Sirius mourned, that of bringing the dead back to life. But he did what was more wonderful, united the soul with the Maker from whom it had been alienated by sin—'bringing back to the joys of eternal life many dead in soul, and by the net of his preaching dragging to the firm and solid shore many who had been submerged in the waves of the great sea. To many sitting in the shadow of Death he showed the way to the heavenly Jerusalem.' [3]

The first of the 'miracles' occurred when Maiolus was at Mâcon. It was a time of famine. Every day the number of the starving increased, and his heart was daily wrung by the sufferings of the poor who flocked round him begging for help. All the resources of the houses could not have relieved them. He therefore betook himself to secret prayer. On rising he saw seven solidi lying on the ground. Fearing that this was a trick of the devil, or that some one had lost the money, he dared not touch it. When he found that it was real, and that no one claimed it, he used it thankfully, not for his own necessities, but for those of the poor.[4]

The *Vitae* give great importance to the story of Maiolus' capture by the Saracens. This occurred on his return to Cluny after his first visit to the imperial court at Pavia. He was accompanied by many monks and clerks who were to escort

[1] *Vita Odilone.*   [2] *Vita Syro*, ii. 10.   [3] Ibid. ii. 10.   [4] Ibid. i. 10.

him part of the way. The passage of the Alps was known to be unsafe, and suddenly the Saracens swooped down on the Christians. Unable to defend themselves, the monks fled. Maiolus, who might have escaped, would not leave his companions, and was taken prisoner. For refusing to admit the power of the Saracens' god, he was bound in chains and imprisoned in a cave. Thinking nothing of his own sufferings, his only thought was to comfort his companions. His virtue was rewarded; he saw one of the apostles standing near him, and his chains fell off. Another sign was granted him. He had grieved at having lost the books with which he always travelled, when to his joyful surprise he found his little volume on the Assumption—proof that he would be rescued before that festival, only twenty-four days distant.[1]

Although the *Vitae* make a great deal of the perils which menaced Maiolus, he was merely held up for ransom. The Saracens questioned him if he were rich enough to pay for himself and his companions He affably replied that he neither possessed nor wished to possess anything in this world, but that under him were many who had ample funds and the money of God.[2] Ordered to write to Cluny he did so in the following words: 'Lords and brothers of Cluny, the roaring bulls of Belial surround me, and the jaws of death yawn for me. Therefore send if it please thee the amount of the ransom our captors require.'[3]

This letter when read in the chapter at Cluny caused great dismay and anguish. 'There was one sound of weeping and one cry of sorrow.' Immediate and spontaneous was the effort to raise the sum required, good men from the neighbouring

---

[1] Ibid. iii. 1. It is not known to what occasion Sirius referred. In the Souvigny *Vita* the story is worked up. A new detail is given that some of the Saracens, fearing there would be an attempt to rescue Maiolus, rushed at him as he stood alone on a high rock. Instead of hurling him from it, they fell themselves and were killed. Maiolus mourned for them.

[2] *Bibl. Clun.* p. 295, ex Rod. Glabro, i. 4. According to the Souvigny *Life* Maiolus knew nothing about the ransom.

[3] *Vita Syro*, iii. 4, *Maiolus miser captivus et catenatus. Torrentes Belial circumdederunt me, preoccupaverant me laquei mortis. Redemptionis pretium si placet, mittite pro me et his qui una mecum capti tenentur.*

district bringing their quota, wealthy men their treasure, and the monks giving up gladly both from the necessaries and ornaments of the monastery. ' For the freeing of such a father each gave what he could, and held himself wretched and unworthy that he could not give more.' All these offerings formed a common fund which was sent to the Saracens. Before the ransom arrived, the hearts of the Saracens had been softened, and Maiolus had converted several of them to Christianity. They affirmed that while the soldiers slept peacefully by night, and Maiolus was engrossed in prayer, they had often heard voices as of a multitude singing. As there was no inn near, this must have been the voices of angels who sang with him! The ransom delivered, Maiolus reached Cluny in time to celebrate the feast of the Assumption.

The Saracen raid was not left long unavenged. ' Nothing happens on this earth without a reason, and this disaster occurred not in opposition to the divine providence but because of it, that by the anguish of the one, the many might be saved.' The men of the district raised a strong force under William of Arles, and set out in pursuit of the Saracens, who, heavily laden with booty, were proceeding to their headquarters in Fraxinetum. The struggle was not long. Hopelessly outnumbered, the enemy soon took to flight. Almost all of them perished, for having taken refuge on a rocky height accessible only on one side, they were cut off by the Christians, and had to choose between death at the hands of their foes, or death from the precipitous rocks. They chose the latter alternative, and to the amazement of the Christians their dead bodies were seen next morning lying at the foot of the rocks. The mediaeval readiness to see the miraculous in great events made men to believe that the completeness of the victory was due to the merits of Maiolus, who though absent in the body had been present in the spirit. Therefore, in gratitude for his spiritual help, when the spoils were divided, the books he had lost were sent to Cluny,—as indeed might have been expected in any case.

Several of the miracles occurred when Maiolus was travelling. Once riding through a wood, 'sunk in deepest meditation broken only by tears and sighs', he fell asleep. His horse went on, but stopped where the huge branch of a tree blocked the way. Maiolus, not knowing his danger, slept, and in his sleep saw a beautiful boy holding the horse's bridle. Awakening, he thanked God with tears for having guarded him from the peril of sudden death.[1] Another time, when he and his monks were travelling in a 'desert region', he ordered for refection *moruclae* which had been given him the day before. The servant, on going to prepare them, found them broken and unfit for use. As this was due to his carelessness he was afraid to tell Maiolus. But the latter already knew through the spirit, and quietly told his companions to search for more. Now, though *moruclae* had never been known to grow there before, this time great quantities were found! [2]

Indeed, the problem of commissariat was easily solved when Maiolus was present. Once returning from Aquitaine, he decided to pay a visit to a monastery, first sending a messenger to say he was coming. The monks rejoiced, but the purveyor was in despair, because for long he had been short of fish. However, he told the fishers to go down to the river and to call on the name of Maiolus. This they did, and to their joyful amazement caught an enormous salmon, a fish never before found in that river. Great was the joy when Maiolus arrived! Another time at St. Paul's, Rome, he found the brothers in a poverty-stricken condition. Having relieved their necessities, he begged the *dispensator* to give them a special gift of a pound of silver, but he, as the monastery was poor, gave only half a pound. Maiolus made no remark. On going out later a man unexpectedly gave him ten solidi, which he handed to the *dispensator*, admonishing him to have more faith in the future.[3]

---

[1] Ibid. iii. 15.
[2] *Bibl. Clun.* p. 1772. *Morucla*, a kind of fungus (Ducange).
[3] *Vita Syro*, ii. 17.

Fearing the sin of pride, he always shunned the gaze of the multitude. At Pavia, where his every movement was watched, he used to go to church secretly at dead of night. One winter night the weather was so bad that the devil tried, but in vain, to dissuade him from going. Maiolus set out ' just as clouds had covered the twinkling stars '. The evil one put his lantern out. This terrified his companions. Maiolus calmed their fears, knowing that God would not forsake them. And indeed, as he arose from prayer his candle of itself began to burn, a lesson to the brothers ! [1]   When William of Provence was dying he sent for Maiolus, convinced that the abbot's prayers would save his soul. Maiolus hurried to Avignon, where he was well known. Wishing to escape the public gaze, he ordered his tent to be pitched on an island in the Rhone. The people, however, determined to see him, crowded on to an old boat and started for the island. In mid-stream the boat began to sink, and men, women, and children, none of whom could swim, were thrown into the waves. Their cries for help reached Maiolus. Great was his distress, and bending his head he prayed. Then all that multitude appeared on the crest of the wave, ' the men and boys swimming, the women, with their babies in their arms, borne along by their inflated garments '. Sailors hastened to the rescue, and all were saved ! Still more miraculous, a servant, sent by count William with loaves for Maiolus, was saved by virtue of those loaves, three of which were untouched by the water ! [2]   Not only did water lose its natural power before the merit of the abbot, but fire also. Once Maiolus, who was in the habit of reading at night, fell asleep with his candle burning and resting on the open page. Awakening with a start, his first thought was for his beloved book, ' a rare copy which could not easily be replaced '. But he found that, though the candle had burnt itself out, and ashes lay on the book, yet it was unharmed. Very joyfully did he thank God for having thus caused the fire to lose its natural energy.[3]

[1] Ibid. iii. 16.   [2] Ibid. iii. 18.   [3] Ibid. iii. 17.

Quite a number of the miracles circle round the healing power of the water in which Maiolus washed his hands. Once at Vallavense a band of mendicants ran to him, ' wise ', as Sirius with a touch of humour puts it, ' in that they managed to live on the morsels which fell from others '. One of them, who was blind, sought, not material help, but the gift of sight, St. Peter having revealed to him that if he bathed his eyes with water in which Maiolus had washed his hands, he would see. Rebuked and dismissed by Maiolus, he tried in vain to get the water from the servants. Still he persevered, and when Maiolus was leaving the town he ran in front of his horse, caught hold of its bridle, and swore that no whipping or punishment would make him leave go until Maiolus blessed water which, with prudent fore-sight, he had brought in a jar slung round his neck. His faith moved the saint, who dismounted, prayed with his monks, and blessed the water. The beggar then bathed his eyes, and saw.[1] The same thing happened when the father of a little blind boy received from the servants water in which Maiolus had washed his hands. The child recovered his sight, but when Maiolus was told he ordered that all such water should in future be poured out before him.[2] Water he blessed had also healing powers.[3] A noble matron, who had long been ill, sent water to be blessed by him. On drinking it she immediately recovered.

Indeed, there was no need of a doctor when Maiolus was present. Once on a journey a monk fell dangerously ill, ' first burning with fever, then turning so cold that it seemed impossible to warm him '. Maiolus took off his coat and covered him. He immediately fell asleep, perspired, and awoke as if nothing had ever been the matter with him ! [4] Another time a German count, who was ill and could eat nothing, sent messengers to beg for some of the abbot's food. It was given. As soon as the messengers started home the count began to recover, and on eating the food, became quite well.[5] In Pavia, Hildebrand,

---

[1] Ibid. ii. 12.   [2] Ibid. ii. 13.   [3] Ibid. ii. 12.
[4] Ibid. ii. 14.   [5] Ibid. iii. xi.

monetarius of a monastery, was very ill. He had spent in vain great sums on skilful doctors and priests, and given much to the poor. Maiolus coming to Pavia visited him. Three days after he recovered ![1] In the case of the bishop of Chur he healed both soul and body. The bishop, who was very ill, confessed to Maiolus that he was afraid there would be no reward for him in Heaven. The blackness of his guilt was so great that any good he had done was done, not for its own reward, but from vainglory. His confession eased him, and when Maiolus prayed for him at High Mass on Easter Day, not only did he recover his bodily health, but was thereafter saved from the sting of vainglory.[2]

Several miracles were worked at his tomb. The majority are of the usual conventional type, though a few are quaint and naïve. One tells of a paralytic who set out to pray at the saint's tomb, sure that by this act of faith he would be healed. He travelled in a cart drawn by two oxen and a horse. The day he started, he found himself a little better and could be lifted on to the horse, and each succeeding day he recovered a little. When his journey was almost done, he came to a church dedicated to God and St. Maiolus. There he left the horse and cart as a gift, and went on his way with the oxen driven before him. At the tomb he prayed and was made whole, so he gave the oxen to St. Maiolus, and also a serf.[3]

A story, which has a pagan touch, tells of an ignorant old peasant woman, who, on a very hot day, cursed the rays of the sun. As a judgement she was struck blind, and not till she went on pilgrimage to Maiolus' tomb was she healed.[4]

Another poor woman, who had an only son, was told in a vision to give the boy to the saint's service. She took no notice, thinking it incredible that a divine messenger would visit a poor woman like herself. Then the boy fell ill, and only when she had taken him to the monks and begged that

[1] Ibid. iii. 13.
[2] Ibid. ii. 16.
[3] *Bibl. Clun.* p. 1812, *Miraculorum Maioli.*
[4] Ibid. p. 1797.

he should be instructed in letters (*literis erudiendum*) did he recover.[1]

The saint, indeed, looked well after his devotees. Once several pilgrims returning from his tomb reached the Loire, which they could not cross as the boat was at the far side, and the boatman refused to come for them. They called on Maiolus, when the boat crossed to them, waited for them to enter, and without earthly rowers or captains bore them to the opposite shore![2]

Another time a pilgrim was robbed on his way to the tomb. Undismayed and unresentful he continued his journey. The robber, struck with contrition, followed and gave him back all he had stolen![3]

The saint, too, would avenge any slight to his dignity, as a woman learnt to her cost. She sinned in that she did not stop weaving to celebrate the vigil of his festival. In consequence, the iron instrument which she was using stuck to her hand, ' as if it were born there '. Only after long and fervent prayer to Maiolus was it removed![4] On one occasion the writer evidently felt that his story was somewhat thin, so he cited as witnesses not only the common people but king Hugh himself, Burchard, count of Paris, and his son, Rainald, bishop of Paris.

Writing 162 years after the death of Maiolus, Peter the Venerable claimed that during that time no saint had healed more sick and sorrowful than he. And could Sirius only have known it, his merit had even called a dead child back to life. A poor woman had a little son who died. She wasted no time in mourning, but gathering up the child in her arms, set forth, replying to all condolences and questioning, ' I bear my dead to Maiolus who will give him back to me.' Arrived at Souvigny, she laid the child's body before the altar. Great was the agitation of the monks and laymen, for though St. Maiolus had cured

---

[1] Ibid. p. 1798.   [2] Ibid. p. 1808.   [3] Ibid. p. 1805.

[4] Ibid. p. 1810, *Maiolus sicut est mitis et propitius suave iugum Domini portantibus, sic castigator manet districtus in incredulitatis duritia permanentibus.*

many cases of disease and sickness, he had never been known to bring the dead back to life. From the first to the ninth hour the body lay before the altar. Then of a sudden the eyes opened and the boy called for his mother, who ran to him. Immediately the people lifted up their voices, praising God and St. Maiolus, ' even the monks who had been resting ran from their beds to rejoice at the miracle '.[1] All the inhabitants of Souvigny crowded around—Souvigny, which, though but a village, was yet inferior in numbers to no town in Gaul, thanks to the fame of the saint.[1]

Rodulf Glaber, writing about the same time (eleventh century), tells of the many miracles which witnessed to Maiolus' virtue and raised Souvigny from a small and obscure monastery to a famous centre of pilgrimage. ' From the whole Roman Empire, men and women, afflicted with disease, came to that tomb to be healed. At the time of the great plague three saints in particular were known to be swift to help, and to them great multitudes flocked. These three were St. Martin of Tours, Odolricus Maior, and Maiolus.' [2]

[1] *Bibl. Clun.* p. 305, ex Petro Venerabili, ii. 31.
[2] Ibid. p. 301, *Rod. Glab.* iii. 5.

CHAPTER XIII

ODILO, FIFTH ABBOT OF CLUNY

ODILO succeeded Maiolus as fifth abbot of Cluny. He was a descendant of an old and wealthy family of Auvergne.[1] His father Berald was so distinguished in 'authority and grace' that he was known to all as Beraldus the Great. In behaviour and dress he was different from any other prince, so eminent in virtue that his word was held as good as his bond. His mother, whose family was equally distinguished, was a woman of deep piety. After her husband's death she gave up her great possessions and riches, left her children, her relatives, and her country, and entered the convent of St. John, Autun, where she took the veil. Jotsaldus, when writing his Life of Odilo, interviewed the few nuns who were old enough to have known her, and 'they, even then sorrowing over her death, told him with sighs of her praiseworthy life and of her gentleness, of her eager desire to help others and of her glorious death'.[2]

Odilo was one of a large family and had several brothers.[3] Of his two sisters, one married. The other, Blismodis, became an abbess and lived to the age of a hundred years.[4]

As a child he was delicate and partly paralysed. He recovered in a manner almost 'too wonderful for belief'.[5] The family had

[1] Migne, 142, *Vita Odilonis Jotsaldo*: *Praefatio.* Cf. Migne, 144, *Vita Odilonis P. Damiano*: *Arvernicæ oriundus ex equestri ordine genus.*

[2] *Vita Jotsaldo*: *Praefatio.*

[3] Bruel, iii. 2788. Eight brothers are mentioned by name: Stephen, Ebo, Berald (*prepositus* of the cathedral of Le Puy), William, Eustorgius, Bertran, Hicterius (2). The grandfather's name was also Hicterius.

[4] *Vita Jotsaldo*: *Praefatio.* Cf. Bruel, ii. 2788, *B. venerabilis abbatisse et Aldegardis secundum seculum nobilissime matrone.*

[5] *Vita*, ii. i, *Quod ne cui videatur incredibile, ab ipsis agnovi quibus ipse solitus erat narrare.* Cf. Damiani, p. 927.

143

been travelling from place to place, Odilo being carried by servants on a stretcher.   One day they came to a church, and the servants went on to get provisions, leaving the boy with the luggage at the church door.   The door was open, and the boy, ' by divine inspiration ', on hands and knees crawled to the altar.   There he caught hold of the pall and tried to stand up, but the tissues of his legs were too weak and he fell back.   He tried again and again, at last succeeded, and even walked round the altar.   When the attendants returned they were terrified at finding the boy gone.   Entering the church they were amazed to find him running about.   With great joy they brought him cured to his parents.   By this incident God showed how grateful and acceptable Odilo was to Him.

Henceforth the boy loved Mary the Mother with all his strength, and when older he entered a church of St. Mary's, where, with God as his only witness, he offered himself to the yoke, saying, ' Oh most pious Virgin and mother of the Saviour of mankind, from this day henceforth receive me into thy service. As a most merciful advocate be present with me in my every deed, for I place none before thee save God alone, and to thy service for all eternity I offer myself.'

From his childhood he was dedicated to the church, and at an early age entered St. Julian's, Brioude,[1] where he was soon distinguished for his humility, charity, innocence, and purity. At St. Julian's, too, he delighted in doing works of mercy as far as was permitted him.   But to his lofty aspirations of holiness the life at St. Julian's seemed strangely inadequate.   St. Julian's was the home of secular canons.   To Odilo salvation seemed only attainable in the regular life, the monastic calling. ' Therefore he began to deliberate whether he should not forsake the flesh-pots of Egypt and enter the land of promise.   Lord Jesus, how sweet is Thy vocation, and how sweet the inspiration of Thy spirit which makes the mind to throb, and which, having

---

[1] Ibid. i. i, *Inter ipsa primordia tanquam alter Isaac Christo consecratus . . . et Brivate clericali sorte est donatus.*   Cf. Damiani, p. 928.

inspired the mind of the young man, made him burn for the true embrace of Solomon!' [1]

At this psychological moment he met Maiolus,[2] then 'an old man and famous throughout the world'. Maiolus, on a visit to Auvergne, was struck by the young clerk's 'elegance of body and nobility of carriage, and pierced with the inner eye to the spiritual grace of which these were but the outward sign'. The two talked long and confidentially, and Odilo decided to enter Cluny. 'The new soldier of St. Benedict then left Romulus and the stronghold of Brioude. Renouncing his ancestral wealth, leaving his relatives and brothers, like Abraham of old who went forth from Ur of the Chaldees, he went to Cluny as to another land of promise. Having thrown off the burden of the old man, he clothed himself in the habit of a monk. Good Jesus, how joyful it was to see the sheep willingly shorn from worldly things, rising from the washing of baptism and going forth with its young twins of either love, bearing nothing sterile within itself and no vain thought.' [3]

As a novice he was distinguished among his fellows and first in good works. Nor when seeking the eternal pastures of truth did he disdain menial tasks—'the cleaning of lanterns and scouring of the floor, the care of the children. But the pearl could not be long hid, nor the strong athlete remain unknown.' [4] He probably entered Cluny four years before Maiolus' death.[5]

---

[1] Ibid. i. i.   [2] Ibid. i. ii.   [3] Ibid. i. iii.   [4] Ibid. i. 3.

[5] Ibid. i. 4, *Evolutis fere quatuor annis.* The first charter in which he is named abbot is dated 994. In 990 Odilo, son of Berald, with his mother and brothers Stephen, Ebo, Berald, Bertran consenting, gave to the sacrosanct monastery of Cluny part of the property to which he had legally succeeded, situated in the province Auvergne, the county Brioude, the vicaria Auratus and the vill Saraciacus. In that vill he gave whatever was his by hereditary right; also a manor formerly ceded by himself, his mother and brothers, for the burial of his brother Hicterius, but which he had bought back for a hundred solidi from his fathers and brothers, the lord canons of Brioude. He gave the property on condition that Maiolus and his successors should hold and order it as they would and never alienate or sell it except to his brothers. This charter has been taken as recording the gift Odilo made on entering Cluny, a hypothesis discredited by the final clauses: if he changed his mind or if his heirs claimed the property a fine was to be paid (Bruel, iii. 1838).

L

From the first the old abbot regarded him with special love, and when he felt death approaching,[1] he, like Aymardus before him, called together the neighbouring bishops and monks, and proclaimed Odilo his successor, or in the words of Jotsaldus, ' Maiolus, after having sweated with great labour for Christ, went forth from the darkness of Egypt, and having traversed the danger of the seas entered Jerusalem, and was gathered to the eternal peace of the Lord.   At the moment of his death he named Odilo his successor, entrusting him and his sheep to God.   Odilo could not refuse the office, which he undertook reluctantly and indeed more unwillingly than could be believed.   The choice was ratified by the unanimous vow of all the monks, and as another Moses he was set over the children of God.' [2]

The charter of election was drawn up at Cluny and signed by king Rudolf, by two archbishops, five bishops, seven abbots, three counts, and eighty-one other signatories.   It ran : Maiolus, an old man worn out by age, exhausted by bodily weakness and unfit for pastoral duties, feared that his ill-health would prevent his watching over Cluny's interests, and that as a result the order might deteriorate instead of being borne to ever higher things. Having summoned a great assembly and many bishops and abbots to Cluny (to prevent the danger of Odilo's refusing the office), he, with all the brothers, sons, and servants of St. Peter, elected Odilo abbot, a choice unanimously acclaimed.   Only Odilo held back : the greater proof that he was worthy : such as he should be forced to office however unwilling, for only the unworthy recklessly aspire to honours.   The charter of election was sent to be signed by duke Hugh and Odo.   Those present at Cluny also signed a copy.

Not long after Cluny's lands were attacked, and Odilo with Vivian, the prior, and many of his monks came to the synod of Ansa (994) to appeal to the bishops of Lyons, Vienne, Autun,

[1] Ibid. i. 4, *Instante vero mortis articulo.*
[2] Ibid., *Ultra quam credi possit invitus.*   The account here does not tally with that of Sirius, p. 113.

Chalon, Mâcon, Valence, Uzès, Maurienne, Grenoble, Auguste, and Tarantaise, there assembled.[1] He begged for a charter of protection, for Cluny was afflicted with many ills and much anguish. The bishops out of reverence for St. Peter and respect for Maiolus, that holiest abbot and magnificent servant of God whose death they mourned, thereupon proclaimed that the monks were to hold their *ecclesiae*, tenths, and dues without molestation. No one was to attack Cluniac land, steal from Cluniac houses, or hold the burg of Cluny on pain of excommunication and anathema. No public judge, nor *exaccionarius*, count, nor any one with his own army, nor *conductucius*,[2] was to make a *castrum*, or fortification within or near Cluny and its *potestates*, or to build there. No secular, no military dignitary, nor men living near Cluny, or Carus Locus, or in Cluny's *castrum* and burg, was to take the monks' oxen, cows, pigs, horses, or other possessions. The heaviest excommunication would be launched on such offenders, for it was not right that a holy monastery should suffer from malignant and proud men.

. . . .

Under Odilo the number of the brothers at Cluny increased. ' He stood the father of many monks, some of whom came to Cluny as boys, some as youths, some as old men, but although they were of different ages, of different character, and of different

---

[1] Bruel, iii. 2255.

[2] *Exactionarius = Exactor = Publicanus* (Ducange). *Conductitius = Procurator plebis* or *minister altaris qui canonica portione minus accipiendo subiectione indebita munus ab obsequio suo conductori persolvit* (Ducange): this species of simony was publicly condemned by pope Gregory. Other points dealt with church discipline. Only a priest was to carry the sacred body and blood to the sick. The ' body of the Lord ' was not to be kept in a church more than a week and always to be renewed on Sunday. Those who came to vigils were allowed to stand and might groan or sigh, but there was to be no talking nor scurrility and nothing done but what was to the good of the soul. No clerk was to hunt. It was to be remembered that priests were not to marry. If they did they lost their priestly office. They were not to believe in nor make incantations nor auguries. No one was to work after the ninth hour on Saturday. No one was to buy or sell on Sunday.

rank, he, cherishing them all with one moderation and virtue of discretion, with maternal love and paternal care, bound them together into one united family.' With joy he could repeat the words of David : ' Thy sons shall be as olive trees around thy table.' To him this increase in his flock was a cause of rejoicing ; to some of the monks it was a cause of anxiety, because of the difficulty of feeding so many. To these pessimists Odilo would say : ' Oh brothers, be not sorrowful at the increase of the flock, for He whose voice called them to this vocation will, by His providence and mercy, provide for their needs.' Joyfully he would precede his flock, and standing in the middle of the choir, with great thankfulness he would look right and left at the brothers around him. Whenever he went on a journey so many brothers accompanied him that he might have been taken not so much as a leader and a prince, but even as an archangel of monks [1]—the name by which Fulbert of Chartres called him.

One result of this increase in numbers was the enlargement of the monastic buildings. The original monastery had been built mainly of wood. Only on the church (rebuilt by Odilo's successor) had expense and care been lavished. When examining the rest of the monastery the foundations were found to be unsafe. Odilo, therefore, undertook the rebuilding on a large scale. ' He marvellously adorned the cloisters with columns and marble brought from the farthermost parts of the province. These were conveyed with great labour to the river, and then carried down by the swift current of the Doubs and Rhone.' When in cheerful mood he was wont to boast over the new buildings, comparing himself to Caesar Augustus, in that he had found Cluny wood and left it marble.[2]

---

[1] *Vita Jotsaldo,* i. xi.

[2] Ibid. i. 13. Some of the funds for the restoration came from Spain. Writing to Paternus, abbot of the Spanish monastery of Pena, Odilo asked him to send on his messengers to St. John's where Bishop Sanchius (who had come from Pampeluna to be a monk at Cluny) had left his possessions. They were to bring back everything belonging to the bishop : with the silver the Cluniacs

Little is known of the first years of his rule. Almost as indefatigable a traveller as Odo, he was probably occupied in those early years in extending the reform, and in supervising the houses already more or less subject to Cluny. During those years Cluny steadily rose in importance and more than ever required protection for her spacious lands and ample privileges. For the first part of this period the little known of the abbey's history comes from the charters of gift and protection which steadily increased in number.

In 999, at Odilo's and Otto III.'s request, Gregory V. granted Cluny a charter. The pope gladly concurred with the wish of the abbot and the ' unconquerable, pious, and august emperor ' that Cluny should be strengthened by the apostolic authority, its freedom and autonomy proclaimed. No one, however great or powerful, was to attack its monasteries, cells, churches, courts, vills, serfs, woods, vines, plains, meadows, waters, torrents, and lands cultivated and uncultivated. No duke, bishop, prince, nor any other person great or small was to molest the monks and their property or dispute their right to tenths. Under pain of anathema no bishop nor priest was to enter the monastery for ordination, consecration of church, or celebration of mass, unless asked by the abbot. Monks were to be ordained by whatever bishop and in whatever place the abbot pleased. The abbot, who was to be chosen by the common counsel of the monks, could ask any bishop to consecrate him. The anathema was called down on any one who dared go against this charter,[1] in which a long list of lands, churches, and monasteries subject to Cluny was given. At a time when Cluny was attacked by the

---

would be able to finish the ' work ' above the altar begun in the name of the bishop and of the dead king; with the gold which the bishop had brought with him they had been able to replace the images to the right and left of the altar formerly destroyed. The bishop also wished his consecrated vessels to be sent to him. The rest of the letter is lost (Migne, 142, *Odilonis Epist.* ii.).

[1] Migne, 137, p. 932, *Sciat se . . . anathematis vinculo innodandum, et cum diabolo eiusque atrocissimis pompis atque cum Juda traditore . . . in aeternum ignem concremandum, simulque in voraginem tartarumque chaos demersum cum impiis deficiendum.*

laity Benedict VIII. intervened, and ordered the bishops of Burgundy, Aquitaine, and Provence to excommunicate the aggressors, and help the monks[1] (1016) (p. 157). The same year he sent similar instructions to the bishop of Clermont[2] (p. 158).

In 1027 John XIX. granted Odilo a very full charter confirming all Cluny's privileges and liberties.[3] In the same year in the presence of king Conrad, then in Rome for his imperial coronation, the pope reaffirmed Cluny's privileges.[4] No bishop was to excommunicate the monks. Again in 1027 John granted his beloved Odilo a *terrula* which had been given to St. Peter's, Rome, some time before. The monks were to pay an annual *census* to St. Peter's for it.[5] In 1045–46 Gregory VI. at Odilo's request confirmed Cluny's privileges and possession of Romainmoutier, as granted by Conrad's royal charter.[6] Clement II. (1046–47) commended Cluny and its possessions to all the bishops, princes, and magnates of Gaul and Aquitaine.[7]

Odilo was also indebted to the Saxon emperors. Otto III. in his short reign gave several charters to Cluniac houses. In 998 at Ravenna he confirmed Peterlingen's charters, and its possession of land in Colmar and Huttenheim, including a manor given by himself.[8] The same year in Rome, at the request of Odilo, two bishops and the chancellor, he decreed that land for long taken away from Ciel d' Oro should be restored.[9] In 999, at Odilo's request, he confirmed Cluny's possession of St. Maiolus', Pavia, with the property given in the past and what might be given in the future. No duke, archbishop, bishop, marquis, count, judge, viscount, nor any one great nor small subject to his imperial power, was to interfere with the monastery and its possessions. Any one who violated the charter was to pay a fine of 100 pounds, half to go to the imperial treasury, half to Cluny[10] (Rome). Next year at Pavia he confirmed the

---

[1] Ibid. 139, p. 1601.   [2] Ibid. 139, p. 1628.   [3] Migne, 141, *Joannis Epist.* vi.
[4] Jaffé, i. 3101.   [5] Bruel, iv. 2798.   [6] Jaffé, i. 3136.
[7] Ibid. i. 3144.   [8] *Mon. Germ. Hist.*, Sickel, i. 273.   [9] Ibid. i. 281.
[10] Ibid. i. 314.

immunity and rights of St. Saviour's placed under Cluny by
Adelheid.[1] In 1001 at Ravenna he confirmed the immunities
and possessions of St. Apollinare in Classe.[2] Odilo also knew
Henry II. well The latter and the emperor Conrad loved and
praised him so much that it seemed as if there were but one
heart and soul between them.[3] Soon after Henry's accession
Odilo visited the royal court at Alsace, when the king confirmed Cluny's privileges[4] (1003). Next year he was in Italy
and present at the royal coronation in the Lombard capital.
The night after the men of Pavia rose against the Germans,
a revolt quickly crushed. The vanquished went to beg mercy
from the king at the monastery of Ciel d' Oro, when Odilo interceded for them.[5] Three years later he was with Henry at Neuberg
on the Rhine. In 1015 the king proceeded to Rome for the
imperial coronation. Odilo spent Christmas with him at
Pavia,[6] and went on with him to Ravenna, when Henry met
Benedict VIII.

After the coronation a great synod was held, the occasion
probably when the pope in the sight of all the Roman people
presented the emperor with a golden apple crowned with a
cross. Henry at once perceived the significance of the gift—
the apple a symbol of the weight of empire, the cross a reminder
that his rule should be moderate. Holding the gift in his hand,
' Oh best of fathers,' he said, ' it is more fitting that this should
belong to those who tread the pomps of the world underfoot
and follow the cross of the Saviour.' Forthwith he sent the
golden apple to Cluny, esteemed the most righteous of all
monasteries.[7] When the emperor died (1024), special masses

---

[1] Ibid. i. 375.   [2] Ibid. i. 400.

[3] *Vita Jotsaldo*, i. 7. Cf. ii. xi., Henry loved him above all others and
humbly adhered to his counsel.   [4] Grandidier, *Hist. d'Alsace*, i. 358.

[5] *Vita Jotsaldo*, i. 7, *Pavia cuius prece et industria liberata est ab excidio
gladii et periculo incendii.*

[6] Coronation, Feb. 14. In March Henry began his return journey. Odilo
was with him at Pavia. In May they were in Verona; at Whitsuntide at
Bamberg. Odilo then returned to Pavia and Cluny.

[7] Rod. Glab. i. 5.

and prayers for his soul were appointed to be said annually in all Cluniac houses.

Odilo was at Mainz for Conrad's coronation. Peterlingen's charters were confirmed soon after. Conrad also put Bremen Novale, Piedmont, under Odilo, a monastery in a particularly evil state. Odilo's nephew was appointed abbot. In 1026 he was at Pavia when the Lombards again rose against the German king, and again he interceded for them. He was with Conrad in Rome (1027) when he may have met Knut of Denmark.

Of his relations with Henry III. little is known. A letter discovered by Sackur definitely proves that contrary to the accepted theory Odilo approved of the emperor's policy in raising Clement II. to the papal throne. ' He was present when the emperor, acting in concert with princes and prelates, judged Clement worthy to ascend the throne. He was present at the coronation and glorified God for having put down those who had stirred up strife, and having strengthened the Roman imperium by the choice of a most just prelate and Catholic head of the state' (1049).[1] When Odilo was ill in Rome, Clement II. visited him frequently. The Cluniacs seem to have regarded the pope as a friend, and far from an imperial catspaw. There is no hint that they disapproved of the emperor's paramount authority in the election. Indeed, the Cluniacs may be said to have welcomed reform from whatever source it came. To Jotsaldus one of Odilo's special merits was that he resisted princes and the great in nothing.

From Rudolf III., king of Burgundy, Odilo received several charters. In the first (994), Rudolf, guardian of the monastery, proclaimed that Cluny was to be left in peaceful and undisturbed enjoyment of its property. As the king could not be in that

---

[1] *Neues Archiv*, xv. p. 119, *In cuius sacra unctione praesens adstitit, dans gloriam Deo qui Romanum imperium electo iustissimo presule et catholico reipublice principe sedatis malorum turbinibus roborare voluerit.* The Cluniacs had been regarded as the opponents *par excellence* of the imperial interference in the papal elections. Gfrörer even stated that Odilo visited Rome with the express purpose of persuading Clement to abdicate!

region to guard the abbey's interests he exhorted all princes, judges, and rulers of counties there, to be a defence and protection in his stead, that the monks might in full security pray for himself and the kingdom.[1] In 998, at the request of 'that most religious abbot and the brothers sweating in the service of God', Rudolf ratified the charters given Cluny by his ancestors.[2] The same year, at the request of his wife, the archbishop of Lyons, and Odilo, he confirmed Cluny's possession of Peterlingen and Romainmoutier, with the cells, churches, vills, and land belonging to them.[3] In 1029, anxious to come to the help of the labourers who worked in the vineyard of the Lord, and to grant his wife's request, he gave Cluny the *ecclesia* of St. Blaise Liens, with hills and plains, and all the property belonging to it.[4] After his death his queen gave Cluny two manors.[5] Odilo also received charters from Robert, king of the Franks. In 999 Robert confirmed Cluny's rights over Paray.[6]

Some time between 1017 and 1025 he and his son, at Odilo's request, confirmed Cluny's possession of the little abbey of St. Cosmo and Dam ani, near Chalon, the *curtis* Belmont, a power (*potestas*) with its churches given by bishop Manasses, and two other churches given of old. The monks were to hold all these without interference from king, count, or any person of inferior rank.[7] Another royal charter was granted when Cluny was hard pressed by neighbouring bishops and nobles.

The duke of Burgundy also extended his protection to the monks (1040). He had spent Easter at Cluny and been received with great reverence and devotion. When he returned home Geoffrey, the prior, and the congregation of Cluny followed him and petitioned that in return for their hospitality and friendship he would grant them in writing the promise of his protection

---

[1] iii. 2270, *Invictissimus cupio esse tutor.*
[2] iii. 2465. A list of vills is given.
[3] iii. 2466.   [4] iv. 2812.   [5] iv. 2892.
[6] iii. 2485. Given by Hugh, count of Chalon and bishop of Auxerre.
[7] iii. 2711.

and help wherever his power extended. Any one who wished to retain his ' favour and friendship ' was never to do harm or injury to any place belonging to Cluny.[1]

Some years before this Odilo had appealed to the duke. The latter, surrounded by the bishops of Autun and Langres, abbot Halinard of St. Bénigne's, and many of his *fideles*, received ' his faithful friend and devoted well-wisher Odilo ', who laid a long complaint before them. A *locus* and the church St. Maurice with its lands, given to Cluny (948) by the bishop of Arles, had been taken by evil men.[2] Not long after, Hugh the Great, duke of the Franks, visited Burgundy. The evil-doers, fearing the monks would appeal to him, waylaid him and cunningly strove to persuade him that the land and church were rightly theirs. The duke knew better and restored the lands to Cluny. After his death the former aggressors and their heirs again seized the lands. Count Otto William restored them, and that such unjust aggression might cease bought the men off with another *benefice*. The monks also paid them a large sum of money. The evil-doers then promised to make solemn and public restitution before the duke and the many princes and magnates with him. Odilo therefore begged the duke to confirm the agreement, which Robert the king also corroborated (1032–39).

[1] Ibid. iv. 2949, *Nullo modo quamlibet torturam aut contrarietatem.*

[2] Ibid. iv. 2888. Odilo wished the duke to know how Cluny had received the lands, how by the negligence of princes and the violence of his enemies it had lost them, and by whose help and zeal it had recovered them.

CHAPTER XIV

CLUNY AN OBJECT OF ATTACK

When Cluny grew in temporal riches and spiritual renown, her position of eminence made her a tempting object of attack, her riches stirring up the cupidity of the lay lords, her independence awakening the jealousy of the diocesan bishops, who saw their authority threatened by the principle of autonomy which Cluny claimed not only for herself but for her subject monasteries. Cluny was attacked by lay lords in 1016 and by the episcopate in 1025. In both cases Odilo appealed to Rome.

Strife with the episcopate arose over Cluny's exemption from diocesan control. The bishop was invested with spiritual power which was supreme over his diocese. In this power St. Benedict acquiesced, and directed his monks to do the same. From the first occasionally, but more frequently after the Cluniac reform, the popes granted particular monasteries charters of protection and immunity from outside control. These seem to have been given for purely practical reasons. The special protection of the papal name might help a small and struggling monastery. Special immunity was an advantage when the spirit of reform within a monastery was checked by a conservative or feudalised bishop, or nullified by lay lords.

But though the popes were actuated by no far-sighted policy, in this they were unwittingly forging a magnificent weapon of offence against the episcopate. In the ultramontane struggle the monasteries proved the papacy's most valuable asset. A statesman like Nicholas VI. may have foreseen what a powerful weapon the monasteries would be. His successors, ignorant and short-lived, had neither the capacity nor the occasion to look so far forward. Nor do the Cluniacs seem to have perceived what a harvest would be reaped from the seed then being sown. Odo, who established the principle of Cluny's autonomy, did so as a means of furthering the immediate and pressing needs of his time. The bishops, equally unseeing and engrossed with their secular duties, were glad enough to have the responsibility for the inconspicuous and poverty-stricken monasteries shifted to the broad if careless shoulders of Rome.

When the reformed monasteries grew in importance and number the bishops began to be jealous of their privileges. As interest in the monastic reform was aroused, the secular church no longer received all the gifts of the faithful. The idea gained ground that monasticism represented the highest Christian life, and that the monks were more detached from worldly interests than the secular clergy, when, paradoxically enough, it was the monks that the laity delighted to enrich.

Nor did abbots and bishops see eye to eye about the provision for those monks who in outlying districts officiated in the country churches. In return for these services the monks asked for church tithes, their argument being that ' if temporal goods were to be divided they ought to be used to compensate those who supported night and day the burden of the priest in the church '. Another grievance was that the secular church like the rest of society had become feudalised. Too often the bishops used their powers over the monasteries as if suzerains requiring services from vassals. The abbots refused to pay dues which might be regarded as services from a fief. As time went on they refused to submit to heavy expenses of forced hospitality, lodging, and purveyance, and demanded their share of ecclesiastical tithes.

On the spiritual side (which was intelligible, seeing they regarded the monastic as the highest calling in the church) the abbots endeavoured to escape from obedience to the bishop. The more the episcopate became secularised the more they redoubled their efforts for independence. Cluny from the first was freed from episcopal control. Other abbots began to protest against the episcopal right of visiting, correcting, and excommunicating the monasteries, and refused the bishop entrance to their buildings. The Cluniacs had early seen that when the bishop's presence was necessary, e.g. for ordination, it was expedient for their position of independence to invite any other bishop than their diocesan or themselves to leave the cloister for ordination. That policy seemed at first to awaken no opposition. Monastery and diocesan appeared to be on friendly terms except for occasional friction over tenths. It was the question of ordination, however, which brought the quarrel with the episcopate to a head.

First, however, came the attack on Cluny's temporal position. In 1016 she was attacked by feudal lords, and immediately appealed to her suzerain and protector, the pope. The answer was prompt. Benedict, on behalf of his foster-child, wrote to the bishops of Burgundy, Aquitaine, and Provence.[1] He reminded them that from its foundation Cluny had been upheld in its freedom from all subjection, save to God and the papacy, by pope, emperors of the Romans, kings of the Franks and of the Burgundians. All his predecessors had confirmed its privileges, so that all who with fervent vow and desire left the world and gave themselves to the regular discipline there, could without let or hindrance be more closely joined to God, and from the offerings of the faithful extend hospitality and care to the poor. But now he had heard from Robert, king of the Franks, and his nobles in Rome, and from the messengers sent by his beloved son Odilo, that evil men, stirred up by greed and madness, had attacked the lands of Cluny, preying not only on the possessions of the monastery but also on those of the poor committed to them. Overcome by great anguish and affliction, the monks could no longer give due service to God, nor extend their

---

[1] Migne, 139, p. 1601, *Epist. Benedicti*, xvi. The archbishops of Lyons, Vienne, Besançon, the bishops of Autun, Clermont, Le Puy, Chalon, Langres, Mâcon, Valence, Uzès, Troyes, Gap, Vaison, Avignon, Riez, Carpentras.

customary care and hospitality to the guests and poor of the monastery. The whole church suffered thereby, as the prayers and masses which Cluny had hitherto offered for all the faithful had to be curtailed. It behoved the faithful to have compassion on Cluny's anguish and to rally to her side. More especially was this the duty of the papacy, to whom after God and St. Peter the care and guardianship of Cluny belonged : hence his letter. Those who had attacked the monastery were then named ; [1] the first offender had not only seized Cluny's property, but when the monks pleaded for justice had mocked at their prayers and disavowed their rights ; others had taken churches and lands, and exacted unjust dues. If the thieves and persecutors did not return what they had taken by a certain date they were to be excommunicated by bishops and priests, and as putrefying and lifeless members cut off from the body of Christ. A tremendous curse was then laid on them.

Benedict also wrote to the bishop of Clermont. By its founder, as the bishop knew, Cluny had been committed to Rome for defence against the insatiable greed of laymen. The shield of the papal might must be opposed to those depraved men who persecuted the abbey. He therefore called on the bishop ' to hurl at those who nefariously attacked Cluniac property and oppressed the monks not a light stone but the heaviest dart of excommunication '.[2]

The next attack was more serious, being directed against Cluny's privileges. It is not known why the bishop of Mâcon chose this particular moment to attack Odilo for exercising a privilege of which his predecessors had availed themselves. But at the council of Ansa (1025) he appealed to the bishops there assembled against Burchard, archbishop of Vienne, who had slighted his rights as diocesan and gone against canonical decree

---

[1] Ibid. One man had seized the church with all its land and property ; two had taken two *potestates* ; other two were raising difficulties about land held *in precaria* from Cluny ; three others claimed a vill ; another was levying unjust dues from a *potestas* and vills. There were many more offenders too numerous to be named.   [2] Ibid. *Epist.* xxix.

by ordaining monks of Cluny without his (Gauzlin's) licence and consent. Burchard cited Odilo in his defence. Odilo rising with his monks immediately showed the charters and privileges granted by the popes, a justification, it would seem, final in itself. The bishops, unable to disprove the fact of the charters, went further and condemned their validity as going against the decrees of the council of Chalcedon (451) and other authentic councils, where it was laid down that abbots and monks were to submit to their diocesan, and that no bishop was to ordain monks without the diocesan's consent. The privilege which Odilo cited was therefore not binding, since not only was it not in accord with canonical decrees, but even went against them.[1] Convinced by this reasoning, the archbishop of Vienne sought pardon from Gauzlin.

Neither Cluny nor the papacy could pass over the insult. Odilo appealed to the emperor and to the pope, who energetically bestirred himself on Cluny's behalf. His indignation and grief were expressed in four letters : one to the bishop of Mâcon, rebuking him for his audacity, another to the archbishop of Lyons condemning Gauzlin, a third to Odilo reaffirming Cluny's privileges and liberties, and a fourth to Robert, king of the Franks. Robert followed the papal example and confirmed the royal charters granted to Cluny.

In the first letter the pope reminded Gauzlin that he held his episcopal authority from Rome whose son and disciple he was. How then did he dare, stirred up by fresh temerity and burning with inextinguishable greed, to spurn his mother, and lift as it were his foot against his master, which he had done by seeking to annul the papal privileges, by attacking Odilo and his monks, and by disturbing the peace of Cluny, a monastery which shone in holiness before almost all nations, which, relying solely on the apostolic privileges, was free from all other authority, and answerable to the papal judgement alone.

---

[1] Mansi, *Concilia*, xix. p. 423, *Decreverunt chartam non esse ratam quae canonicis non solum non concordaret sed etiam contrariet sententiis.*

Gauzlin's attempted tearing asunder of the papal members could end only in ruin to himself. Let him beware, and leave Rome's special monastery to Rome! The papacy would guard it from him and all others. If he had any real case against Cluny, let him seek the papal judgement which suffered prejudice to none.[1]

In the letter to Burchard, the pope expressed his grief at Gauzlin's having arrogated to himself the right, against the apostolic privileges, to ordain the monks of Cluny. By his greed he had made himself liable to the papal ban. The pope, grateful to Burchard for having defended the monastery for so long, begged him to continue to do so. As metropolitan he was to forbid the bishop of Mâcon to consecrate, ordain, or claim any other right in ' this our monastery '.[2]

In the charter to Cluny John dwelt on the close relationship which had always existed between monasteries and the see, a union which made his predecessors ready to hear the petitions of the monks, more especially those of their beloved sons of Cluny who had ever encouraged true religion and piety. In reply to Odilo's petition, strengthened as it was by the emperor and the empress, he reconfirmed the monastery's charters and privileges. For the Holy See did not suffer liberties once granted to be rescinded. Under pain of excommunication no bishop was to enter Cluny for ordination, consecration, or celebration of Mass, unless invited by the abbot, who could send his monks to receive ordination wherever he pleased, and himself be constituted by any bishop. Also, under pain of excommunication, no bishop was to excommunicate, interdict or anathematise the monastery, or excommunicate or lay malediction on monks of Cluny wherever they happened to be. For it did not seem fitting that without the papal judgement a son of the apostolic see should be anathematised like a disciple of any subject church. If a complaint against Cluny arose, the apostolic judgement was to be humbly requested

---

[1] Migne, 141, *Joannis Epist.* xii. 1027-33. [2] Ibid. *Epist.* xiii.

and patiently submitted to. Cluny was the gate of mercy, of piety, of salvation, ever open to the sinful, the needy, and the sorrowful. There the just would find a resting-place, and the sinful, seeking pardon, not be repelled. There to the innocent would be offered brotherly love, and the hope of salvation not denied to the wicked. Any one bound by the chain of anathema and fleeing to Cluny was not to be excluded from the pardon and mercy he hoped for. The anathema was pronounced on any one who went against the charter.[1]

The letter to king Robert (1027) opened with a sombre if conventionally worded picture of the times. The love of the many waxed cold, iniquity abounded, the church was oppressed not only by strangers but by those who called themselves her sons. Religion decreased, justice was dishonoured, the apostolic privileges and royal precepts were scorned. It behoved both papal see and royal power to be vigilant. Especially did the pope grieve over the luxury and avarice of the bishops in France. He begged the king to assist him in restraining the rage and insolent fury with which the bishops had attacked places subject to the Holy See, and particularly Cluny, the especial child of Rome. He recapitulated the monastery's privileges in a charter which he forwarded to Gaul to be read aloud to all the ecclesiastics and princes of the kingdom, to be authorised by the king and sealed with the royal seal. All were to know that the anathema would be launched against any one who dared go against the charter.[2]

In the same year Robert, in order to ' check the insolence of evil men ', granted Cluny a charter. All were to know that by the royal charters and apostolic privileges of old, Cluny was freed from the authority of all men. Within the confines of its boundaries, from Chalon to Mâcon, from Mt. Algoia to Chedrelense and Mt. St. Vincent, no man, nor prince, nor duke, was to build either fortress or fortification. Any bishop, count, freeman, or serf of either sex or different grade who offered a gift to the altars

[1] Ibid. *Epist.* vi.   [2] Ibid. *Epist.* xi.

M

of Cluny was assured of royal commendation. All gifts were
to be held in perpetuity. On any one who disobeyed the decree,
in whatever part of the kingdom it might be, the king himself
would take vengeance.[1] The attack of the bishops had thus
shown how energetically papal and royal power was prepared
to act for this ' special child '.[2]

Another dispute between the Cluniacs and the episcopate
arose over the monastery of Vezelay, the condition of which
was so bad that the count of Nevers expelled the abbot and
monks. A monk of Cluny was appointed abbot without the
bishop of Autun being consulted. Having been present at the
council of Ansa he probably knew that he could rely on the
sympathy of his episcopal brothers. At this disregard of his
diocesan rights he threatened to interdict all the ' altars ' in
his diocese at which the Cluniacs officiated, and ordered the
Cluniac monks, on penalty of excommunication, to leave Vezelay.
They appealed to Rome : unfortunately it is not known whether
or what the pope replied.

A letter to Odilo from William of St. Bénigne's [3] showed how
much ill-feeling had been aroused over Vezelay. ' The bishop
of Autun ', William wrote, ' is so much infuriated against yourself, myself, and our monastery that he threatens to do us all
the harm he can, to take from us the monastery of Magabrense,
to put under his episcopal ban all our altars in his diocese, and
to stir up bishops, clerks, and laymen of every rank against us.
He has excommunicated the monks of Vezelay and ordered
them to leave. They, relying on the privileges of the abbey,
paid no heed,[4] spurned his letter, and trampled it under foot.
This had stirred the bishop to greater wrath, and told far and

---

[1] Bruel, iv. 2800.

[2] A story from a later and unknown source (*Gall. Christ.* iv. 1060) and
difficult of credence states that several years later Odilo proceeded to Mâcon, and
after giving gifts to the cathedral prostrated himself before each of the canons
in turn and acknowledged that he had sinned over the question of ordination.
The incident is quoted as proof of his humility.

[3] Bouquet, x. p. 505.

[4] Ibid., *Per nihilo eius sententiam computaverunt.*

near has aroused much ill-feeling against them. Those who before seemed our friends ', William continued, ' have made this an excuse to turn against us. They blame us for unheard-of presumption and horrible greed for secular possessions. They maintain that the abbot ought not to have been expelled, as no abbot can be deposed without canonical procedure and sentence passed by the bishop of his diocese '—criticisms William had heard not only from those whose opinions he discounted as arising from envy, but from those formerly well disposed to the Cluniacs. As the bishop had pronounced the anathema against the monks and would not remove it till they left Vezelay and returned with all their belongings to Cluny, he believed it would be best for Odilo to recall them lest any of them died under excommunication. Yet he did not know if the count of Nevers would allow this, or if they themselves would be willing to leave. He wished he could have thought of better advice, but had felt it right to tell Odilo all the circumstances and leave the matter to his judgement. Unfortunately further details are lacking. Eventually the king intervened, took over the monastery, and the monks left.

John XIX., who had bestirred himself so vigorously on behalf of Cluny, was equally vehement in his denunciation of Odilo when the latter refused the archbishopric of Lyons. On the death of Burchard of Lyons ' great dissensions arose, for many coveted the see, though their only claim was not merit but vainglory '. Burchard's nephew, a man proud beyond all measure, left his own see and snatched that of Lyons. After committing many crimes he was captured by the imperial soldiers and exiled. Next a count seized the see for his little son, who soon after fled, ' a mercenary rather than the shepherd of his sheep '.[1] The pope was then appealed to, and asked to appoint Odilo, whose nomination had been enthusiastically acclaimed by clergy and people. The pope sent the ring and the pall to Cluny. Odilo, who had already refused the see,

<hr>

[1] Rod. Glab. v. 4.

wrote to Rome that he would hold the ring and the pall
for a worthier candidate. This reply infuriated the pope.
Odilo must obey or he would learn with what bitterness,
with what severity, Rome could chastise him who did not
do her bidding. There was no virtue more praiseworthy than
obedience, for which God asked rather than for sacrifice, and
which, as he need not remind Odilo, Benedict praised most
highly in his monks. He, the pope, could let pass the insult
to the cathedral of Lyons, though Odilo had as it were
spat in the face of that church; he could overlook the
injury to the *sancta plebs* whom, that his strength might
be spared, Odilo had refused to govern; he could be silent
at Odilo's rejection of the request of so many great men
(*praesules*); but what he could not, what he ought not to
pass over unavenged was the disobedience to Rome and to
himself.[1] Odilo's reply is unknown. The pope died soon
after, a circumstance which automatically brought the incident
to an end.

The see was next offered to another Cluniac, Halinard, abbot
of St. Bénigne's, Lyons. He protested that he, a monk, was
not fitted to uphold such a burden,[2] all the more as Odilo had
deemed himself unworthy. Finally, the see was offered to the
insignificant Odulrich, archbishop of Langres. To his nomination king Henry, grieving that there had been so much discord,
gladly consented. Odulrich only enjoyed his dignity till 1046,
when he was poisoned. At his death the see was again offered
to Halinard, who again refused it. Gregory VI. was asked to
intervene, and to his express command Halinard bowed. But
when receiving investiture at the imperial court at Speyer (1046)
he refused to give the customary oath of fealty, maintaining that
he could not go against the precept of St. Matthew's Gospel, nor

---

[1] *Joannis Epist.* xvi.

[2] Migne, 142, *Vita Halinardi*: *Obtendens se monachum ad tantum onus
nequaquam fore idoneum.* According to Sackur, Odilo refused the see because
he could not take the oath of fealty to the emperor. There is no such statement
in the original authorities.

the command of the Benedictine rule.[1] Notwithstanding the consternation of the German bishops and the outcry of the courtiers, he held to his decision. The difficulty was finally settled by compromise. This refusal to take the oath is an interesting sign of sentiment against imperial control in ecclesiastical affairs, the more significant as the emperor in question was the especial friend of the church.

. . . .

Twice Odilo and his abbey were vehemently attacked, once by the Southern bishops at the council of Ansa, and again by the scurrilous satire of Adalbero of Rheims. Both attacks may be regarded as signs of a larger movement, the growing jealousy and mistrust of a certain section of the secular church for the regulars.

Jealousy was heightened on the accession of Hugh Capet's pious son, who became king at the time when Cluny had carried through much of her reform, and stood unchallenged as the first reforming house of the age. Robert, a true Capetian in this, favoured the church and especially the monks, a policy in the circumstances far from unsound. By favouring the regular church he might hope to check the overgrown power of the bishops. Besides, the monks probably represented the best spirit of the age, for which reason the more progressive of the bishops had been glad to favour them. To the more conservative, however, it was galling to see honours which they regarded as their prerogative passing to the monks, many of lowliest birth. The prevalence of these grievances made possible the writing of the satire. Not that Adalbero [2] can be taken as representative of the better section of the conservative school, his record even for that age being a black one. Yet behind his personal

---

[1] 'Give no oath, and have no connection with temporal affairs.' Richard of St. Vannes and Poppo of Stablo also protested against this oath. William of St. Bénigne's when appointed abbot refused to give the oath of fealty to the archbishop of Lyons. The abbots of Fleury also fought long with the bishop of Orleans over the taking of the oath.

[2] Adalbero's life was far from edifying : he had changed sides and mingled in intrigues in a way that was barefaced even for that age. Finally he had

animosity against the monks, some idea may be formed of the valid criticism to which the movement was subjected.

The satire [1] was addressed to king Robert, whom Adalbero hoped to win from the side of the monks. The exact date is not known. In choosing the form of satire Adalbero followed the taste of his age, which delighted in pamphlet warfare. Unfortunately the dialogue is very obscure, and the style so involved that it is often almost impossible to follow. Many of the allusions are now unintelligible. The satire may be divided into four sections : Adalbero's description of the change and deterioration in church and state ; his burlesque of the Cluniacs ; his theory of ecclesiastical hierarchy and social caste ; his programme of reform. The central thought that runs through all four, giving a certain unity to the whole, is Adalbero's hatred of the changes transforming society which are attributed to monastic influences, and contrary to the traditions and laws of the fathers and popes. The evils of the movement are exposed, by invective, satire, and ridicule.

Adalbero begins by expressing his grief at having to write what he was about to write. He then passed to criticism of the monastic leaders, who, in order to carry through their reform, falsely asserted that they were reviving the principles and customs of old. ' They formulate new theories which they call old, writing above them " *lex antiquissima* ".' [2] But should a great error in the holy faith arise, they would never think of attacking it. One of the most pernicious of their innovations was their teaching the unconditional obedience of the monk to his abbot, ' so that what a monk would refuse to do of his own free will, he was compelled to do by force '. The order of society was being changed for the worse by the admission of

---

to retire to Laon, and there in his bishopric, away from the intrigues of court, watched from afar the new course of events which he bitterly resented. A discredited prelate, he never learned to adjust himself to the times.

[1] Migne, 141, p. 773, *Adalberonis Carmen.*

[2] Ibid. Perhaps a reference to Abbo of Fleury's canons.

the monks,[1] men of lowly birth thereby penetrating to the higher ranks of the church and state. The peasant, lazy, coarse, deformed, shameful (*turpis*), was enriched with a thousand beautiful crowns studded with gems ; the magistrate was forced to wear the cowl and to follow the Cluniac hours of prayer, of genuflection, of silence, of communication by signs, and kissing of the forehead. Bishops were deprived of their sees, and found themselves obliged perpetually to follow the plough, cracking their whips while they sang the songs of exile of our first parents. If a see fell vacant, at once a sailor, a shepherd, or any common person was raised to it. The only persons who need not aspire to high office in the church were those skilled in the divine law. Sufficient qualification for a bishop was to know nothing about the Scriptures, never to have devoted a day to study, and, as his sole scholastic qualification, to be able to count the alphabet on his fingers. Such ignorant men rose to be heads and teachers, celebrated throughout the world and reverenced even by kings. He next attacked the hypocrisy of the monks, who preached one theory in public but practised another in secret. They had departed from the traditional virtues of monasticism, and secretly revelled in luxury, incest, theft, and crime. Monks only in name, they took to themselves wives, engaged in warfare, and considered themselves outside the laws of their country.

Perplexed by these changes and disconcerted that the king encouraged them, Adalbero talked the matter over with his friends. They advised him to lay his difficulties before Odilo of Cluny, ' reminding him that Gaul still possessed monks nourished in the rules of the fathers, and that Odilo would assuredly be able to clear up his perplexities '. Accordingly he sent a messenger to Cluny a monk of the old school, sober, responsible, obedient, and learned in the rule, who had never ceased to obey the laws of the fathers. He set out in the evening and returned next morning, an impossibly short time—i.e. probably meant as a gibe at the rapidity with which the Cluniacs carried through

---

[1] Ibid. As they command, so is the order of society changed.

their reforms. And what a change in his bearing! He who formerly had been engrossed in spiritual things now leaped off his foaming steed and called for his wife and children. He was no longer clothed in the monastic habit, but in such weird accoutrements that his former companions scarcely recognised him. His shoes, with their pointed and upturned toes, were in the latest fashion. His spurs pricked the ground, and he skipped jauntily forward on the points of his toes. He called for the bishop, and having clenched his fists, stretched his arms, raised his eyebrows, twisted his neck and rolled his eyes, he burst into a torrent of speech.

'I am a soldier now,' he cried, 'and if a monk, a monk with a difference. Indeed, I am no longer a monk, but fight at the command of a king, my master Odilo.'

The bishop attempted to quell this untempered zeal by reminding him of the rule about silence, but shamelessly he replied, ' I may remember knowing it in the past, but your rebuke will not keep me from speech. I must deliver the message of my master.'

The message told of a fight between the monks and the Saracens. The monks had been defeated, and the safety of Cluny being in jeopardy Odilo resolved to petition the king for help. When he announced this decision his monks crowded round him in protest, and shouted that none but he should be their captain and lead them to victory. Odilo, thereupon, took over the command and issued his orders. The young and the strong were to travel in chariots, and to proceed as slowly as possible. The old and infirm were to mount on horseback, or advance rapidly on foot. Horses were scarce, so two had to ride on a donkey, ten on a camel, and three on a buffalo. Bucklers were to be tied round the neck, garlands to adorn the head, casquettes to be tied to the waist-belt, javelins hung on to the back, and the sword held between the teeth. The absurdity of the commands was probably meant to typify the topsy-turvydom into which the monks were bringing society.

The company, thousands and thousands of warriors (*millia mille*), set out for a three days' battle, described in mock heroic vein. Whether there was a reference to a real incident or not, the intention was evidently to satirise the huge train which followed Odilo when he travelled. The monks were put to flight, but resolved to fight again. The defeat took place on December 1. Revenge would follow on March 1. Odilo called on the bishop to take part on that great day. Far better to die arms in hand than to live cultivating his fields. The satire ends with the messenger's being chased ignominiously away, and Adalbero warns the king, ' Believe me, oh my king, all that I say is truth. The discipline of the church is transformed in thy kingdom.'

CHAPTER XV

CLUNY AND THE PEACE MOVEMENT

ONE of the most interesting movements of Odilo's day was the peace movement in which he took an active part.[1] From the earliest times the church had regarded it as her duty to further the interests of peace. That duty became more particularly hers after the dismemberment of the Empire, when with no central authority in the State old institutions had passed away and new ones had not been born. In the resulting dislocation of society, the church as the one stable institution became a preponderating influence in the struggle for order as against lawlessness, stability as against unbridled licence. Her efforts for peace culminated in the *Treuga Dei*, that first ' week-end ', by which it was agreed that from Saturday night to Monday morning private warfare should cease.

Other movements for peace preceded the *Treuga Dei*, the *Pactum pacis* or *Pax Dei* being one of the earliest. The inception of the latter may be traced to the council of Charroux (989),[2] when three decrees were drawn up in the interests of peace and order. The anathema was to be declared (1) on any one who attacked or took prisoner an unarmed traveller, a priest, deacon, or clerk who was not bearing a shield, sword, buckler, or helmet, and was either at home or peaceably travelling. (2) On any who stole from a church. (3) On any who stole an ox, ass, cow, goat, deer, or pig from the poor, or from tillers of the soil (*agricolae*). The council was attended by the bishops and clerks of the province, as also by the laity, both men and women.[3]

---

[1] Pertz, *Scriptores*, vii. p. 403, H. Flaviniac.   Cf. Mansi, xix. p. 593.
[2] Mansi, xix. p. 89.   [3] Ibid., *Omnis uterque sexus.*

In 990 two important councils were summoned by the bishops, the first at Narbonne, the second at Le Puy. The decrees of the first were directed against nobles who had overrun church property and attacked ecclesiastics. At the second the bishops proclaimed that all church property was to be held inviolate, and appealed for the security of the peasant, the labourer, and the travelling merchant. Three points are striking about these councils : (1) Their inception came from the church, a fact which gave the church a certain preponderance throughout the movement ; the penalties imposed were ecclesiastical ; the church's aim, while *a priori* to defend her property, soon developed into the wider ideal of extending protection to the defenceless and the weak. (2) The movement originated in Southern Gaul precisely in those provinces where Roman civilisation had been most firmly established, and where a lingering tradition of more settled times may have brought about this revival of the desire for peace. The South had suffered less than the North from the attacks of barbarians, the conditions of society had changed less. Trade and commerce continued here where the great roads made by the Romans allowed communication between the Moors in Spain and the Christian world. If these were to flourish, peace was necessary. (3) Women as well as men were present at these councils.

These three councils were the first of many held to promote unions of peace. The higher ecclesiastics took the most important part at them, but the nobles co-operated in calling them together. In Aquitaine bishops, princes, and nobles together drew up resolutions against disturbers of peace, in a *carta de treuga et de pace* (990).[1] All men were exhorted to be the ' sons of peace, because without peace no one will see the Lord '.[2] The peace clauses here were more numerous, and more clearly defined than before. (1) No one was to break into any church situated in the dioceses

---

[1] *Gall. Christ.* ii. p. 825.

[2] Ibid., *Quia scimus quia sine pace nemo videbit dominum, ammonemus . . . ut sint filii pacis.*

or territory of those present, and no one, except the bishop when he came for tribute, was to enter the enceinte of the fortifications.   (2) No one was to steal horses, oxen, cows, asses (nor the burdens with which they were laden), fowls, eggs, goats, nor swine from the sees or provinces of those present.   (3) Clerks were not to carry secular arms, and monks and the defenceless were not to be attacked unless by the command of a bishop when collecting dues.   (4) No one was to capture or hold a villein in order to force him to buy himself free again.   (5) No one was to carry home or to use in defence of his, what was not his.   (6) The *Pax Dei* was to be extended to merchants, who were not to be plundered when travelling.   All those present were exhorted to come to a *placitum Dei* in October that they might swear to the peace.

In 997 a *pactum pacis* was inaugurated.   In that year, in the hope of assuaging the wrath of the Lord, manifest in a terrible pestilence which had swept over the land and decimated the people, a three days' fast was proclaimed at Limoges by the abbot of St. Martial's, bishop Alduin, and duke William.[1]   The bishops of Aquitaine assembled at Limoges, relics of the saints were borne in procession, even the body of St. Martial being brought from the tomb.   Nor did they fast in vain, for thereafter disease ceased, and all hearts were filled with great rejoicing.   In gratitude an oath of peace and justice was sworn.[2]   The council of Poitiers, summoned by William of Aquitaine, marked a further development in the movement (1000), hostages being given for the restoring of peace and justice.[3]   Any dispute about theft in the past five years was to be examined before the chief men of the district.   If justice was not enforced, the disputants could appeal to the nobles and bishops who had attended the council, who would meet again and pass sentence on the guilty.   Cumbersome as this machinery was, the idea underlying it is plain :

[1] Bouquet, x. 147.   [2] Pertz, *Script.* iv. p. 132.
[3] Bouquet, x. p. 536.   Mansi, xix. p. 267, dated 999, *Firmaverunt per obsides et excommunicationem dux et reliqui principes huiusmodi pacis et iustitiae restaurationem.*

the system of self-help to be put down and one law enforced on all. The example was followed later by the men of Amiens and Corbei (1030).[1]

After the year 1000 the work of peace was continued and with greater enthusiasm. Till then there had been a vague foreboding that the end of the world was at hand. What need, then, for peace? But when the fatal year had passed, and the world still went on, it was more urgently felt that if life was to continue, the conditions of society would have to be ameliorated. In the last years of the century humanity had suffered very terribly. There had been famine throughout Europe, and incursions by the Saracens caused further misery. But when the first years of the eleventh century were safely over, then ' in almost all the world, especially in Italy and Gaul, Christians vied with one another in rebuilding and restoring churches. It seemed as if the church had thrown away age and clothed herself in the white garments of the saints, the faithful restoring almost all the churches of their respective dioceses, the monasteries of the saints, and the *oratoria* of the smaller vills.' [2] The hearts of men were thus more attuned to peace when a new impetus was given to the movement by Robert the Pious, who in 1010–11 called a general assembly at Orleans to debate on the question. Fulbert of Chartres, in a letter to the king, rejoiced at the good news.[3] Unfortunately, nothing is known about this council. Henceforth the king was a zealous supporter of peace councils, his ideal indeed going so far as to embrace the possibility of a general cessation of private warfare throughout all Europe, a chimerical Utopia for those times. He approached the emperor Henry II. with his project. In 1023 the two rulers met at Ivois on the Meuse to discuss the peace problem, and agreed to call a council at Pavia in a year's time, when peace

---

[1] Bouquet, x. p. 379.   [2] Migne, 142, p. 651 ; Rod. Glab. iii. cap. 4.
[3] Bouquet, x. 454, *Audito inter alia quod concilium habiturus sis, cum principibus regni de pace componenda, gaudeo.* Cf. 467, *Si ergo de iustitia, de pace, de statu regni, de honore ecclesiae vultis agere, ecce habetis me parvum satellitem pro viribus opitulari paratum.*

measures were to be drawn up and a scheme of church reform
brought forward : Benedict VIII. was to preside, the princes and
prelates of Germany, France, and Italy to attend. With the
death of pope and emperor within the year the scheme was
abandoned.

The next development of the peace movement came from
Burgundy, a province not long incorporated in the Frankish
kingdom. Hoping to heal the many wounds his numerous
campaigns had inflicted, the king asked Hugh, bishop of Auxerre,
to call a council to discuss measures of peace. Not only the
bishops, but also an ' innumerable multitude of nobles and the
common people ', men and women, attended. The importance
of this council lay in the fact that the king definitely placed
himself at the head of what till then had been an ecclesiastical
movement. Next, in Northern France (1023), the bishops of
Soissons, Beauvais, and Cambrai in the interests of the State
(*respublica*) followed the example of their Burgundian brothers,[1]
because they recognised that the solemn sentences of the church
would become a dead letter if the barons did not swear to cease
their pillages. This council was interesting for two reasons :
(1) that for the first time the oath of peace was taken by each
noble individually ; (2) that this innovation aroused the strong
disapproval of Gerald, bishop of Cambrai, who protested against
the procedure as pernicious and dangerous : if every one took the
oath it would undoubtedly lead to perjury, for it was impossible
that every one should keep it : the oath infringed on the royal
prerogative and would lead to a confusion of the spheres of the
ecclesiastical and temporal powers which ought to be kept
strictly apart, the function of the one being to pray, of the other
to fight. His episcopal brothers censured this bold speaker as
the enemy of peace, while his own retainers and the abbots so
eagerly begged him to take the oath that he reluctantly consented.

[1] Bouquet, x. p. 201, *Videntes episcopi . . . prae inbecillitate regis,
peccatis quidem exigentibus, statum regni funditus inclinari, iura confundi,
usumque patrium et omne genus iustitiae profanari, multam reipublicae succurrere
arbitrati sunt, si Burgundiae episcoporum sententiam sequerentur.*

'Nevertheless, his foresight was justified by the event, and very few escaped the sin of perjury.' After this councils were held in every *civitas*. At Héry, in the diocese of Auxerre, king Robert was himself present when an 'innumerable multitude' of the common people of every age and of either sex assembled,[1] relics of the saints were carried among them, and oaths sworn on the relics (1024). Two years later, at the council of Poitiers, the bishops of Burgundy and William of Aquitaine drew up new measures for protecting churches, monasteries, and their property. Again an 'innumerable multitude' met, male and female, rich and poor, ecclesiastical and lay. In 1028 William of Aquitaine called a second council at Charroux to discuss questions of faith and to confirm peace. Similar meetings were held in Dijon, Beaune, and Lyons.

A further development in the movement came from the North when the men of Amiens and Corbei mutually swore to an agreement for peace (1030). Vengeance had come on them from on high because they had never sworn to that peace which God ordains. For such is the character of the men of Gaul that more than the men of any other nation they always want to fight.[2] To the chronicler there seemed little call for internecine strife. Pestilence and famine were already killing men off in hordes, and the world could no longer bear the anger of its Judge. The men of Amiens and Corbei therefore resolved to placate the God they had offended. A council was held, the relics of the saints brought forth, and on the relics an inviolable pact sworn, the men of the two towns, after consultation with their lords, agreeing to keep peace for a whole week. They further promised to return every year to Amiens on St. Firmin's day to confirm their oath ; to strengthen their resolve they received the holy sacrament. If strife arose among them no revenge by destruction or fire was to be taken until a day was appointed,

---

[1] Ibid. p. 375.
[2] Bouquet, x. p. 378, *Talis quippe consuetudo naturaliter innata est regno Gallorum, ut praeter ceteras rationes semper velint exercere rabiem bellorum. . . . Non necesse est velle mori in bello quia catervatim moriuntur famis et pestis gladio.*

and notice given before the church in the presence of the bishop
and count.   John XIX. confirmed this agreement.   As a result,
a new and salutary custom arose by which the men of the
two towns annually met to exchange a reciprocal oath of
peace.   Eight days were set aside for prayer, disputes were
settled, the unruly recalled to peace, and an opportunity given
for mutual deliberation.   Unfortunately this state of things was
too good to last, familiarity bred contempt, and an innovation
which had at first been greatly venerated began to be as greatly
despised.[1]

Throughout the rest of the kingdom the movement for peace
continued.   Terrible evils from on high had again forced men
to think.   The outburst of prosperity after the year 1000 did
not last long, and as the ' fateful year approached which marked
the thousandth anniversary after Christ's death ', a terrible
famine ruled in the land.   Such storms raged that the crops
could not be harvested.   So persistent was the rain that for
three years it was almost useless to sow seeds.   Famine arose in
the East, depopulated Greece, spread to Italy, to Gaul, and
finally to England.   Every class suffered : ' not only the poor
but even the higher and well-to-do classes grew pale with hunger,
many fled from place to place, stayed at inns where they watched
by night, and turned those who had received them into food.'
Then, as if humanity had not suffered enough, after the famine
came pestilence, and for three years the sound of weeping, of
grief, and of sorrow was heard in the land.   Society seemed to
have fallen into perpetual chaos, and the human race to be
brought to destruction.[2]

The aggravation of all these horrors by private warfare was
indeed a mockery, and the church was not slow to preach that
such evils must befall a lawless generation that sought not
peace.   She persevered in her work, aided by the king, who
presided at the council of Bourges, called in the interests of

---

[1] Ibid., *Coepit res ipsa usu vilescere et irreverentia fieri ex multa veneratione.*
[2] Rod. Glab. iv. 4.

peace (1031). In the same year, at the council of Limoges, bishop Jordan brought an indictment [1] against the barons and the laity of his diocese, who had attacked churches and church property, molested priests, clerks, and the poor, and shown no desire for peace, although he had pronounced a general peace for his diocese. The offenders were excommunicated, and a motion carried that their lands were to be laid under interdict if they continued in their evil doing. The sentence must have been most impressive, for at the words ' As these lights (*lucanae*) are extinguished before your eyes, so let their joy be extinguished before the angels,' bishops and priests dashed their lighted candles to the ground, and the heart of the people being greatly moved, all cried aloud, ' So let God extinguish the joy of him who is not willing to keep peace and justice.' [2]

The prosperity and abundance which reigned from the thousandth year after the death of the Saviour also made for peace. A feeling of gratitude and relief was awakened throughout all classes. Peace assemblies were called more enthusiastically than ever, all rejoicing at the prosperous times, being ready to obey whatever measures the chiefs of the church deemed advisable. ' It was as if a voice from heaven spoke down to earth ',[3] and men, remembering the times of adversity through which they had passed, were chastened in spirit and terrified lest those evil days returned. The following decrees were drawn up : (1) Any person who took refuge in a church was to be in sanctuary ; (2) clerks, monks, and nuns were not to be oppressed. It was also agreed that wine would not be drunk for six days after the council, nor meat eaten for seven. So great was the fervour which filled all hearts that, when the bishop raised the ring to heaven, the multitude shouted ' *Pax, pax, pax !* ' as if hailing in the ring a symbol of perpetual peace between themselves and God.[3] That the harvest was good that year, and that there

---

[1] Labbe, ix. p. 870, *Clamorem de secularibus potestatibus parochianis meis.*
[2] Mansi, xix. p. 530.
[3] Rod. Glab. iv. 5. Cf. Hugh de Flavigny, ii. 27, anno 1033.

was great plenteousness of food and wine seemed a direct reward of good resolutions. In 1034, synods were held in Aquitaine, Arles, Lyons, Burgundy, and in the North of France, at one of which one bishop even affirmed that he had received letters from heaven exhorting him to renew peace on earth.[1] In Poitiers an important council was called by bishop Isembertus and a great peace proclaimed (1036). At the council of Bourges a further step was taken, in that all present pledged themselves to attack disturbers of the peace (1038). This was proposed by archbishop Aimo of Bourges, who, anxious to have peace established in his diocese, consulted his suffragans, and on their advice ordered that all the men in his diocese above fifteen years of age should pledge themselves to be the enemies of those who disturbed the peace, and, if necessary, to take up arms against them.[2] The oath pledged each to proceed, without gift or favour of person, against those who seized church property, stirred up rapine, oppressed monks, nuns, and clerks, or attacked the church.[3]

The priests on several occasions took banners from the churches and led the people against disturbers of peace. In one encounter (according to the chronicler) the archbishop's men and seven hundred clerks were killed. A new cause of strife had arisen.

Finally came that interesting branch of the peace movement,

[1] Mansi, xix. p. 530, *Unus eorum caelitus sibi delatas dixit esse litteras, quae pacem monerent renovandam in terram. Quam rem mandavit ceteris et haec tradenda dedit populis.*

[2] Huberti, *Studien zur Rechtsgeschichte der Gottesfrieden*, p. 217: *Pacem sub iurisiurandi sacramento in diocesi voluit sua . . . ut contra violatorem compacti foederis unanimi corde hostes existant, et distractioni rerum eorum nullo pacto se subducant; quin etiam, si necessitas posceret, armis exturbantes appeterent. Non excipiuntur ipsi sacrorum ministri, sed a sanctuario domini correptis frequenter vexillis, cum extera multitudine populi in corruptores invehuntur iuratae pacis.*

[3] Ibid. p. 218, *Ego Aimo archiepiscopus hoc toto corde et ore Deo Sanctisque eius promitto . . . toto impleam animo. Hoc est, ut pervasores ecclesiasticarum rerum, incentores rapinarum, oppressores monachorum, sanctimonialium et clericorum, omnesque sanctae matris ecclesiae impugnatores . . . totis viribus venire promitto.*

the *Treuga Dei*. The aim of the *Pax Dei* was to protect certain persons and property from the violence of the powerful. The aim of the *Treuga* was to stop private warfare for short but fixed intervals of time. The *Pax* took under its protection clerks, monks, pilgrims, women, children, labourers and their instruments of work, monasteries and cemeteries. These were to be undisturbed and in ' perpetual peace '. The *Treuga* was an attempt to put a check on the lawless barons who regarded private warfare as their prerogative.[1] In this movement Odilo took an important part.

The *Treuga Dei* seems to have been first definitely mentioned at the council of Elne [2] (1027). At that council many bishops, priests, the God-fearing of the dukes, and a multitude of the faithful, men and women alike, met together, and having prayed God to direct their judgement, drew up the following decrees : (1) No one in the retinue or diocese of those present was to attack an enemy from the ninth hour on Saturday till the first hour on Monday. This would allow all to pay due reverence to the Lord's Day.[3] (2) No monk nor clerk without arms was to be attacked, nor any man walking with a woman, nor any man going to or returning from church or council. (3) No one was to attack, violate, despoil, nor enter by force a church or a house situated thirty paces from the church. The *Treuga* was drawn up because the divine law and Christian religion were no longer observed, iniquity abounded, and charity grew cold. Breach of the *Treuga* was to be visited by ostracism and excommunication ; none of the faithful were to eat or drink with any one who broke it, nor to talk with them unless to convince them of the evil of their ways : no priest was to bury them, nor were the faithful to pray for them.

Thus once more men had begun to build up peace, and in

---

[1] Luchaire, *Histoire de France Lavisse*, ii. 2.

[2] Mansi, xix. 483, *Caterva quoque fidelium, non solum virorum sed etiam foeminarum.*

[3] Ibid., *Ab hora sabbati nona usque in die lunis hora prima, ut omnis homo persolvat debitum honorem die dominico.*

that very region where once the *Pax Romana* had done its civilising work and reigned supreme, and from the modest and tentative proposal that from Saturday to Monday private warfare should cease. This indestructible idealism in the heart of humanity is an interesting phenomenon. Material force had brought society almost to destruction, yet at the very moment of its greatest triumph men looked to moral force to reconstitute society. And humanity's instinctive, if unconscious, faith in idealism was justified. From the thin wedge of the one day's peace, the larger European movement was to grow. In Gaul the principle of the *Treuga* seems to have made rapid progress, for in 1041 an appeal went forth from the church in Gaul to the brethren in Italy. The appeal was headed by the names of Reginald, archbishop of Arles, Benedict, bishop of Avignon, Nithard, bishop of Nice, and Odilo, venerable abbot of Cluny, who with all bishops, abbots, and clerks living in Gaul appealed to all the archbishops, bishops, priests, and clerks of Italy ' to receive and keep ' the *Treuga Dei*, which, transmitted to them by the inspiration of the divine mercy, they had received and did firmly keep.[1] The *Treuga* was to extend from sunset on Wednesday to sunrise on Monday, that men might meditate on the significance of those days : Thursday the commemoration of the Ascension, Friday the Passion, Saturday the Adoration at the tomb, Sunday the Resurrection. During these four days and nights firm peace and stable truce was to obtain among all Christians, friends and foes, neighbours and strangers.[2] All were to be secure (*securi*) at every hour, and to do whatever was fitting, free from all fear of enemies because confirmed in the tranquillity of the *Pax* and *Treuga*.[3] If theft was committed in

---

[1] Ibid. xix. 593, *Recipite ergo, et tenete pacem, et illam trevam Dei, quam et nos, divina inspirante misericordia de caelo nobis transmissam iam accepimus et firmiter tenemus.*

[2] Ibid., *Inter omnes christianos amicos et inimicos, vicinos et extraneos, sit firma pax et stabilis treuva.*

[3] Ibid., *Omni hora securi sint et faciant quidquid erit opportunum ab omni timore inimicorum absoluti et in tranquillitate pacis et istius treuvae confirmati.*

those days, the loser was not to seek his own, lest cause of strife should be given [1] During them rural labour was to cease.[2] Any one who committed homicide during the *Treuga* was to be driven from his province and go on pilgrimage to Jerusalem. For any other breach of the *Treuga* the offender was to be examined by the secular law and forced to make reparation, after which double penance would be laid on him according to the holy canons.[3] Nor were the framers of the appeal exempt. ' We think it right that if we break our promise we too shall be doubly condemned—both by secular and spiritual judgement.'[4] Any one who took vengeance on those who broke the *Treuga* would be held guiltless and blessed by all Christians as the *cultores causae Dei.*[5] All who observed the *Treuga* were assured of absolution from Father, Son, and Holy Spirit, and of union with Mary and her choirs of virgins, with St. Michael and his angels, with St. Peter, chief of the apostles, and with all the saints and faithful then and for ever. Those who swore to keep the *Treuga* and wittingly broke their oath would be excommunicated by Father, Son, and Holy Spirit, cut off from all the saints of God, and if they did not make amends, then and for ever excommunicate, damned, and accursed, with Dathan, Abiram, and Judas who betrayed the Lord. Like Pharaoh who sank to the bottom of the Red Sea, they would sink to the depths of Hell.

In the life of the bishop of Autun there is a reference to Odilo's work for the *Treuga.* The aged bishop was wont to tell that by divine revelation the *Treuga* was instituted by Odilo of

---

[1] Ibid., *Si vero residuis diebus aliquid sublatum fuerit, et in diebus treuvae obviaverit, omine non teneatur, ne occasio inimico data videatur.*

[2] Ibid., *Ab omnibus rurale opus in ea omnino non fieret impositum.*

[3] Ibid., *Si vero in aliis cuibuslibet rebus supradictam treuvam . . . fregerit, examinatus per decreta legum secularium iuxta modum culparum cogatur persolvere et per sanctorum canonum regulas duplicata poenitentia iudicabitur.*

[4] Ibid., *Quod ideo dignum cucimus ut si promissionem illic factam in aliquo corrumpere praesumpserimus mundano et spiritali iudicio dupliciter condemnemur.*

[5] Ibid., *Cum autem evenerit cuiquam vindicare in eos, qui hanc chartum, et Dei treuvam irrumpere praesumpserint, vindicantes nulli culpae habeantur.*

Cluny, and that all agreed to receive and keep it.[1]   But, alas,
as Rodulf Glaber mourned, the human race soon forgets.   Old
sins revived and the efficacy of a movement that had started
with such high hopes and noble enthusiasm died down.

In what was destined to be another world-wide movement
Odilo also took a chief part, for according to our authorities
it was by his inspiration that a day of special intercession for
the faithful dead was set apart.   The legend of All Souls' Day
ran as follows : [2]

A monk of Rodez was returning from a pilgrimage to Jerusalem.   When crossing the sea from Thessaly to Sicily a storm
broke and drove the boat on to an island or rock.   There a
hermit had lived for many years, and with him the monk talked.
The hermit, learning that he was a native of Aquitaine and knew
Odilo of Cluny, gave him a message for the monks.   Near the
island where he lived great fires belched forth, into which, by the
manifest judgement of God, rows of tortured sinners were thrust.
A multitude of demons received them and renewed their torments
and unbearable sufferings.   But often the hermit heard the
demons lament, that through the prayers and almsgiving of the
monks so many of the damned went free, and more particularly
through the prayers of Odilo and the monks of Cluny.   He
therefore implored those virtuous ones to be more and more
instant in prayer, vigils, and almsgiving.   By these means they
would cause the angels to rejoice and the devil to rage.   When
the monk returned home he sent the message to Cluny.   Great
was the joy and amazement of the brothers.[3]   In their gratitude

---

[1] Pertz, *Scriptores*, viii. 403, Hugo Flaviniac : *Superest adhuc Iduensis
episcopus, . . . qui referre solitus est quia cum a sancto Odilone et ceteris ipsa
divinis revelationibus instituta treuga Dei appellata, et ab Austrasiis suscepta
fuisset, et voluntas omnium in hoc esset una et ubique servaretur, negotium hoc
impositum.*   [2] *Vita Jotsaldo*, ii. 13.

[3] *Ibid., Ad Cluniacum admirationem non parvam cum maxima cordis
letitia sumpserint.*   Rod. Glaber gives a slightly different version of the legend,
the monastery in question being Maior Monasterium and the meeting-place
Africa.   There in the desert an anchorite had dwelt for twenty years, living on

to God, they added prayers to prayers, and alms to alms, until
Odilo bethought himself of setting aside a special day of intercession for the souls of the faithful, to be observed in all the
houses under him, i.e. 2nd of November, the day following All
Saints' Day. Special psalms, prayers, and giving of alms were
appointed.[1] After the meeting of the chapter, the deacon and
cellarer were to distribute bread and wine to the poor who had
been at mass ; the poor were also to have for dinner what
remained over from the brothers' refection. The office for the
dead was to be read, a *tractus* sung by two brothers, and the
monks to say private prayers and public masses for all the faithful dead. At night twelve poor men were to be given food.
Silence was to be enforced during periods of the day. ' By the
throwing of this dart it was hoped that the adversary would
suffer more and more.'

Another story was specially treasured at Cluny as showing
the value of those prayers to offer up which the monk thought
it his highest privilege to dedicate his life. Benedict VI., a
pope who delighted in Odilo's society and loved him with great
affection, died. For long his soul remained in purgatory, God
having resolved by this means to make manifest the merit of
Odilo. One night Benedict appeared to John, bishop of Porto,
and two of his friends, lamenting that he was still held in the
shades of purgatory, and not advanced to the realms of light.
He begged his startled hearers to send to Odilo, and implore
him to pray that his (the bishop's) soul might be saved from
torment. John and his friends immediately hastened to the
pope, who, sorrowing greatly for his brother, sent John to Cluny.
On his way the bishop stopped at St. Maiolus', Pavia, where

---

herbs and seeing no man. Finally, one bold seeker found out his retreat, and
was told that before all monasteries in the Roman kingdom, the prayers of
the monks of Maior Monasterium were most efficacious in freeing souls from
damnation, and that on All Souls' Day at Maior Monasterium mass was
celebrated from daybreak till the hour of refection, with such dignity and
reverence, that it seemed rather divine than human.

[1] *Bibl. Clun.*

he told the story to the great excitement of the abbot, who begged to accompany him. However, they decided that a letter would arrive sooner. 'By the divine providence' the letter found Odilo at Cluny.

After reading it, Odilo called the brothers together, and earnest prayers were offered for the soul of the pope. 'After prayers alms were distributed, a charity the burden of which was very dear to the *seniores*.' Odilo next appointed fixed hours for the offering of special prayers and giving of alms, not only at Cluny but also at all the Cluniac houses. Not long after, a monk of Cluny saw a form conspicuous in light enter the cloisters, followed by a great multitude in white robes. All proceeded to the chapter where Odilo sat with the holy senate. There the first figure humbly bent his head on the knees of the father. The monk asked who the shining one was, and learned that it was Benedict, humbly giving thanks to Odilo, by virtue of whose prayers he had escaped the depths of hell, and soared to the blessed on high. Next day, remembering all with tenacious memory, he told the brothers. All feared with holy awe, and all rejoiced that it had been so clearly manifested how great Odilo's favour with the Trinity was, 'since by his merit even the prey caught in the jaws of death was enabled to escape'.[1]

[1] *Vita Jotsaldo*, ii. 14. Jotsaldus adds the caution 'that it is most vain to be always observing signs and dreams'.

CHAPTER XVI

INCREASE OF CLUNIAC INFLENCE

OF the monasteries which came under Cluny when Odilo was abbot, one of the first was St. Victor's, Geneva, the gift of bishop Hugh. The bishop had often deliberated with himself, and discussed with his friends how the religious houses of his diocese might be restored : his opportunity over St. Victor's came in this wise. The empress Adelheid, on a visit to Geneva, entered St. Victor's to pray, and was so struck by the suitability of the site for a monastery that she mentioned the fact to the bishop. Soon afterwards the bones of martyrs were discovered on the very spot. With great ceremony the bones were raised from the ground, and buried under the altar of the church in the presence of king Rudolf, queen Agildrude, and a great company of bishops, religious, monks, and noblemen. After further consideration the bishop decided to build cells for the monks round the church, but as the monastery thus formed did not have enough property to support an abbot, after consultation with king Rudolf, his brother Burchard, archbishop of Lyons, the counts, and other noblemen of the district, the bishops begged Odilo to undertake the duty. St. Victor's monastery and church was thus committed to him and his successors to be held in perpetuity from the bishops of Geneva, for the bishop did not wish to take any power from his cathedral, but only to establish religious life there, and most excellent love between his successors and the abbots of Cluny (993–99).[1]

From the bishop of Liez Cluny received the church and

[1] Bruel, iii. 1984. Cf. *Vita Jotsaldo*, i. 13, *Locus sancti Victoris Genevensis praeter suam antiquam et nobilem ecclesiam ex toto suo tempore constructus. . . . Quia non erat in eodem loco tanta facultas possessionis, ut aliquis ibi potuisset ordinari loco abbatis.*

altare of Valensolle, for he felt that as earthly fathers ought to lay up treasures for their sons, so those called fathers in the spirit should advance their sons' interests in material as well as spiritual things. Therefore in answer to the request of the congregation of Cluny sent by Rainald, the prior, he gave the church on the conditions agreed between them, i.e. the monks were to pay eighty solidi to the funds of his church and synodal service annually—ten denarii in May and ten in October. They could hold, order, or give away the church. Neither the bishop, his successors, nor the archdeacon when visiting the parishes of the diocese were to require hospitality or build little houses there (*mansionaticos*), lest this should be a burden to the monks. The 'writing' was drawn up *pro signo socialitatis* that the members of his church and their monastery might, alive or dead, mutually share in each other's good deeds.[1] Later, Odilo asked the bishop's permission to build a monastery near the church of Valensolle. The bishop assented, having received from the monks four pounds of denarii, eight measures of wheat and of wine.[2] Neither the bishop, his successors, nor any other men were to have authority over the monastery, nor ask oblations and burial dues from it.

Walter, bishop of autun (994–1000), on the advice of his clerks and other sons of the church, gave the Cluniacs the monastery of Magabrense, in the hope that his church and Cluny might remain bound by the chain of love as in the time of Maiolus, and continue 'untroubled' for all time.[3]

In 998 a new monastery was founded at Bévais above Lake Neuchâtel, and given to Cluny by a certain Rudolf,[4] who had learned from the Scriptures that the wicked would receive pain, but the good would be granted pleasant homes in heaven. Anxious to atone for his sins, he could think of no better way than to found a monastery, where daily due service might be rendered to God. When the monastery was built, the monks of Peter-

---

[1] Bruel, iii. 1990 (993–1031).
[2] Ibid. iii. 1991.
[3] Ibid. iii. 2276.
[4] Ibid. iii. 2453.

lingen advised him to ask the bishop of Lausanne to dedicate it,
which he, being good and noble, did. Rudolf then richly
endowed the monastery with a church, lands in various districts,
ten manors, thirty-five serfs with their wives and children, and
placed it under Odilo and his successors, who were to pay Rome
two solidi annually, so that (*ea ratione*) any one who disputed
the charter might be bound by the chain of anathema. That
the gift might remain firm and stable he wished to appoint one
of his heirs to be *advocatus* after his death, and to rule and govern
according to the will of Odilo and his monks. In succeeding
ages that office was always to belong to one of his descendants.

In 999 Hugh, count of Chalon and bishop of Auxerre, gave
Cluny Paray with its churches, vills, manors, fields, vines, mills,
and serfs.[1] His father, advised by Maiolus, had founded the
monastery, adorned it suitably, and loved it beyond all places.
He had declared it free from all local authority and lay domination,
that the monks might serve God there under their own pastor.
But, alas, iniquity abounded, charity grew cold, and the bishop
saw that the monastery could not of itself remain in that state
which his father intended. Therefore, on the advice of king
Rudolf and his fellow bishops, he gave it wholly to Cluny, with
its churches, vills, lands, and serfs. The king confirmed the
charter. About the same time, through count Otto William,
St. Cyprian's, Poitiers, came under Cluny.[2] An abbot was
appointed who had such difficulties with his monks that Abbo
of Fleury wrote asking Odilo to exercise his authority and enforce discipline (1004). In the same district St.-Jean-d-Angély
was subjected to Cluny. Great excitement had been aroused at
St. Jean's by the discovery of a head in the wall, which abbot
Alduin hailed as the head of John the Baptist (1010). The
discovery was celebrated with much ceremony in the presence of
the kings of France and Navarre, the count of Gascony, many

[1] Ibid. iii. 2484.
[2] Sackur, ii. p. 68, Migne, 139, p. 438, *Abbonis Epist.* xii. *ad Odilonem* :
Quem locum postquam reperi vestrae subditum ditioni nostrum credidi.

bishops and abbots.   Odilo reformed the abbey, over which he appointed one of his monks abbot.[1]   In 1011 Le Moûtier de Thiers became Cluny's.[2]   It had belonged to a secular lord Wido,[3] ' very rich and noble, and though a layman praiseworthy for many things ' (*per multa laudabilis*).   He, seeing that the condition of men was going from bad to worse and to headlong and daily ruin, consulted his wife and three sons, and resolved to reform Thiers, which ' had been neglected by his forefathers more than was fitting '.   For a time his scheme had no success ;   the abbot he appointed died, and the monastery, deprived of its father, seemed destitute of all human help.   Then the monks, with the consent of Wido and his retainers, chose as abbot a certain Peter, a man of distinguished birth and of blessed simplicity.   But though he did his best to uphold discipline, his influence was rendered negligible by the malice of men.   So, remembering how it is written, ' Woe unto him who is alone when he falleth ', he begged Odilo of Cluny to bear the burden with him.   With Wido's joyful consent   it was arranged that he was to hold the monastery, ruling over it with Odilo's help, and on his death Odilo and his monks were to rule, order, and dispose it ' in the same way as Sauxillanges, Souvigny, and not a few other distinguished houses, which for long had firmly belonged to the noble Cluny '.   Wido then richly endowed the abbey with land and serfs, and at the same time gave up his right to all the evil and importunate exactions which his predecessors and even he himself had unjustly demanded.

La Volta,[4] in the diocese of Auvergne, was built by Odilo and his relatives (1025).   His brothers had thought of founding a monastery, a project which death cut short.   Their sons, with Odilo and his other nephews, relatives, and many of the faithful, met to discuss what they could do for the dead men's souls. There seemed to them nothing better than to carry out the deceased's intention of building a monastery.   Neighbours

---

[1] *Gallia Christ.* ii. 1097 ; Ademar, iii. cap. 56.   [2] Bruel, iii. 2682.
[3] Probably Guy II., viscount of Thiers.   [4] La Voute-près-Chilhac.

and friends heartily approved, and on the little hill of Volta,
near the river, the foundations of the church were laid. The
bishop of Clermont was asked to consecrate the oratory. At
the dedication, Odilo, his nephews, brothers, and sisters ' offered
to the hierarchy of heaven property which, gained worthily
by their ancestors, had descended to them from their parents
by hereditary right ' ; i.e. the hill Volta, surrounded by a river,
across the river a church, with its lands and tenths, three vills,
part of two others, two little vills, a manor, and two churches.
The monastery was adorned with skilful work, and suitably
provided with books and ornaments. Exempt from all dues,
it was placed under the protection of Rome and the direction
of the abbots of Cluny.[1]

In the same year Amadeus I., count of Savoy, and his wife,
in order to participate in the prayers of the monks, gave them
the church of St. Maurice, Malaucène, reserving for themselves,
their children, their descendants the rights of patronage and
presentation.[2]

In 1029 Rudolf III. of Burgundy, at the request of count
Rainald, confirmed Cluny s possession of the monastery of Vaux,
near Poligny, Besançon, with its lands and tenths, three vills
in different districts and their churches (one the vill Mantes),
vineyards, alods, fisheries, serfs, salt pits, and four large vessels
for cooking salt (*ferreas cældarias*), everything the count and his
father, count Otto William (who built the monastery), had given,
and everything the monks might in the future gain in the *burg*.[3]

In the same year Isembertus, bishop of Poitiers, wished to
make known that viscount Kadolein and his son, grieving over
their past life and converted to good, with pious mien and humble

[1] Ibid. iii. 2788. The charter is written in the first person, Odilo addressing
all foreigners and citizens of the region and county. It seemed only right that
Cluny should gain something from the family's poverty, since by the reverence
and merit of that holy place, one of them had gained honour before God and
before men. Cf. *Vita Jotsaldo*, i. 13.

[2] *Bibl. Clun.* p. 412, *Quod vocatur ius patronatus, et ius praesentandi.*

[3] Bruel, iv. 2817 ; cf. 2890. The monastery had been built by count Otto
William, consecrated by the bishop of Autun, and put under Cluny in perpetuity.

countenance, begged him by his ecclesiastical authority to grant in writing a privilege to the *ecclesia* of Molgon. He, not compelled by greed, but moved by their humble prayer, consented, and decreed that it and its property should never again be sold or bought, nor pay dues, nor be in subjection to the lay power, but be under his authority and the rule (*regimen*) of the monks of Cluny. To this the consent of his canons, of the abbots of Poitiers, and of the princes of Aquitaine had been given.[1]

In 1031 Bernard, bishop of Cahors, and his brother gave Cluny St. Sernin's, Carennac, with everything belonging to it, except a third of a rivulet, which the brother retained. The church had belonged to the cathedral of Cahors, and lest any one objected to this alienation, the bishop gave the cathedral another church which was his by hereditary right. The agreement was signed in the chapter at Cahors before the whole body of canons, abbots, priests, archdeacons, clerks, and other men.[2]

In 1032 the archbishop of Besançon, at the request of the distinguished abbot Odilo, gave Cluny the *altare* of the monastery Vaux, near Poligny, Besançon. The bishop recalled that Christ committed His church first to the apostles, then to the bishops, many of whom with fervent zeal had watched solicitously over the clerks and monks of their flock, until at the end of the last century, iniquity abounding and charity growing cold, they had become lax. He called on his episcopal brethren, therefore, to awake from sleep, and to follow his example by doing good, joyfully and with more generous hand, to those houses of the saints where they knew the grace of the Spirit most fervently to abound. As a reward for sharing their temporal goods with such houses they would participate in the merits of the monks. Besides the *altare*, he gave to the little monastery tenths, burial dues, and oblations from the vill Mantes, and two chapels with their tenths, burial dues, and oblations, on condition that at the synodal season the monks of Poligny should pay to his cathedral, as had been done in the past, a fourth of the *paratae* and *eulogiae*.

[1] Ibid. iv. 2816.　　　　　　[2] Ibid. iv. 2856.

To all this wealth of almsgiving, the bishop ended with conscious
virtue, he added *bagarna*[1] in Graus, for which the monks were not
to neglect to pay his successors three measures of salt annually.

In 1037 Aymar, count of Valence, his wife and five sons,
gave Cluny the abbey of St. Marcel's, Sauzet, with land,
woods, meadows, vineyards, waters, mills, pasture. For long
the abbots of St. Marcel's had been careless and neglectful of
the cure of souls, and the viscount wished to see the spiritual
life of the abbey restored.[2] Four years before Odilo's death,
St. Saviour's, Nevers, which belonged to the jurisdiction of
bishop Hugh of Nevers, was put under Cluny (1045).[3] Famous
in former times, St. Saviour's had been so much neglected by
the bishop's predecessors that 'almost all knowledge of the
Benedictine rule was lost' (*eliminatam*). Wishing to see it
restored to its former greatness, the bishop on the advice of its
abbot, his clerks, and the faithful of the diocese, ceded it to
Cluny, that by the prayers of the monks his and their names
might be written in the book of the living. The canons of St.
Cyr, who had rights over St. Saviour's, gave their consent to the
gift. In the vill Sarrians, given to Maiolus by William, duke of
Provence, a Cluniac monk (*frater et monachus*) built an *ecclesia*
to which he gave a manor as endowment.[4]

Cluniac influence spread to Spain through the reforming zeal
of Sanchius the Great. Sanchius held himself responsible for
the secular and ecclesiastical welfare of the kingdom. His task
filled him with fear and awe, but he had prayed to God for
strength, intelligence, and wisdom. He felt that his prayer had
been heard when God granted him to expel many of the Moors
from his kingdom 'as all the world knew'. Wishing to show
his gratitude, he could think of no better way than to revive
monastic life, which was unknown in his kingdom, though the
most perfect (*perfectissimus*) of all ecclesiastical orders.[5] He

---

[1] *Bagerna* (Ducange)=vessels for cooking salt.   [2] Ibid. iv. 2921.
[3] Ibid. iv. 2961.   [4] Ibid. iv. 2866.
[5] Ibid. iii. 2891. The charter is addressed to the pope, archbishops,
bishops, all ecclesiastics, and all Christian people.

himself had wished to be a monk, remembering that it was written, ' Go, sell all that thou hast, and follow Me.' He had sorrowed greatly that the command was not for him, but had prayed God to give him help to illuminate the darkness of his kingdom with monastic virtue. Having consulted the prudent and religious men of the kingdom he learned that Cluny shone more brightly in the regular life than any other monastery. He therefore sent Paternus with a devout company of religious companions to study the perfect monastic life at Cluny, and to bring back to the thirsty the drink of the monastic profession. On his return, Paternus was appointed abbot of St. John's, Pena, a monastery favoured with royal gifts and many privileges.

Next the bishops, clerks, nobles, and common people begged the king to reform Ona (Castile), a monastery founded by count Sanchius, once richly endowed with lands and goods, but fallen into decadence. Paternus was consulted, Ona was put under the Benedictine rule, the women expelled,[1] and monks brought there, one of whom Paternus instructed in the duties of abbot.

The king granted the monastery a royal charter. It was autonomous. No king, duke, count, bishop, secular nor ecclesiastical person was to disturb or enter it without the abbot's consent. The monks were to elect their abbots, whom the bishop of the diocese, if he was a Catholic and would do so without payment (*sine pretio*), was to consecrate : if not, the metropolitan was to be approached : failing him, Rome. The abbot had full power over the monastery's land and property. Only he could expel or admit a monk. He could not be deposed nor suspended except for a capital and venal offence, and after canonical sentence passed in a general and Catholic council. Interdict laid on the province was not to apply to the monastery. A terrible anathema was called down on any one who violated the charter.

---

[1] Ibid., *Depulsisque mulieribus monasterio sine aliqua reverentia habitantibus.* Cf. *Vita Enecorus*, cap. 3, *Pulsis ex eo monialibus quarum vita parum monasticae regulae respondebat.* Count Sanchius had originally founded a double monastery, inhabited by monks and nuns (Gams, *Kirchengeschichte von Spanien*, ii. 2, p. 419).

During this period there were not so many gifts from bishops, and those mostly monasteries put under Cluny. Several churches were given, and land, e.g. the bishop of Grenoble (996) gave half a *castrum* with his house to Cluny, the whole of a burg with its church and all belonging to it, also another church with tenths, cemeteries, and oblations.[1] In 1006 Liebald, bishop of Mâcon, ' willingly obeying the voice of Odilo and his monks ', gave two little serfs (*servulos*) to the Doorkeeper of Heaven.[2] In 1019, when presiding at a synod he was asked by Odilo and his monks to grant Cluny the church of St. Sulpicius, with its tenths and all belonging to it, in perpetuity. After consultation with his canons he consented, reserving for the cathedral synodal service, *paratae et eulogice*.[3] Geoffrey, bishop of Chalon, sitting at the general council with his canons, was humbly asked by Odilo for the *altare* and tenths of a church at Juilly, for which he was to receive another church. He consented and decreed that no future bishop of Chalon was to dispute the gift, nor demand any dues from the monks, except synodal service,[4] Hugh, bishop of Autun (1019), gave half a *curtis* and praised his sister and her husband for giving the other half. In gratitude the monks gave him a censer weighing five pounds gold.[5] Walter, bishop of Besançon, at the request of the monks and because he had always been bound in special friendship with Cluny and hoped to participate in the monks' good deeds, gave them the *altare* of St. Stephen, Porto, tenths and other dues, saving *eulogiae et paratae*.[6] Gauzlin, bishop of Mâcon, exchanged lands with Odilo (1023).[7] Walter, another bishop of Mâcon, confirmed a gift of land made by his mother to Cluny (1047).[8]

Certain other charters are of interest. One is somewhat quaint : A certain man, speechless and at death's door, was carried by his relatives to Cluny, where he died. In the first flush of their grief the relatives decided to give the *seniores*

---

[1] Ibid. iii. 2307.
[4] Ibid. iii. 2692.
[7] Ibid. iii. 2783.

[2] Ibid. iii. 2636.
[5] Ibid. iii. 2722.

[3] Ibid. iii. 2721.
[6] Ibid. iii. 2746.
[8] Ibid. iv. 2965.

part of a vill, a freehold (*franchisia*) in another vill, a field, and a female serf for the good of the dead man's soul. Eleven of the relations, i.e. a mother with her six sons and four daughters, and four of the friends signed the deed of gift. After a time the six brothers, ' blinded by greed ', threatened to take the serf back, maintaining that they had never really given her. Odilo immediately summoned the malcontents to the cloisters at Cluny, and before the font, on the festival of St. Paul's, showed them the charter of gift. Of those present some acknowledged it, but others denied it. Partly by his sweet speech, partly by a gift of 23 solidi, Odilo persuaded all to sign a second time.[1]

Another charter contains a *clamor de malis*.[2] A certain lord Bernard did harm to Odilo and his monks by giving them a wood for their own (*in proprio*) and then putting his pigs to feed there. The monk in charge took some of them as pledges. Bernard put them back. The monk retaliated by killing them. Bernard then made him pay for them. In the same wood he gave a vill to the monks, then took the dues and they had nothing. Besides, men who had no right to be there held the land of St. Mary's, Bernard taking their services : daily they did the day's work from their *castellum*, fed the dogs, did much damage, and carried off wood. The monk Odo received dues from the land of St. Mary's. Bernard made him return them. These and other unheard-of ills he did, too numerous to be written down.

A dispute over meadow land between Odilo, his *prepositus*, and Elizabeth, abbess of Balma, was amicably settled at Cluny before the abbots of St. Bénigne's, St. Evre's, St. Stephen's, the *prepositus* and deacon of Langres, Erluin skilled in human and divine wisdom, and other clerks and noblemen. The decision of these able men was to be final, ' for the dispute had continued long, though not in anger, nor bitterness, but in peace, tranquillity, and legitimate reasoning '. However, they were not called on to give judgement, for the abbess and her nuns, that good fellowship might continue, preferred to give up the pasture

[1] Ibid. iii. 2009.   [2] Ibid. iii. 2142.

land in question which indeed was useless to them. The monks, for the great love they bore the nuns, presented them with a small gift (*parva satis munuscula*), i.e. 100 solidi of public money.[1]

One charter records a slanderous attack on Cluny, when (1020) before Odilo and count William, at Mâcon, the sons of a certain Heluin accused the monks of having taken their lands and manors, and of having carried off some silver vases. All present swore that this was false, a lie, and unjust. A few charters deal with compensation for murder; e.g. for the murder of a *miles* at Cluny the monks were given a manor, a serf living there with his wife and children, and a *curtilus* in the vill Carsiniacus.[2]

In another case where a man was killed before the very gates of Cluny, the murderer and his accomplices were brought before Rainald the prior by Walter the clerk. Besides paying the customary 60 solidi (for which sureties were given) the criminal ceded to the monks land which he had long held *in beneficio*, and swore on the holy relics never to disturb Cluny's possession of it. He also gave the monks a manor, the possession of which he had long disputed with them.[3] 'It is pleasing to add that, on the day of his funeral, his wife and son acknowledged the agreement before many witnesses, and sealed their testimony with a stone'—a scrupulous fulfilment of liabilities evidently rare! Another case of murder where the victim was only one of Cluny's serfs was more lightly settled, the dead man being replaced by the son of his murderer. The statement of the owner ran : ' I, my wife and children, give Cluny a serf Dunarrunus, son of Dehonus, in place of another serf whom Dehonus killed '— a case of the child indeed paying for the sins of the father. The monks of Cluny were to do what they would with Dunarranus.[4] One charter gave the formula by which the father of

---

[1] Ibid. iii. 2043. [2] Ibid. iii. 2784.
[3] Ibid. iv. 2848. The accomplices, one a priest and one a *miles*, had to stand security each for a hundred solidi. *Pro malefitio infra salvitatem perpetrato iuxta consuetudinem.* [4] Ibid. iv. 2849.

the bishop of Mâcon enfranchised a serf (a clerk), proclaimed him free from all servitude save that of God and the monks whose *seniores* he begged to love and defend and with all honour guard and keep him.[1] After Odilo's death, once when his successor Hugh was at Chalon the gift was confirmed again by the donor, his two sons and grandson. In gratitude to Odilo who had rescued him from captivity, a man gave his paternal inheritance to Cluny and proclaimed himself Odilo's ' man '. Of his three brothers, two became monks. The third, still a minor, was to hold his share of the paternal inheritance *in beneficio* from St. Peter. On his death it reverted to Cluny. Several other charters may be quoted. Archimbald, viscount of Mâcon, before setting out on pilgrimage to Jerusalem, gave the monks an *ecclesia*, a manor, and a wood, to be held in trust until he returned. On his return, in generous mood he gave them the manor and its serfs.[2] Two years later (1039) he gave the *ecclesia*, having reflected that if they who throw grain on the earth to receive back a hundred-fold are wise, much more so are they who give earthly things to receive eternal. All he had formerly given the *ecclesia* was to serve for the use of the monks who were to have a perpetual habitation there, subject to the will of the abbot of Cluny.[3] He also confirmed a charter by which his father left a *curtis* to Cluny.

A man and his brothers ceded to Cluny in perpetuity their dues from a vill with the stipulation that on the anniversary of their father's death the *seniores* would always give a very generous refection to the monks that they might the better bear the anniversary in mind ![4] A woman, who had just married a second husband, gave the monks land, a female serf, and her children, for the soul of her first husband.[5]

---

[1] Ibid. iv. 2869, *Dono mei iuris servum clericum ut ab hac die a mea sit servitute et omnium parentum meorum extorris, extraneus et alienus et liber quatenus nullius mortali homini servire cogatur nisi Domino, SS. Petro et Paulo et monachis de Cluniaco tali tenore tali ratione ut seniores illum pro Dei honore et amore diligant.* [2] Ibid. iv. 2922.
[3] Ibid. iv. 2932.   [4] Ibid. iv. 2940.   [5] Ibid. iv. 2946.

A ' noble woman ' who wished to enfief land given to the
monks came to Cluny with her request.   The land was granted
her for her own and her son's lifetime at a yearly rent of 35 solidi,
which if she failed to pay one year was to be doubled the next.
In goodwill she also agreed to give 40 solidi, a mule valued at
100 solidi, and a saddle.   After her own and her son's death the
property reverted to Cluny.[1]   A man at his death left property
to Cluny.   His wife and sons, who had not consented to the gift,
showed their ill-will by doing as much harm (*injurias*) as they
could to the monks.   This injustice the latter bore so meekly
that the sinners returned to a better state of mind, and before
the count of Mâçon and other nobles made a large gift of property
to Cluny.

Count Otto himself, knowing that *pervasores* and other
persons who unjustly held church property were an abomination
to the Lord, restored to Cluny two vills which he had devastated.
A more cogent reason may have been the fact that Odilo, ' a man
loved by all ', was suing him before duke Henry and his counts.
One transfer of a grant of land, in the presence of bishop Walter
and the monks, was made good by the giving of a stone.[2]

Churches in those days seem to take the place of the modern
company, and their dues that of the modern investment ; e.g. a
donor who held two-thirds of a church gave *in hereditario* a
third to Cluny and his son, a monk, and a third to his wife and
daughter ; the other third belonged to his sister.   A man and
his wife gave Cluny a church with the cultivated and uncultivated
land belonging to it.   They were to hold it for life, and in
investiture were to give the burial dues in their entirety, and
without delay, and annually two measures of wine, and one-
tenth ' of the fruit of their labours '.[3]   A repentant sinner who
had made unjust claims on property and land adjoining his,
thereby stirring up much mischief against the monks, begged for
pardon.   He renounced the evil and unjust dues he had taken
from a church, its grounds and cemetery, and promised not to

---

[1] Ibid. iv. 2883.   [2] Ibid. iv. 2870.   [3] Ibid. iv. 2914.

support the priest there if he annoyed the monks or took *ser-vitium* which belonged to them. To make his pardon doubly sure, he also gave up whatever rights he had in four manors, two given to the monks by his sister, that the love and benevolence which had existed between them and his parents should remain firm and uncorrupted, and descend to his successors. The monks could always rely on his fidelity. He commended his body to them for burial.[1]

A repentant sinner, remembering the injuries he had done the monks, the dues he had exacted from them, and the unjust claims he had stirred up against them, thereby having for long afflicted the servants of St. Peter, and roused the apostle's anger against him, confessed his guilt before Odilo and his monks. The charter of his misdeeds was drawn up because he wished to have it put on record that his conduct had been without justification.

[1] Ibid. iv. 2905.

CHAPTER XVII

ODILO'S DEATH—CHARACTER AND MIRACLES

LONG before Odilo died he longed for death, life being to him a burden and death the reward. In the last five years of his life he suffered very. terribly.[1] Once thinking the end near, he hastened to Rome, hoping to die there protected by the apostles. But man's fate is not in his own hands. After four months' illness he recovered and returned to Cluny, where he lived ten months longer.[2]

He often stayed in the Holy City for weeks and months. During his last visit, at the time of the papal election and the imperial coronation, he spent all his time in praying at the different churches of the city and in giving alms to the poor. He passed the Epiphany sorrowful that he must leave Rome. He spent his last day in St. Peter's still hoping that he might be allowed to die in Rome. At last he tore himself away, but returned to fall before the altar in prayer. Then, his face so ravaged with grief as to be unrecognisable, he fled.[3] Accompanied by his monks he started on his journey. The roads were bad, and Odilo, who was still weak, fell from his horse and was struck by its hoof. The monks carried him to St. Pancratius' and next day to St. Mary's, Aventine. Rome, the greatest city in the world, was moved by a wave of grief : no one without a breast of iron could have refrained from mourning. Many visitors came to that bedside : pope Clement, alone or with the chief men of the city, often with wonderful kindness and sweet words consoled the sufferer,[4] and archbishop Lawrence of

[1] *Vita Jotsaldo*, i. 14.
[2] Ibid.
[3] *Neues Archiv*, xv. p. 121.
[4] Ibid. cf. *Vita Jotsaldo*, i. 14.

Amalfi, learned in Greek and Latin, the charm of whose eloquence and affability of whose great genius were as medicine to the sufferer. Odilo wrote to tell his monks of his accident and begged them to pray for him, ' guilty in that he had not been careful enough of their spiritual guidance '. Masses were said till March, when he began to recover, and meant to leave Rome. Pope Clement persuaded him to stay for Easter. On Palm Sunday he grew very ill again : ' the floors of the grief-stricken house were wet with tears ', and his life despaired of. On Easter day, to the amazement of all, he went to St. Paul's, and afterwards had refection joyously with his monks. Five days later he returned to Cluny.

He lived ten months longer, afflicting himself with fasts and vigils, praying with fervent prayers and exhorting his monks with great earnestness. Then, old as he was, he decided to visit all the houses he had reformed, and where his health failed to await his call. He did not get farther than Souvigny. ' Lord Jesus, what sighs and groans the saint uttered, with what fervour he confessed his sins, glorified Thy majesty, invoked Thy name, dwelt on Thy passion and our redemption. With eyes raised and tears running down his cheeks he gazed on Thy image and sorrowed over Thy face as if he beheld Thee again crucified. With Mary Thy Mother he stood in anguish at the foot of the cross, the sword of sorrow piercing his heart. With his corporal or incorporal eyes he saw the evil one approach. His cry rang out, " By the virtue of Christ and the standard of the Holy Cross I withstand thee, thou enemy of the human race. Turn thy machinations from me and cease thy secret and hidden ambushes before the Cross of my Saviour whom I have always adored, always blessed, and into whose hands I commend my spirit." '

Christmas approached, the festival Odilo always loved the most. On Christmas Eve he went with the brothers to the chapter-house, heard the glad tidings, fell on his knees, adored and prayed, then gave an address, the best he had ever delivered ! He comforted the sorrowing brothers, and told them that he hoped to be present at the festival after his death. Too weak to be present at the council, he was carried to the chapel of St. Mary, and left there with some of the monks. Then, a joyous precentor, he ordered psalms and antiphons to be sung, and forgetting his own suffering joyfully repeated all the Christmas offices. Joy was the keynote of his death. Daily he was carried to mass, and at last it was revealed to him that his call would come on the day after the Circumcision, at which he rejoiced the more, because that perfect man, William of St. Bénigne's, had received his divine crown on the day of the Circumcision. Wrought up by this expectation, he lived for days almost without food or drink, and making little of the pain he suffered, put all his public and private affairs in order, and gave directions about his funeral.

St. Sylvester's Day passed, the vigil of the Circumcision approached. More and more terribly did the pains of death assail him. In agony he asked for the sacred Body and Blood, which faithfully he recognised and devoutly received. Ever he adored his Christ, and ever he repulsed the prince of darkness. All day long the brothers read to him. Then, for the last time they gathered round him. They asked him whom he wished to be his successor. He replied : ' I leave that to the dispensation of God and the choice of the brothers '.

Day drew on to vespers. He was carried to St. Mary's chapel, where he rallied again, chose the psalms, and, though dying, himself sang with the brothers. When they in their grief forgot a verse he corrected them. He then bade them leave him alone. When he was being carried back to the dormitory, he asked what had happened at the council, and suddenly in the bearers' hands he seemed as dead. In haste a cloth was spread on the ground, ashes sprinkled on it, and his holy body laid thereon. But his spirit returned, he asked where he was, and on learning that he lay on the cinder and ashes, gave thanks to God. He next inquired if the children and the conventus of the monks were present, and was told they were.

Seeing the Cross near him, he fixed his eyes on it. From the movement of his lips it could be seen that he was repeating the prayers for the dead. Then, without any twitching of the body, he closed his eyes and passed away in peace. The brothers whom he had chosen washed and anointed his body. His limbs were composed in their old familiar attitude, and his body laid before the holy altar, where as to a shrine for three days monks came hastening from far and near. His funeral was attended not only by the whole town, but also the whole province. All who came were weeping, some with joy that they had been given such a father, some with sorrow that he had been taken from them. He was eighty-six years old, and for fifty-six had been abbot of Cluny.

Wonders marked his passing. On the night of his funeral he appeared to a certain Gregorius, a monk of simple nature and innocent life, who had come from afar to the funeral. Having kept vigil before the altar, he retired worn out to his cell. In his sleep he saw Odilo stand before him. To his question, ' How is it with thee, oh master ? ' he received the answer, ' Very well, oh brother, Christ Himself deigned to come and meet His servant. In the hour of my death He pointed out to me a fierce and terrible figure which, standing in a corner, would have terrified me by its huge monstrosity had not its malignancy been annulled by His presence.' The vision vanished, and the brother rose and told his companions. Forty days after, Odilo appeared again, this time to a clerk, of Teutonic race, of very good family, a relative of pope Leo and a beloved friend of Odilo's. The clerk was at Rome for the funeral of archbishop Lawrence, and after the ceremony fell asleep. Roused from his sleep by the appearance of Odilo, the trembling and fearful brother asked, ' Master, why art thou here ? ' Odilo answered, ' I come from the funeral of our brother Lawrence, and I did not wish to go away without seeing thee '.

Odilo had not that beauty of person which marked Maiolus. He was of middle height, very thin and pale. From his dead-

white face his eyes blazed with a splendour which was the terror
and admiration of beholders. His voice was strong and beautifully modulated : his speech suave and always apt ; his expression tranquil and cheerful ; his every gesture marked by authority
and gravity. To the proud and offensive he could be so terrible
that they shrank.[1]

In analysing Odilo's character Jotsaldus took as his standard
the four cardinal virtues, prudence, justice, fortitude, and
temperance. In prudence [2]—search for truth and desire for
fuller knowledge — he excelled. Nothing gave him greater
pleasure than reading. He was learned in the Scriptures, from
which he could quote by heart. He always had a book of divine
contemplation in his hands. His own eloquence was great,
as was seen in his letters and sermons, ' sweet as richest honey,
redolent of prudence, eloquence, suavity, and grace '.

In justice [3]—rendering to each his due, not taking what
belongs to another, and neglecting his own interests for the
common good—he also excelled. He gave due honour to men
of every age and rank. According to the word of the apostle,
he resisted princes and Christian dignitaries in nothing. Four
popes, Sylvester, Benedict, John, and Clement ' of pious
memory ', regarded him as a brother. Robert, king of the
Franks, the empress Adelheid, the emperors Henry and Conrad,
loved and venerated him. Between him and the two latter it
seemed as if there were but ' one heart and mind '. Stephen,
king of the Hungarians, and Sanchius, king of Spain, though
they never saw him, knew of his holiness and delighted in his
letters and admonitions. Sanchius, bishop of Pamplona, came
from the far west to be his monk. Italy rejoiced in his presence,
more especially Pavia, which he twice saved from destruction by
fire and sword ; so too did Rome, mistress of the world. He was
not proud, and was the friend of all, regarding old men as fathers,
the young as brothers, old women as mothers, and virgins as
sisters. To all, as was commonly said, he was dear as an angel.

---

[1] *Vita Jotsaldo*, i. 5.   [2] Ibid. i. 6.   [3] Ibid. i. 7.

Strangers coming to Cluny found him profusely generous, so sure was he that Christ would never let him lack. Anything offered to him he took, that he might have the more to give to the poor. He gave away so much that often he had nothing for the necessities of the brothers, but always, however unexpectedly, ' sufficient blessings ' would arrive for their needs. In a time of famine he melted down many of the church vases and ornaments for the poor—not grudging even the imperial crown.[1] Gold, he would say, was less precious then Christ's blood so freely shed for them. During another famine he went round many vills and churches and by his sweet speech and promise of absolution persuaded princes, the rich, and the well-to-do (*mediocres*) to give alms, thereby saving many thousands of the poor from starvation. He was compassionate to all,[2] so much so that sometimes the prudent chided him for lack of discrimination, when he would jokingly say, ' I would rather be mercifully judged for having shown mercy, than be cruelly damned for having shown cruelty '.[3] He even received the murderer of a bishop who fled to Cluny to take vows, and who, as he could read and sing like a skilled clerk, Odilo thought in time might be ordained. But the pope, whose consent he wrote and asked, replied that no such criminal could become a priest nor offer oblation at the altar lest through him the wrath of God descended

[1] Ibid. It was perhaps at this time that he wrote to make known to Garseas of Spain—though not without a blush (*sine rubore*)—the necessity and need which had afflicted Cluny for two or three years past. And not Cluny only, for the general poverty of the kingdom was such that hunger and want oppressed all their neighbours. He begged for help. *Epist. Odilonis*, 3 Migne, 142.

[2] Ibid. Once when going to St. Denis he saw the bodies of two boys lying on the road dead from starvation and cold. He dismounted from his horse, found gravediggers, wrapped the bodies in his own woollen coat, and said the funeral service over them. If St. Martin is celebrated throughout the world for giving half his cloak to a beggar, surely Odilo should be so also since he gave away his whole coat, and that not to a living man but to two dead boys. Many similar stories could have been told had not Jotsaldus' poor genius succumbed.

[3] Ibid. i. 8, *Eleganter illudere solitus erat. Ego inquit magis volo de misericordia misericorditer iudicari quam de crudelitate crudeliter damnari.* Jotsaldus once saw him kiss a leper, *nobis qui videbamus valde mirantibus.*

on others : he was not even to receive the sacraments. Yet when he died Odilo in his pitiful mercy did not refuse him the *viaticum*. His humility was great. It was nothing to him to be officially received with honour and ceremony. He only accepted the *obsequium* of his monks because he could not refuse it without causing scandal to many. When he visited Monte Cassino his humility and love of St. Benedict made him climb to the monastery on foot.[1] In the chapter he asked as the greatest of favours that he might kiss the brothers' feet. Nor would he say mass nor carry the pastoral staff on St. Benedict's Day, considering it unfitting for any one to do so except the abbot of Monte Cassino, the father of all abbots. On leaving he promised to send the brothers a relic of St. Maur, and seven years later sent the whole bone of the arm, which, enclosed in a silver shrine and crowned by a tower, beautifully worked, was borne by six monks from Cluny.

Fortitude [2]—a mind acting without fear, bearing adversity and prosperity with courage, and afraid of nothing except disgrace—was his. Even his holy soul endured attacks and vile reproaches from near and far, but he fearlessly withstood his enemies and patiently bore adversity. He was tireless in working for the peace of churches and the welfare of his neighbours, preserving peace for others even at peril to himself. Since he had swum to felicity it may be told, what God alone knew, that he bound his limbs with chains and iron bands, causing himself agony almost too great for human endurance, and under his garments wore a rough hair shirt.

Temperance—preserving the mean and order (*modum et ordinem*)—was his in every word and deed. He moderated his fasts, as St. Jerome advised, according to his health. He ate and drank whatever was set before him, enough to avoid remark but not too much for temperance. His dress was neither too

---

[1] *Bibl. Clun.* p. 337.

[2] *Vita Jotsaldo*, i. 12, *O quantas infestationes et quam gravissimas insectationes a domesticis et extraneis ipsa sancta anima sustinuit.*

slovenly nor too fashionable. His manner was grave, but tempered by cheerfulness. He was severe when necessary, but gracious in granting pardon, preferring rather to be loved than feared. An example of every virtue was found in him. Whoever heard anything displeasing about him ? Whoever if he heard believed, for was he not greater than malice and scandal ?

Jotsaldus is careful to explain that he did not himself witness all the miracles of which he wrote. Many he heard when collecting material for his *Vita*. He had sifted his material most carefully, only retaining what was vouched for by true and faithful witnesses. His chief authorities were Robert *prepositus* and Sirius, abbot of St. Maiolus', Pavia, who quoted largely from notes made by Boso, a monk of wonderful simplicity and innocence. Robert and Sirius, trustworthy men, intimate friends and confidants of Odilo, for long had been companions of his work and troubles. Whatever they told about him was worthy of belief, since it was what they had heard with their ears, seen with their eyes, and remembered with prudent memory.[1] The ' miracles ' are far removed from the charming naïveté of the stories about Odo. A point that is striking about them is their materialism : many being instances of the miraculous increase of food and wine. The simplicity of the earlier abbots had vanished. Odilo travelled with many attendants, his domestic belongings, bed, and books (p. 210). Adulation of the abbot has become fulsome : e.g. it might be said of Odilo that even God obeyed him : St. Peter's deed paled before his (p. 209). A sinister note is struck in the story of the madman who was not healed till his relatives laid a gift on the tomb and promised to renew it annually (p. 216). The ' miracles ' do, however, give some picture of the daily round of monastic life.

Jotsaldus' style is involved at any time, and quite hopelessly so when he tries to rise to the occasion ; e.g. ' Odilo, when staying

---

[1] Ibid. ii. 1, *Absit enim me nisi visa et experta, et a fidelibus personis sive idoneis testibus relata, de tanto viro aliquid mendaciter fingere vel narrare.*

at St. Denis, ministered the food of life and drink of salvation
with eloquent mouth. Lent was almost over, the day of the
mystic supper and the saving Passion of Christ approached,
when the triumphant light of the joyful Resurrection would
illuminate the world : and the sterility of the waters yielded no
affluence of fish ! The divine providence was to ordain, however, that at this new festival a new guest of the waters should
be sent to the new man renewed in the spirit.' [1] The story con-
tinues : At dawn on the great day the *prepositus* called the most
skilled fishers, lamented the scarcity of fish, gave them many
hints, and reminded them that the brothers would be worn out
with the Easter celebrations. ' Go ', he said, ' throw your
nets in the Seine, call on the merits of Odilo, invoke the name
of Christ, and I believe your hope will not be in vain.' They
went and caught an enormous fish (of a kind scarcely ever seen
there before) which Christ had sent direct to His servant. Odilo
was amazed and called the boys of the school (*infantes scholae*)
to come and see it. *Laetantur heroes novitate rei peractae meritis
tanti viri.*

Near St. Denis was the little monastery of St. Martin,
where the monks of St. Denis went when ill or for rest. Once
when Odilo stayed there the stewards of St. Denis sent supplies
for him, but not much fish, which was very scarce. Odilo did not
have much rest, for as usual many men came to see him, among
others two abbots with several monks whom he invited to dinner
to the dismay of the monks, who protested that there was very
little food. But when the guests lay at table a wonderful thing
happened. The fish, either in the hands of those serving, or
the hands of those eating, began to increase. All partook
abundantly, nay superabundantly, and much remained over for
the servants ! ' Boys,' said Odilo, ' you promised little and
have given much. See that you keep enough for yourselves.'
To this they, joyful of heart, replied, ' Lord, enough remains
even for others should they arrive. Henceforth, when your

[1] Ibid. ii. 8, *Ut in nova festivitate novus hospes gurgitis, novo etiam homini.*

holiness asks us to do anything, we will know that it can be done.' [1]

Odilo loved to stay at St. Mary's, Aventine, where cool breezes made the heat of summer tolerable.[2] Once when he was ill he asked the abbot at refection for a certain wine. There was only enough for one left, but the abbot, who loved Odilo greatly, with cheerful face and placid mind ordered it to be served. Odilo, always generous, shared it with the abbot, who lay next him. The monks who were stronger in health drank another wine. Odilo, noticing that his little bottle was not empty, said blandly to the brothers, ' I have not yet shown all my love to you ', and poured the wine for each of them in turn— about twelve altogether. Then happened a marvellous thing (*res stupenda*)—the bottle remained partly full ! The monks marvelled and rejoiced, but Odilo said, ' Our host overflowing with love has caused the wine to abound even in this little bottle ', i.e. his humility attributing to the grace of another the deed divinely accomplished by himself.

A similar miracle occurred at the ecclesia of Toulon.[3] No one in future ages—for what is written endureth—can doubt its truth, for it was told by Abrald, one of Odilo's monks, a true and faithful witness. Odilo arrived unexpectedly, was welcomed with joy, embraced and kissed but a little chided— though humbly and submissively—for not having given notice of his coming. Supplies were low and Alrald sent far and near to beg for necessaries. Odilo with his usual suavity said that he expected no sumptuous preparations. The vine season had been bad that year, so that only the rich could afford wine, and the considerate father, not wishing to burden the monk, offered to buy wine—' which was not to be thought in what was his

---

[1] Ibid. ii. 8.

[2] Ibid. ii. 9, *Qui prae ceteris illius urbis montibus aedes decoras habens, et suae positionis culmen in altum tollens, aestivos fervores aurarum algore tolerabilis reddit.*

[3] Ibid. ii. 23. Subject to Paray, cf. ibid. 3. Paray, a monastery famous for the holiness of its monks and belonging to Cluny.

own house'! At dinner 'sufficiency and even abundance of food was served, though not beyond what their discreet order allowed'. The wine was brought in a small and almost empty bottle : the monks were to drink twice, the others once, but this measure was exceeded and all drank largely! When Odilo left, the *dispensator* found the bottle still full. In amazement he looked again, but there was no mistake. He told Alrald, who thought him mad, till the testimony of his own eyes convinced him, and he could only exclaim, ' *Mirabilis Deus in sanctis suis.*'

A miracle one Ash Wednesday [1] at Paray reminded Jotsaldus of the feast at Cana of Galilee. At nine, when the brothers left their reading to have a little food, Odilo secretly took a handful of ashes, which he ate, and signed for a drink of water. When he put the cup to his lips the odour of wine arose. He put it aside and signed for water again. The brother protested by signs that he had brought water, emptied the cup, and refilled it. Again, when Odilo raised it to his lips, the odour of wine arose. Recognising in this the grace of God, he took with humility what was sent.

On yet another occasion Odilo was miraculously provided with wine. Descending the Juras he met a group of poor men who begged from him. He ordered the skins of wine to be emptied for them. Yet not long after, when he and his monks sat down to eat, the skins were found to be full of excellent wine. All were amazed and gave thanks.[2]

Twice by a miracle Odilo crossed a river on foot. Once when hastening to Pavia, he found no boat at the Ticino. He ordered one of his servants to walk across, and followed himself. The others came after, and, without the help of rowers, arrived unhurt! Nothing could be more worthy of praise : St. Peter once walked on the sea, but Odilo crossed the waves! Some horsemen who had seen the miracle, rashly concluded that it was ebb tide, and spurred their horses into the water. They

[1] Ibid. ii. 3, *In quo et cineris super capita impositio suscipitur et arduae inceptio abstinentiae a fidelibus inchoatur.* [2] Ibid. ii. 11.

P

were submerged.[1] A man who had watched all with awe fell at Odilo's feet and begged him to visit his house. In the night a terrific wind blew out the lantern and awakened the chamberlain. Terrified at the darkness he prayed, ' Oh, divine light that illumines the world, hear me unworthy as I am, and for the sake of Thy Odilo take from this house the horror of darkness.' Immediately a light appeared from the air, and filled him with joy and the house with brightness.

On the second occasion Odilo was travelling from the ' delectable monastery ', Peterlingen, by the mountains to Cluny. He stayed all night at Lions-le-Saunier,[2] so as to start at dawn. ' The sky was dark, the rain poured down, but could not turn the strong minds of the men of God from their journey.' After plodding on all day they came to a river so swollen with rain as to seem impassable. Odilo sent a servant to try. He crossed safely and came back for the others. As they passed through the vast flood, the water which came up to their thighs never rose beyond the holy man's shoes. Wet and miserable they reached St. Marcel's, Chalon, at midnight. Seated round a huge fire they warmed themselves and changed their garments while the gentle father, knowing what they had come through, soothed their afflicted breasts with improvised verses.[3]

At another time when coming from a monastery at Mantua which he had been asked to reform, his luggage was saved by a miracle. When crossing a river, the mule that carried his bed and his books got out of its depth. It managed to reach the bank, but when one of the servants tried to catch its head it swerved and swam to the opposite bank. A magnanimous hero

---

[1] Ibid. ii. 6. Every gift cometh from God, as they learnt to their cost. If this story seems incredible, let faithful men and Christian brothers remember the marvellous power of the Creator who wished to glorify Odilo that the light of his merits should be diffused throughout the world. [2] Ibid. ii. 7.

[3] Ibid. *O quondam fortes per multa pericula fratres !*
Ne vestra vestris frangatis pectora rebus ;
Per varios casus per tot discrimina rerum
Tendimus ad regnum coeli sedesque beatas ;
Durate, et haec olim meminisse iuvabit.

advancing over the plain watched what was happening, made no
mortal sound, lifted the cap which covered his white hair, and
was proceeding on his way, when Master Peter (the most agitated
of all, for he was responsible for Odilo's luggage) shouted to him
to catch the mule. He immediately dragged the animal from
the water. Quickly unloaded, not a trace of damp on the bed,
books, or luggage could be found. When Odilo was told, he was
sceptical that anything immersed in water should not be wet ;
yet at night he found it was so. ' Beloved,' he said, ' how
wonderful is the goodness of God. He has kept untouched what
we could not have restored (i.e. the luggage), while what could
be touched without harm (i.e. the mule) He allowed to get wet.'
Indifferent to the praise of men, he ascribed nothing to his own
merits but all to God who worked in him.[1]

Another time, when travelling in the Juras, a heavily-laden pack
horse fell from a height on to jagged rocks in the valley beneath.
The servants descended and found most of the luggage, but not
a book of the sacraments written in letters of gold nor some
crystal vases of rare make. Odilo stayed the night at the *cella*
St. Eugenius, and in the morning sent searchers to look for the
book and vases. There had been a heavy fall of snow, so nothing
was found. ' Then for two months snow covered the hills, and
harsh winter denuded the face of the mountains.' The loss
was almost forgotten, when one day a priest found the book
untouched by the mist and the snow, and the vases unbroken.[2]

Thieves were powerless before the merits of Odilo, as two
stories show. When Henry II. went to Rome for his coronation,
Odilo accompanied him and spent Christmas with him at Pavia.
The table where he had his meals was covered by a beautifully
embroidered cloth, which one day was stolen. When the theft
was discovered the servants murmured, but the generous father
merely told them to bring another cloth, ' and silence covered
the deed '. After the royal party left, the thief three times took
the cloth to market, and vainly tried to sell it. The third time

---

[1] Ibid. ii. 16.   [2] Ibid. ii. 18.

a flush of shame covered his brow.   Nor was the divine justice
slow to avenge him.   Suddenly his hands and feet dried up !
He was carried to the church of St. Maiolus, laid on the floor,
and covered with the cloth.   Crowds filled the church, marvelling
at the merits of Maiolus and Odilo.[1]   At last the sinner recovered, and glorifying God returned home.   Another time in
Pavia Odilo's horse was stolen.   Knowing it would be suspect
in Pavia, the thief took it to Lodi, but no one would buy it,
' God having turned the hearts of all against the purchase '.
Struck with contrition, the sinner returned the horse.   Wishing
to return good for evil, Odilo would not let him be punished.[2]

The ' miracle ' of the broken vase, told at great length,
evidently impressed Jotsaldus very much—why, it would be
difficult to say.   He reaches the story in a more roundabout
way even than usual.   To make sure of the details he had
questioned bishop Richard,[3] who asked him if he remembered
the quarrel between the bishop of Comensis and Odilo's nephew
over the monastery of Bremen.   Meeting the bishop at the time,
Richard asked how he could have acted so unjustly, knowing as
he did that the emperor Conrad had put Bremen under Odilo,
whose merits had so often shone forth, as for example in the
case of the broken vase.   The bishop of Comensis not only knew
of the incident of which he had been a witness, but many fresh
details, to which Richard eagerly listened and diligently stored
up in his mind.   This was the story.   Once at court the emperor
Henry ordered two young clerks (one of whom was the bishop,
and the other Landulf, afterwards bishop of Tours) to place on
Odilo's table a very precious vase of Alexandrine work.   They
obeyed the Caesar's command, humbly inclining themselves before
the abbot.   The monks—human nature being always curious
over anything new and rare—wishing to inspect it more closely
passed it from hand to hand, when it fell to the ground and was

---

[1] Ibid. ii. 4.   [2] Ibid. ii. 5.
[3] Ibid. ii. 12.   Formerly a Cluniac monk and one of Odilo's greatest
friends.   *Patris Odilonis nutrito et monacho . . . sibi valde familiarissimus suorum
secretorum conscius itinerisque vel laboris socius.*

broken. 'Brothers,' said Odilo in great distress, ' you have not done well, for by your carelessness those young clerks to whom the vase was entrusted may lose the imperial favour. Let us hasten to church and pray that the loss be not visited on the guiltless.' When they returned, not a crack nor a mark could be seen on the vase, and Odilo indignantly said : ' What was the matter with you, oh brothers ? Surely a mist obscured your sight.'

They dared not tell him it was a miracle, but the emperor was told *sub silentio*. The latter, who loved Odilo beyond measure and humbly adhered to his counsels, was filled with wonder and great jubilation, and held him more and more worthy of veneration.[1] Not only bishop Richard but many others assured Jotsaldus of the truth of this story.

Other miracles tell of deeds of healing. At Besorniacum he noticed the son of one of his serfs, a child beautiful [2] but blind. He prayed silently, signed the boy's eyes with the sign of the cross, and sent him home healed. Nor was this incredible : did not Christ say, ' He who believeth in Me, shall do My works ' ? At Peterlingen he healed a little boy-monk (*puerulus monachus*) who had a disease of the throat, very common in those parts. A tumour began to grow, and the child could scarcely speak. Odilo touched the sore, signed it with the sign of the cross, and from that moment the tumour began to decrease, just as before it had increased. It finally disappeared, and the boy was well when Jotsaldus wrote.[3]

At the monastery at Nantua he noticed a little boy-monk who suffered from a horrible disease, had lost the use of his limbs, his voice, his memory, and was almost dead. Odilo prayed, and gave him holy water from the chalice of St. Maiolus. Immediately he recovered.[4]

The *senior* of the Albigensians was lying under a tree when a

[1] Ibid. ii. 12, *Supra modum eum diligebat, illiusque consiliis humiliter adhaerebat.*
[2] Ibid. ii. 2, *Puerum cuius faciei effigiem pulchra manus superni opificis decoram effecerat.*   [3] Ibid. ii. 15.   [4] Ibid. ii. 17.

particle of bark fell into his eye. He could not get the bark out, use his eye, eat nor sleep. He came to Odilo, who was travelling through that district. The abbot signed the eye with the sign of the cross and said mass. He fell asleep, and on waking the bark had gone, and he could enjoy his food! Ever after he held Odilo in great veneration.[1] Another time when returning from Rome he met at Lucques a canon of St. Martin's, Tours, who suffered from a growth in his arm, which seemed likely to prove fatal. Odilo cured him, but would not let him tell any one. For he feared publicity as deadly poison, and praise as a pestilential evil.[2] Jotsaldus himself witnessed the healing of a madman at Nantua, who when he escaped his keepers wandered naked and miserable, emitting strange sounds, and living without food, as his kind do. Odilo and his monks prostrated themselves before St. Peter's altar, then he sprinkled the madman with holy water and made him drink. When he left for Cluny, the young man followed him, ' not mad but sane, not bound but free, not compelled by others but of his own free will '. At Cluny he made an offering of fish, a gift of love, and returned home. Next year he revisited Cluny, and not finding Odilo there, went on to Souvigny, arriving the day of his death. The thanks he was unable to give to the living he gave to the dead.[3] The nephew of the abbot of Ebreuil, a strenuous *miles*, for long deaf and dumb, learnt in a vision that if he drank water in which Odilo had washed his hands he would be healed. He came to Souvigny, received the water, mixed it with water from the chalice of St. Maiolus, changed his garments, entered the church, fell in prayer, drank the water, and was healed.[4]

Odilo worked many other miracles, but in secret, so that the people never knew of them. In fever cases he always used St. Maiolus' chalice, and then attributed the merit to that saint. Yet there was no doubt that he, the disciple, co-operated in his master's work.[5]

[1] Ibid. ii. 19.   [2] Ibid. ii. 20.   [3] Ibid. ii. 21.
[4] Ibid. ii. 22.   [5] Ibid. ii. 23.

In the third book of the *Vita*, Jotsaldus tells a few out of the many miracles worked after Odilo's death. All of them he had learnt on excellent authority.

The first is quaintly told. Four miles from Souvigny a poor woman lived with a daughter, insane, deaf and dumb. Three times when she was asleep, a beautiful and pleasant person told her to take her daughter to Odilo's tomb, and see what would happen. She did so. Passing through a wood near Souvigny the daughter suddenly spoke : ' Mother, mother, I hear a great sound of bells ', i.e. the bells of the monastery. Next she cried, ' I hear the lowing of oxen, and the bells round their necks '. At the tomb the mother gave what thank-offering she could, and returned with her daughter healed.[1] From the vast Alps in the interior of Aquitaine two young men came to the tomb, one deaf and dumb, the other leading him. At the tomb the latter took some of the water in which Odilo's corpse had been washed, poured it in the deaf man's ears, and some in his mouth. Next day the afflicted man laid a gift on the tomb, for he could speak and hear.[2] Another man, dumb for seven years, regained the power of speech at the tomb, and joyfully told all and sundry. Several persons, out of curiosity, sent to make inquiries. Jotsaldus heard the story from the latter.[3]

A priest who was dumb went to Odilo's tomb and humbly prostrated himself, praying to regain his speech. When no answer came he sadly returned home, whereupon he spoke. Solomon, a rich merchant, and several others witnessed to the truth of this.[4] A blind old man was led to the tomb by a boy, and before reaching the crypt saw. Swiftly preceding his leader he ran to give thanks.[5] A blind woman was also led there. For long she remained in prayer, but as no sign was vouchsafed her, asked the saint's permission to depart. ' As she spoke, sighing profoundly from the depths of her sad heart, her eyes long evilly closed were opened, the hoped-for light returned, and she went home guided by the light of her own, not others',

[1] Ibid. iii. 1.   [2] Ibid. iii 2.   [3] Ibid. iii. 3.   [4] Ibid. iii. 5.   [5] Ibid. iii. 6.

eyes ' ! [1] A blind old man from Tours was led by his daughter to
the tomb, and given water with which the corpse had been washed.
He arrived at night, and being poor could find no inn nor food.
He therefore spent the night hungry and without shelter.   In the
morning he returned to the tomb, when he received his sight.
Hastening into the church, which was crowded with men, clerks,
and priests celebrating mass, with loud voice he gave thanks to
God.   Hearing him, all flocked round him and glorified God.[2]

A merchant of Souvigny who had long been ill, lost his memory
and his reason.   His brothers and relatives brought him to
Odilo's tomb and tried in vain to make him sign himself with
the sign of the cross.   They then laid a gift on the tomb and
promised to pay a certain sum annually if the sufferer was
healed.   Immediately he regained health and sanity.[3]   A peasant
(*ruricola*) belonging to the monastery of St. Maiolus went mad.
Fighting with all his strength he was dragged by his son and
relatives to Odilo's tomb where they offered a gift.   He recovered.   A peasant of Autun who was paralysed, heard of the
virtue of the saint.   Seated in a cart, he was drawn to Souvigny
by his wife and brothers, and bathed his limbs with the water
of which he had heard so much.   Gradually the pain left, and in
a few days, not seated in the cart, but firm on his own feet, he
went to the tomb to give thanks, and having given to all proof of
his cure, returned home.[4]   A young clerk of Flanders who suffered
from dropsy, could eat and drink only with great pain : ' His
stomach swelled so much that his skin was extended beyond
measure, and seemed likely to burst.'   He could scarcely walk,
and yet to stand or sit was dangerous.   He longed for death,
as preferable to so wretched a life.   At last he dragged himself
to Odilo's tomb, with feeble voice told how far he had come, and
with tears begged his help.   There was no delay.   ' A stream of
clotted blood burst from his mouth ', and rising from his knees he

---

[1] Ibid. iii. 7.   [2] Ibid. iii. 8.
[3] Ibid. iii. 9, *Hoc itaque pacto quem adduxerant amentem et insanum . . .
ex integro sanum ad domum reducunt.*   [4] Ibid. iii. 10.

declared himself healed. Gathering up his voluminous garment, which (as his unnatural size was reduced) hung limp around him, he showed the onlookers how far his skin had extended.[1] An old man of the people was likewise healed of the same disease.[2]

A captive though bound and imprisoned in a cave which was barred and closed by a heap of stones, yet never lost faith, and in the dark depth begged Odilo to intercede for him. One day he heard some one approach and bid him come forth. His chains fell off, the bars burst asunder, the stones flew hither and thither, and he emerged from darkness to light. Rejoicing he gave thanks at Odilo's tomb.[3]

A girl paralysed for many years was told in sleep to go to Souvigny. Carried to the tomb, she there found she could walk. She started home, but on reaching the outskirts of the vill could go no farther. Carried back to the tomb, her strength returned, and never again did she go beyond the vill.[4] A merchant's daughter in Souvigny suffered from the same weakness. Carried to the tomb, first she stood, then gradually she walked, and as long as she remained there could stand and walk quite well.[5] Another girl was healed in the same way. These three miracles took place on Sts. Peter and Paul's day, when the church was crowded. Great was the amazement. Monks and clerks sang psalms in jubilation. Men and women raised their voices in thanksgiving at miracles of 'such stupendous novelty'. All told how wonderful Christ was in His saints, and what grace, thus verified by signs and wonders, must abound in his most faithful servant [6] Odilo.

With the death of Odilo the first phase of Cluniac activity came to an end. The work of reform had been carried through, and Cluny stood pre-eminent as the first reforming house of the age.

In those early years the essential sanity of the Cluniac movement is very attractive. For that sanity much must be attributed to the character of her first abbots. The note is struck

[1] Ibid. iii. 11. [2] Ibid. iii. 12. [3] Ibid. iii. 17.
[4] Ibid. iii. 13. [5] Ibid. iii. 14. [6] Ibid. iii. 15.

when Odo, ' a learnéd man with his hundred books ', stood at
the gate of Baume, so repelled by the tale of Berno's harshness
that he was ready to flee. For it was no intolerant fanatical
life that he sought, but a community where, with men like-minded
to himself, he might develop his love of religion, holiness, peace,
learning, literature, architecture, and art. There is a human
touch in his distress at the thought of his father and mother,
enmeshed in the snares of the world. There is charm in the
humane nature that could advise the unbalanced young zealot,
worn out with self-inflicted penances, either to learn or teach ;
in the mystic temperament of Maiolus to whom nevertheless
the mean in all things was praiseworthy ; in the characteristic
readiness of Odilo to risk censure for judging others mercifully.
Cluny, essentially Western, stood for moderation.

In an age of coarse materialism Cluny sought to recall to
men that interest in spiritual and mental things that seemed to
have been lost. To attain her end, she took every means that
lay to her hand. In her reform she accepted help from whatever
source it came. Founded by a secular prince, and in her development owing much to emperors, kings, and nobles, from her
foundation she was in close relation to the temporal power.
Autonomous, from her origin she looked beyond the bishop to
Rome, and by so doing, as her influence grew, enormously
strengthened the power and prestige of the papacy.

In that she acted unconsciously, for so intensely self-engrossed ·
was the life of the Cluniac community that her sons seldom
looked beyond their monastic walls. Very rarely do the bio-
graphers of the early abbots spare a thought for the outside
world. If they mention their abbots' participation in an historical event, it is not because the outside connection interests
them, but that the outside world's connection with them serves
to glorify their monastery.

True to monastic tradition, they looked on monasticism as a
higher calling than that of the secular church, the monk as alone
fulfilling literally the words of the Gospel. They reaped their

reward, in that Cluny was regarded as the great intercessory house *par excellence*, by the prayers of whose sons the souls of the damned went free, to the intercessory merits of whose abbot even a pope owed his escape from purgatory.

But for the larger issues of Cluniac history one has to look beyond the Cluniac chroniclers. It is from other sources that one learns what enormous power lay in the hands of the abbots. Under Odilo's successor Hugh that power reached its culmination. In Hugh's sixty years of office the Cluniac congregation was built up, the Cluniac power consolidated. Cluniac houses were to be found in France, Germany, Italy, Spain, England, even in Jerusalem. In those subject houses the will of Hugh was supreme : to him alone Cluniac abbots and priors were subject : from those houses revenue flowed to Cluny, and from Cluny emanated the policy that directed them. Hugh was head of a vast institution, of an international system. He lived through the stormiest period of the struggle between empire and papacy. In those years of stress, true to Cluniac tradition, his influence seems to have made for moderation. He never wholly broke off relations with Henry IV., who clung to him ' as his only refuge, his one consolation in his misery '.[1] At Canossa, Hugh may have acted as intermediary between pope and emperor.

Under Urban II., former monk and prior of Cluny, Hugh's influence and that of his monastery reached its highest point. Further privileges were showered on the abbey, honours heaped on the abbot. To Cluny again and again Urban's longing for his former master's presence went forth. To Hugh, ' as Christ on the Cross committed his mother to the belovéd John, so Urban committed the church '.[2] And at the apogee of Cluny's splendour, when the altars of her great church—one of the glories of Europe—were consecrated by the pope himself, Urban called to his former brothers and comrades, ' *Vos estis lux mundi* '.

[1] Migne, 159, p. 937.   [2] *Neues Archiv*, vii. p. 164.

INDEX

THE END

Printed by R. & R. CLARK, LIMITED, *Edinburgh.*